THE GOLDEN AGE
OF THE CANADIAN COWBOY

Riders on the Stuart Ranch, Jumping Pound, AB, late 1880s. *Glenbow Archives/NA–1939–2*

THE GOLDEN AGE
OF THE CANADIAN COWBOY

AN ILLUSTRATED HISTORY

HUGH A. DEMPSEY

FIFTH
HOUSE
PUBLISHERS

SASKATOON & CALGARY

Front cover photograph, "Charlie Cockburn, cowboy,"
courtesy Glenbow Archives / NA-3811-85
Hand colouring by Laurel Wolanski
Back cover photograph, "Alex Gladstone and Dan Nault, Pincher Creek cowboys,"
courtesy Glenbow Archives / NA-102-5
Cover design by Sandra Hastie/GDL

The publisher gratefully acknowledges the support received from
The Canada Council, Heritage Canada, and the Saskatchewan Arts Board.

Printed and bound in Canada by Friesens, Altona, MB
95 96 97 98 99 / 5 4 3 2 1

CANADIAN CATALOGUING IN PUBLICATION DATA

Dempsey, Hugh A. 1929–

The golden age of the Canadian cowboy

ISBN 1-895618-69-X (bound)
ISBN 1-895618-76-2 (pbk)

1. Cowboys - Canada, Western - History. 2. Ranch
life - Canada, Western - History. 3. Ranchers -
Canada, Western - History. I. Title.

FC3209.R3D44 1995   971.2'02   C95-920154-8
F1060.9.D44 1995

FIFTH HOUSE LTD.

620 Duchess Street   #9 – 6125 – 11 Street S.E.
Saskatoon, SK   Calgary, AB
S7K 0R1   T2H 2L6
                CANADA

CONTENTS

ACKNOWLEDGEMENTS

In writing this book, I have had constant support
and encouragement from the Glenbow Museum,
particularly Lindsay Moir and Catherine Myhr in the library,
Doug Cass in the archives, and Ron Marsh,
who made such excellent prints from the vast photo collection.
Also, my wife Pauline was very helpful,
providing criticism when asked and leaving me alone to write when needed.
I am proud to say that my wife comes from a ranching and rodeo family,
so I have been privileged over the years to absorb something
of the ethics and ethos of cowboy life.
Perhaps that's why I'm so much of an admirer.

INTRODUCTION

THE COWBOY HAS BEEN AN INTEGRAL PART OF WESTERN CANADIAN LIFE
FOR OVER A CENTURY. HE CAME WITH THE GREAT HERDS IN THE 1880s,
WORKED FOR OUTFITS LIKE THE BAR U AND COCHRANE,
AND CONTRIBUTED MUCH TO THE HISTORY,
ROMANCE, AND CULTURE OF THE WEST.

Frank Lowe, of the Oxley Ranch, was typical of early western cowboys. He is seen here on *Polecat* at a roundup camp in the 1880s. *Glenbow Archives/NC–19–6*

Over the years, the American cowboy has been both romanticized and vilified by movies, television, and novels to the point where the image and the reality have little in common. In the middle part of this century, he was presented as a hero of the downtrodden, often strumming a guitar and wearing a white hat to distinguish him from the bad guys. In the revisionist years of the last two decades, he is sometimes depicted as a degenerate and psychopathic killer.

Of course, none of these images are accurate. The Canadian cowboy was, to all intents and purposes, a hard-working man with special skills. He was deft with a rope, handy with a branding iron, and had an intimate knowledge of cattle, horses, and his surroundings. As a rule, he was tough, hardy, and fiercely loyal. Often an itinerant, the cowboy had few roots and those he had, he preferred to leave behind on the trail. Sometimes he was from a well-to-do family in England, but he could just as easily have been a farm boy from Iowa or raised on a ranch in Texas.

The golden age of the cowboy on the Canadian prairies extends from 1880 to the disastrous winter of 1906-07. The cowboy continued to thrive long after that date, but the influx of settlers and breakup of the big ranches changed his role forever. This book looks at those early years, extending when necessary to the first Calgary Stampede in 1912. That event is singularly significant, for it was to be a tribute to a bygone era, an admission that the golden years of the cowboy had passed.

The cowboys of British Columbia have not been included here. Their history may be as impressive and exciting as that of their prairie counterparts, but to include them would be like telling two separate stories. They originated at different times for different reasons; their intermontane locale presented unique challenges and obstacles; and their separation from the American frontier

Charlie Millar was an experienced American cowboy when he came to Canada in the 1880s. Here he joined his more famous brother, Herb Millar, horse breaker and foreman of the Bar U. *Glenbow Archives/NC-17-1*

saved them from the cross-border problems that plagued Alberta and Saskatchewan ranches. On the Canadian prairies, there was easy access between the lush foothills, the arid regions to the east, and the Great Plains of the United States, so the history of this region has a certain unity that did not extend across the mountains. There is a wealth of excellent published material on ranch life and cowboys in Canada's westerly province by such authors as Richmond Hobson, Thomas Weir, Alex Bulman, and H. Lavington.

The Canadian cowboy inherited much of the Spanish heritage from the American cowboy, wore the same clothes as his counterpart across the line, and spoke the same lingo—often with the same Texas drawl. In these ways they were alike but with a Canadian perspective; the most obvious difference between the two was caused by the presence of the North-West Mounted Police. Unlike the western United States, the Canadian West had law and order before it had settlers. When the Mounties arrived in 1874, the land was still the territory of the Indians and buffalo. By the time the first American cowboys came, the rule of law was well established, and the cowmen accepted this fact just as easily as they had adapted to the lawless American frontier. These men were willing to live under Canadian laws and to accept them. As a result, the Canadian frontier tended to be more orderly and law-abiding, so that the lynching of horse thieves was unknown, gunfights were exceedingly rare, and serious range wars never occurred. The best Canada could do was to experience a certain amount of friction between homesteaders and ranchers.

This is not to say the life of the Canadian cowboy was dull; it was not. As with his American counterpart, there were roundups, stampedes, horse thieves, cattle rustlers, heroes, and villains. The location of ranches close to the American border offered many tempting opportunities for gangs of thieves to operate on both sides of the line.

Today, the image of the cowboy is a fascinating mix between Canadian conservatism and Hollywood ballyhoo. There is pride in the old-time cattle drives, some of which are reenacted annually, and the modern cowboy is admired for his virtues of hard work and resilience. Yet the historical picture is inevitably affected by American stereotypes created by movies, television, advertising, and western novels. Over the years, Canada has been flooded with stories of the fight at the OK Corral, range wars, bounty hunters, and shoot-outs on Main Street. A number of Hollywood movies about the American West were filmed in western Canada as early as the 1920s and the Calgary Stampede was the locale for more than one "shoot 'em up" western.

As a result, Canadians expect the lawmen in western movies to be sheriffs, not Mounties, and the centre of action is always Deadwood or Abilene, not Calgary or Moose Jaw. So while the media-driven cowboy image has tumbled across the border into Canada, it is that of an alien American cowboy, not a Canadian one.

The most enduring and positive depiction of the cowboy through the years has come through rodeo. While the big-time shows in Calgary and Edmonton are dominated by American cowboys, the dozens of rodeos in smaller centres are purely Canadian events. Here, local cowboys from ranching communities as far north as Peace River and Prince Albert display their skill as calf ropers, bull doggers, bronc busters, and bull riders. The chuckwagon race is seen as a Canadian invention, and there is pride in the fact that Canadian rodeo stock is in demand throughout the continent.

Another positive representation has come through country music. Canada has taken a leading role in fostering cowboy ballads and promoting a concept that is universal and positive. From Wilf Carter of the 1930s to Ian Tyson of the 1990s, Canadian singers have helped keep alive a romantic and sometimes soulful picture of the Canadian cowboy.

Ranching remains an important part of prairie life and despite the inroads of farming, it has flourished and prospered. The cowboy may have exchanged his horse for a four-wheel drive but his goals are the same—to look after the cattle and horses under his care. His riding ability and skill with a rope are equally at home on the ranch or at the rodeo ground. Second- and third-generation ranching families are proud of their skill as riders, ropers, and wagon drivers. And, like their counterparts of the golden age, they possess those same unique qualities of hardiness, independence, and determination so identified with western life.

The camp cook is obviously the centre of attention for this Walrond Ranch crew. The cowboys were photographed at a roundup in the spring of 1901. *Glenbow Archives/NA–1035–4*

BEGINNINGS

———

THE PRAIRIES BECKON

BY THE SUMMER OF 1880, THE CANADIAN PRAIRIES HAD LOST
THEIR GREAT BUFFALO HERDS. MILE AFTER MILE OF LUSH GRASS LAY IDLE
IN THE SUMMER SUNSHINE. HERE AND THERE, BLEACHED BONES WERE STARK REMINDERS
OF THE MILLIONS OF SHAGGY BEASTS THAT HAD ONCE COURSED THE PLAINS.
NOW THEY WERE GONE.

The prairie wolf, lean and haggard, hunted the timid white-footed mouse instead of fat buffalo calves. Eagles, hawks, and other raptors found no freshly killed carcasses to sate their ravenous appetites; instead they had to settle for tiny creatures like prairie dogs.

The land varied from flat, arid plains to rolling short-grass prairie, all interspersed by countless coulees. Many valleys were wide and deep, with grassy knolls folding into each other along their bottoms, sometimes capturing small ponds within their slopes. Other valleys were shallow and grass-covered, with little shelves of rock protruding from the slopes to interrupt the symmetry of the landscape.

In summer, flowers of yellow, purple, and red dotted the prairies. Overhead the sky was an intense blue sprinkled with white clouds. Sometimes a lone antelope on a distant hill sensed danger and bounded away in a series of graceful hops, disappearing from view. Meadowlarks called out in the Blackfoot language, *ahkito-tsito-tsin-aiee*, unaware that the days of freedom for that Indian nation had tragically passed. In winter, snow might carpet the land one day and be swept away by the warm breezes of a chinook during the night, or a savage gale might drive all living things to shelter during a raging blizzard. It was a land of moods, but like a fickle woman or bold lover, the moods were never predictable.

In 1872 an English writer described the western prairies as a succession of undulating hills and shallow basins. He added,

No sound broke the stillness except the chirp of the gopher, or prairie squirrel, running to his hole in the ground. The character of the soil every few yards could be seen from the fresh earth that the moles had scarcely finished throwing up. It varied from the richest of black peaty loam, crumbled as if it had been worked by a gardener's hand for his pots, to a very light sandy soil. The ridges of the basins were often gravelly. Everywhere the pasturage was excellent.[1]

By 1880, the vast buffalo herds that once roamed the Canadian plains had been gone for less than a year. Yet the prairies were too fruitful a land to lie fallow and unproductive for long. There was too much succulent grass, too many streams, and far too much fertile soil to be ignored. Some saw the area as a desolate "Great Lone Land." As early as 1821, a missionary at Red River wailed, "When will this wide waste howling wilderness blossom as a rose, and the desert become a fruitful field?"[2] A half-century later, William F. Butler commented, "No solitude can equal the loneliness of a night-shadowed prairie; one feels the stillness, and hears

the silence, the wail of the prowling wolf makes the voice of solitude audible, the stars look down through infinite silence upon a silence almost as intense."[3]

This is not to say that cattle raising was unknown on the Canadian prairies before 1880. Far from it. The Red River colonists had started with a few head in the Winnipeg area after 1811, and many of the Hudson's Bay Company trading posts had small herds of dairy cattle. Most of these forts were in the woodlands, beside the great rivers. But Canada's potential prime ranching area was along the foothills, and east to the Cypress Hills and Maple Creek regions. These lay beyond the white man's voracious appetite for land until treaties were made with the Indians and the buffalo no longer dominated the range.

The Methodist mission on the Bow River, seen in this early engraving, was the site of the first cattle-raising attempts in western Canada. Missionary John McDougall purchased a few head of cattle in Montana in 1874, and a year later John Shaw wintered almost five hundred head in the foothills near the settlement. *Glenbow Archives/NA-1406-182*

Until these matters were resolved, the ranching empires of North America were confined to the Great Plains region of the United States and south to Mexico. The end of the Civil War in 1865 found the Texas plains overrun with cattle, and the construction of transcontinental railways brought thousands of longhorns streaming north. By the 1870s, the great cattle drives had extended into Wyoming but the working cowboy was still a stranger to the Canadian West.

However, cattle ranching did gain a small foothold in the West, in spite of buffalo and Indians. Probably the first attempt to bring range cattle to the region was undertaken by a gold prospector. In the summer of 1874, he travelled to Fort Benton, in Montana, with Methodist missionary John McDougall and his brother David. While there, the miner invested his savings in twenty-five head of Texas steers to take to the mission station at Morley, west of Calgary. At the same time the two McDougalls "each bought a couple of cows, with the calves."[4]

On their way home, they managed to ford the St. Mary and Belly Rivers, but when they got to the Bow, their animals wandered away during a storm. The would-be ranchers tracked them for two days as the steers seemed determined to go back to Montana. During the chase, McDougall and his companions encountered a war party of Sarcees who mistook them for American whisky traders. The Indians were preparing to attack when one of them recognized the missionary and raised his hands in friendship. The relieved travellers then followed the cattle past the Little Bow River and Mosquito Creek, finally catching them on an island on the Belly River. There they were rounded up, turned north again, and ultimately set loose in the rolling foothills near the Morley mission.

A year later, they were joined by an even larger herd. In August 1875, a man named John Shaw drove 450 head of cattle through the mountain passes from British Columbia and stopped at the Morley mission. "His intention was to have gone in to Edmonton to sell them," reported trader John Bunn, "but he was told that there was no sale for more than 30 or 40 head at most & therefore he has decided to winter them here."[5] When Shaw tried to sell them for thirty-eight dollars a head to the Hudson's Bay Company trader at Morley, his inventory included 200 cows, 187 steers, 60 spring calves, and 9 horses. When he was unsuccessful, he decided to winter the animals on the upper waters of the Bow. Later, he received a sub-contract to supply beef to the Mounted Police at Fort Calgary and gradually sold off the herd. In 1876, when the last animals were gone, Shaw moved to Edmonton and out of the ranching business.

Meanwhile, a dairyman at Fort Benton, Joseph McFarland, saw an opportunity for providing milk and beef to the newly arrived North-West Mounted Police. In the spring of 1876 he drove a small herd of cattle to a river bottom just east of Fort Macleod where he established the Pioneer Ranch. Initially he was in partnership with Henry Olsen, but they soon split up, Olsen becoming a squatter on land farther west near Pincher Creek. A year later, ex–whisky trader Fred Kanouse brought twenty-one cows and a bull from Montana and successfully wintered them on the open range, and within a short time, former trader William Henry Lee also had a few cows nearby. Similarly, at Fort Walsh, Metis settlers brought in dairy cattle to supply the local traders and police.

However, as long as there were buffalo, it was impractical to consider any major ranching schemes, for there was always the danger that the livestock would drift away with their shaggy relatives. In 1876, Mounted Policeman Cecil Denny witnessed such an occurrence near the Blackfoot Crossing of the Bow River. A huge prairie fire had swept through the area and dozens of buffalo had stampeded over a cutbank. Next morning, Denny went to examine the place where Indians were butchering the fallen creatures.

More than a hundred animals lay in a great pile, many still living, and the moaning of these poor animals was most pitiable . . . We noticed [the Indians] were in the act, with many grunts

Two of Alberta's earliest ranchers are seen in this rare 1882 photograph. Posed with a friend in front of the Mounted Police barracks at Fort Macleod are Ed Maunsell *(left)* and Joe McFarland. *Glenbow Archives/NA–1071–2*

of astonishment, of dragging out from underneath what we at first thought to be the long talked of white buffalo ... But on the head coming in sight it was seen to be a domestic steer, and a Texas [longhorn] at that, having only one long horn, the other having been broken off. How it had come to run with the buffalo is a mystery, no doubt having joined a herd as a calf, probably in Texas or some southern country.[6]

By 1878, a number of Mounted Policemen had served their five-year terms and decided to stay in the West. They became, to all intents and purposes, Canada's first cowboys—along with a few Americans who had gravitated to the western frontier. Among the ex-policemen was Edward Maunsell, an Irishman who had been fascinated by the excitement created in Britain when the first shipments of live beef cattle had arrived from the western United States. "This decided my future life," he recalled. "I reasoned that when the Mounted Police had established law and order, it would not be many years before settlers flocked in and we would have railway communication. It appeared to me, judging from the condition of the buffalo ... that domestic cattle could be raised here at a minimum cost."[7]

In the summer of 1878, Maunsell travelled to Fort Benton to see if he could buy some cattle but "there was none in northern Montana, as ranching had not yet started there."[8] A local trader agreed to get him one hundred cows and three bulls, but to avoid carrying them over the first winter, Maunsell would not take delivery until the spring of 1879.

Others joined in ranching enterprises of their own, and by the summer there were more than one thousand head of cattle in the Fort Macleod and Pincher Creek areas. Among the early rancher-cowboys were ex-policemen Jim Bell, Bob Patterson, and John D. Miller, while officers still serving in the force who began ranching as a sideline included Sam Steele, Percy Neale, William Winder, and Albert Shurtliff. There were also a number of small-time operators like Olsen, Lee, McFarland, "French Sam" Brouard, Billy Hyde, J.B. Smith, and Mrs. Annie Armstrong; the latter had a mixed herd of beef and dairy cattle and hired O.H. Morgan as her foreman. Some of these cattle had been driven into the country by an American cowboy, Tom Lynch, who later figured in some of the major cattle drives as foreman of the Bar U Ranch.

By 1879, the buffalo had virtually disappeared from the Canadian prairies, but while that problem had been resolved, another became more pressing and tragic. Although the government knew the herds were being destroyed, it made no adequate provisions to feed the Blackfoot Indians, who, until recently, had relied solely on that animal as their source of food. Now, starving Indians had no recourse but to roam the country in search of food, some even trapping gophers in an attempt to feed their families.

On one occasion, after Ed and George Maunsell had been checking their newly acquired herd, they returned to find that their cabin had been ransacked by hungry Indians. "But at least they had been decent enough not to clean us out," Ed told a reporter. "They had left enough bacon, tea, sugar and flour for a couple of meals."[9] Soon, cattle started to disappear, and the ranchers never knew for sure whether the loss was the result of hungry Indians, wolves, or natural dangers such as quicksand, or whether the stock had simply wandered away on the unfenced prairie. The ranchers were convinced that starving Indians were the main culprits, so Colonel James F. Macleod, commissioner of the NWMP, was asked what could be done about it.

"If we corral our stock every night, can we shoot any Indians we find killing them?"

"If you do, you'll probably hang," said Macleod.[10]

"Then, will we receive compensation for the cattle killed by Indians?"

"No, this country is not open for settlement, and you brought the cattle in entirely at your own risk."[11]

In the summer of 1879, when the ranchers rounded up their cattle, they learned the extent of their losses. After scouring the ranges, they discovered they had lost almost half their stock. Two months later, a delegation of stockmen presented their grievances to Indian Commissioner Edgar Dewdney, who was visiting Fort Macleod. They told him that southern Alberta was not yet ready for ranching and offered to sell their entire herds to the government to be used for beef rations for the Indians. Failing that, they would take their herds to Montana until Canada's situation improved.

Robert Patterson was among several Mounted Policemen who became cowboys or ranchers after their discharge. Patterson went into partnership with fellow constable Jim Bell in 1879 and started a ranch near Slideout. In 1911, Patterson was elected to the Alberta legislature. *Glenbow Archives/NA-329-2*

Dewdney was not impressed by their losses. "I asked them if they were sure that the Indians had killed them. They all stated most positively that they had, but were unable to bring a single proof . . . One man stated he had lost one hundred, another fifty, another thirty, making an aggregate of between two hundred and three hundred."[12] In fact, the police were able to give several examples showing that cattle reportedly killed by Indians had simply strayed away and were discovered after the complaint was made. As for buying the cattle, the government already had a contract with Montana merchants to supply all the beef needed for rations.

In disgust, most of the ranchers rounded up their cattle and began the long trail drive to Montana. Arriving at Willow Rounds on the Marias River, they left the livestock under the care of Jack Miller, one of their crew. Mrs. Armstrong and her foreman also settled nearby. The arrangement was that Miller would tend the herds until the Indian situation was under control, at which time the cattle could be returned to the southern Alberta ranges.

It took two years, but by 1881 the Canadian government finally had an effective system of rationing in place. This meant if starving Indians wanted beef and flour, they had to stay on their reserves to be close to the ration houses. This, in turn, meant they would no longer be wandering the ranges in search of food.

The news may have been good for some of the ranchers, but it came too late for Mrs. Annie Armstrong and her foreman. While in Montana, they became victims of the lawlessness that was so prevalent on the American frontier.

Late in June 1881, a cowboy named Brackett E.

Stewart arrived at the Armstrong Ranch on the Teton River, supposedly in search of some strayed horses. He was invited to stop over, and on the second night he went upstairs, where he killed Morgan, then went downstairs and shot and killed Mrs. Armstrong. He didn't realize that two young girls from the ranch—Maggie, aged twelve, and Annie, aged six—were outside checking their horses. When they heard the shots, they hid. Meanwhile the murderer looted the house and then set it on fire.

When it was safe, the girls rode to a neighbouring ranch and next morning were taken to the Old Agency where storekeeper Alfred B. Hamilton was the deputy sheriff. His store was full of cattlemen from a local roundup, and as Maggie was telling her story she suddenly screamed and pointed to a cowboy who had just walked in the door. "There's the man who killed my mother!" she cried.

Stewart was searched and besides a sizeable amount of money, the sheriff found a gold watch that was recognized as belonging to Morgan. Sheriff Hamilton immediately placed the man under arrest and locked him in one of the storerooms until a judge could be summoned. This, however, proved to be unnecessary. According to a Fort Benton newspaper:

> . . . a party of masked men rode up to Mr. A.B. Hamilton . . . levelled their guns at him, and demanded his prisoner. These men were immediately joined by about twenty more, and they took the prisoner by force from Mr. Hamilton, and hung him to a tree . . . [13]

When the Canadian ranchers went to recover their cattle, they suspected another crime had been com-

Besides the huge spreads like the Cochrane, Bar U, and Oxley, there were many small ranches scattered through the foothills. This is a typical small outfit, photographed in the early 1890s. *Glenbow Archives/NA-237-23*

mitted, but they couldn't prove it. When the stock was rounded up, there were fewer cattle than two years earlier, and no yearlings. Jack Miller explained that an epidemic of blackleg among the calves the previous year had virtually wiped out the Canadian crop. However, the ranchers couldn't help but notice that Miller himself had suffered no such loss. In fact, his herd seemed well stocked with yearlings. But without evidence the Canadians could only round up their stock and head for Canada as quickly as possible.

By this time, the Canadian frontier was ready to give them a friendly welcome. Surveyors were travelling through the countryside, laying out lines for the Canadian Pacific Railway and marking the township lines. The Indians were on their reserves, and the millions of buffalo had now been reduced to a few score that stampeded in fright at the sight of a hunter.

In short, the land was ripe for exploitation.

COMING OF
THE COWBOY

"I have become well acquainted with the cowboys," commented a Calgary newspaperman in 1883, "and have found them as a class the best fellows in the world, good hearted and generous and always ready to assist a man in trouble."[1]

In the early 1880s, cowboys were a new phenomenon on the Canadian prairies. Until then, the area had been known only to Indians, fur traders, Mounties, and missionaries. The newly arrived cowboys were usually American, frequently young, and often lean and tough. And when they came, they not only brought cattle and horses with them, but also customs and traditions that could sometimes be traced back to Old Mexico and Spain. Yet within a short time, these men absorbed some of the uniqueness of the Canadian prairies and its people, thus creating a new breed of men—the Canadian cowboy. They were much like their American counterparts in many respects, yet they could not help but be affected by Canada's land leasing and marketing methods, the presence of British mores and values, and the West's unique system of law and order. For many years, the Mounted Police combined the duties of arresting officers, magistrates, and jailers so that the law could be strictly enforced. An early rancher noted that "American cowboys, coming to work on Alberta cattle ranches, shed their six-shooters at the boundary as trees shed their leaves in the fall, and were glad to do so."[2]

Canada's unique system of issuing grazing leases was a factor that drew many American cowboys across the border. With the signing of Indian Treaty Four in 1874 and Treaty Seven in 1877, all the potential ranching country had become Crown land, available for utilization. Measures were put into place that allowed eastern and British investors to acquire huge leases in this vast region at relatively little cost, thus encouraging rapid use of the vacant lands, and, at the same time, giving the friends of the government a chance to make a little money.

The terms were indeed generous. By order-in-council passed in 1881, a person or company could lease up to one hundred thousand acres of grazing land for twenty-one years at the rate of a cent an acre per year. The only requirement was that there be one cow on the land for every ten acres under lease. If an investor had the full one hundred thousand acres, he needed a herd of ten thousand cattle.

These were the kind of regulations that encouraged large-scale ranching and required the importation of thousands of cattle from the United States. And who could better trail in these herds than the American cowboy? Once he arrived, he often liked what he saw and stayed.

The Canadian herds were purchased in Montana and Idaho at the northern terminus of the trail drives from Texas and Arizona. In 1880 about one thousand head were imported, with well over six thousand arriving in 1881, and sixteen thousand in the following year.[3] Each time they came, the

John D. Norrish.

Range, Spring Creek and Porcupine Hills.
Address, Mosquito Creek.

Horse Vent,

RL

on left thigh.

Cattle Vent.

RL

on left shoulder.

Ear Mark, over half crop right, under half crop left

In 1880, John Norrish made one of the first cattle drives to Alberta. He later established a ranch in the Porcupine Hills. His horse and cattle brands are displayed here. *Glenbow Archives/NA-2286-1*

bawling herds were accompanied by veteran cowboys and a number of greenhorns who were seeing the Canadian West for the first time.

One of the first drives occurred in 1880 when John Norrish brought a herd of forty-three cattle across the mountains from Fort Steele. His two cowboys were local Indians who had about as much experience as he did. When they got to the Elko River, the animals refused to cross a narrow bridge. Norrish roped a small yearling steer and tried to drag it across, but it frantically plunged through the guard rail and was killed in the raging current. The rest of the stock were crossed on a sandbar several miles downstream, and after weathering a windstorm in the Crowsnest Pass, the animals were finally delivered safely to the Highwood River range.

But this was a minor drive compared to the efforts of the big outfits. In the early 1880s, the Cochrane, Bar U (or North-West Cattle Company), Oxley, Walrond, Military Colonization Company, and other newly formed ranches brought in thousands of head.

There were two kinds of range cattle readily available. One was the rangy Texas longhorn that one rancher described as having "such lean racks of frames and bony backs that not even the wonderfully nutritive grass of their new range with its powerful assistants of ample water and bracing climate could transform it into a great beef producing animal."[4] This stock had been moved through the Great Plains of Nebraska and Wyoming into Montana. The second group available to Canadian ranchers consisted of a Durham-Shorthorn cross that came through the Pacific North-West and provided a much better range animal. Yet both types would benefit from the purebred bulls imported from the east by the big ranchers in order to improve the quality of beef.

When Fred Stimson, manager of the Bar U, went to Montana in 1881 to purchase a foundation herd, he hired one of the most notable drovers of the day—Tom Lynch—to ramrod the outfit that would bring them north the following spring. Born in Missouri, Lynch began working on the cattle drives from Oregon to Montana while still a teenager. In the late 1870s he began taking his own herds into Alberta, selling them to settlers as far north as Edmonton. Then, in 1879, he established a ranch on the Highwood River where he adopted the TL brand.

After looking over the available livestock, Stimson decided to buy three thousand head of Durham-Shorthorn cattle from ranchers in the Lost River area of Idaho. Lynch then hired a crew of American cowboys, giving preference to those with experience. One of the applicants was Bill Moodie, a seasoned cowhand, but he would not join unless Lynch also took his partner, a black man named John Ware. Lynch was dubious but, being short of hands, he took him on as night herder. Befitting his perceived inexperience, Ware was given an old saddle and a docile nag. The cowboy

Many of Canada's early cattle herds were imported from Montana. This view of the open range of eastern Montana, taken by L.A. Huffman in 1880, shows the type of cattle found in that region. *Glenbow Archives/NA-207-74*

took one look at the gear and immediately asked for a better saddle and a worse horse.

Although the cowboys rounded up a decent saddle, they decided to test Ware by giving him the worst outlaw in the herd. According to L.V. Kelly, a reporter for *The Calgary Herald* with an interest in ranching history, the black cowboy "swung up to the top of the wicked mustang and rode him from ears to tail."[5] Ware proved to be such a skilled horseman and cowman that during the trek he was placed in charge of one of the herds and later became one of Canada's noted bronc riders.

On the drive from Lost River, the Bar U crew travelled only a few miles a day, trailing the herd northwards over the Monida Pass and along the Madison River. According to historian Grant MacEwan, "To begin the day, a trail herd would be grazed for a couple of hours, being eased along lazily in the proper direction. Then the cattle were driven along at reasonable walking speed until noon when there was a two or three-hour rest."[6] In the early afternoon, the process was repeated as the cattle grazed and were driven northward until

nightfall. As the day riders gathered around the chuckwagon for their evening meal, the next shift, the "night hawks," took over. They rode around the herd all night in two-hour shifts, often serenading their bovine charges to keep them calm and settled. They watched for prairie wolves and other predators and hoped that a thunderstorm or other unusual occurrence would not frighten the cattle into a frantic stampede. But the whole drive went off without incident; in fact, Sam Howe, an eighteen-year-old cowboy, said, "The worst thing about it was to keep awake."[7]

When the Bar U outfit reached the Canadian border in August 1882, there were 3,014 cattle in the herd. They were now in Canada, but would spend another month on the trail before arriving at the Highwood River. However, because the cattle had been nursed along, allowed to graze along the way, and set their own pace, their losses had been minimal.

Earlier, in 1881, while the cattle were being rounded up at Lost River, the Bar U owners were taking steps to improve the breeding stock. Stimson travelled to Chicago in the fall where he visited the stockyards and bought twenty-one young Polled Angus bulls. While there, he was approached by a twenty-year-old farm boy, Herb Millar, who was eager to work on a ranch. Stimson hired him and gave him the task of bringing the herd by rail and steamboat to Montana in the spring of 1882. In spite of his inexperience, Millar got the animals safely aboard a Missouri River steamer and offloaded them at Fort Benton. There he found a freighting outfit that was travelling to Fort Macleod. Acting under orders, he bought his own bull wagon, filled it with supplies for the Bar U, and joined a train of other outfits going north. At Fort Macleod, he discovered the local bullwhackers were on strike, but, undaunted, he learned the gentle art of driving oxen and reached the ranch a few days later. There he found men "engaged in erecting crude rough log buildings, corrals, etc., for the accommodation of the cowboys and rangemen and the breeding stock, which were then being slowly herded across the prairies."[8]

Millar was destined to remain at the Bar U for the next fifty years as cowboy, bronc buster, and later as foreman. He had become sufficiently adept as a cowboy to take part in the 1882 fall roundup, and in spite of an unexpected snowstorm, all the Bar U stock came through without a single loss.

From this humble beginning, Millar developed into one of the best riders on the Canadian range. When he became foreman of the ranch, he trained many novice cowboys, some of whom became well-known ranchers and stockmen. Among his "graduates" were Billy Playfair, Charlie McKinnon, Bert Sheppard, and Billy Henry.

The movement of Bar U cattle into Canada may have been free of problems, but not so with the Cochrane outfit. Formed in 1881 by Quebec interests, the company hired ex–Mounted Policeman James Walker as its first manager but retained rigid control in Montreal. The company's first purchase was three thousand head of mixed Hereford and Aberdeen Angus cattle, as well as Texas longhorns. The second herd, some four

thousand head, were bought in Idaho and were "judged to be among the finest cattle in Montana Territory."[9]

Frank Strong, foreman for I.G. Baker & Company's ranching operations, was given the task of bringing the Cochrane herd to Canada. A veteran cowboy, he later operated the Strong Ranch east of Fort Macleod and was known as an excellent rider. Perhaps he was anxious to get back to his new bride when he took the Cochrane contract. Or perhaps he was acting under orders. But whatever the reason, Strong jeopardized the entire future of the Cochrane Ranch by the speed with which he drove their six thousand head from Montana to the Bow River. He hired thirty Montana cowboys, gath-

Frank Strong was already a veteran cowboy when he came to Canada for I.G. Baker & Co. in 1880. A year later, he was criticized for pushing the Cochrane herd too quickly to get to the Bow River range before winter. As a result, many weakened animals died along the way. *Fort Macleod Museum/80.1681*

ered a remuda of three hundred horses, and moved the cattle along the trail at the rate of fifteen or more miles a day. To hurry the animals along, he split the herd in two, sending the steers ahead and following with the cows and calves. As a result of this mad rush, hundreds of cattle were left to die along the way. And when Strong delivered the herd to the Cochrane foreman in the late fall, the cattle were hungry and weak from their ordeal.

Then, as luck would have it, the snows came early and there was no time to properly brand the stock. That meant they went into the winter of 1881-82 with no markings to identify them as Cochrane cattle. Not only that, but the winter was a long one and scores of weakened cattle died. By spring, the company had lost almost two thousand head. And more disappeared into the herds of small ranchers who were quick to brand the drifting stock.

The tragedy was repeated during the following season when another forty-three thousand head were imported from Montana. Through a series of blunders, the stock, which was supposed to have been delivered in July, did not arrive until October—right into an Alberta blizzard. William Kerfoot, a Virginian and veteran cowboy, was put in charge of the weakened herd, but interference from Montreal plagued the enterprise. Kerfoot suggested that the animals be allowed to drift onto the open plains where the snow was light, but headquarters demanded they be close herded on the Cochrane range, where drifts and heavy snowfall made grazing virtually impossible. During the winter of 1882-83, the cowboys had the thankless task of working out of tent camps along the Elbow River and Fish Creek, driving back cattle that were trying to reach the grassy plains.

The following spring, according to L.V. Kelly,

Dead bodies were heaped in every coulee, thousands of head having perished. Some of the long ravines were so filled with carcasses that a man could go from the top to the bottom, throughout its entire length, and never have to step off a dead body ... Out of the

12,000 head that had been purchased and placed on the Cochrane range, there remained now but a scant 4,000, counting natural increase.[10]

Discouraged by the conditions along the Bow River, the Cochrane Ranch owners took a new lease near Waterton Lakes in the southwest corner of the North-West Territories. They also hired a new manager, who succeeded in getting the stock to the new ranch without serious loss. This in itself was a remarkable feat, but even more so in that the manager was a Mexican and had to deal with discrimination as well as cattle on the long drive south. On the frontier, anyone who was not racially of European origin was considered inferior. This man's leadership under the circumstances was an indication of his ability as a cowman.

Everyone knew him simply as Ca Sous but his real name was Jesus Lavarro. (The Spanish pronunciation of "Jesus" is "Hay-sous," which was corrupted to "Ca Sous.") His family had moved from Mexico to Idaho several years earlier with the cattle drives, and there Ca Sous had become a skilled horseman. He was with the crew of cowboys who had brought the stock to the Cochrane range and had helped close herd them over the winter. During this time, Ca Sous was accompanied by his Peigan Indian wife, Almost An Owl Woman, and their nine-year-old boy, Joe.

One of the crew driving the cattle to Waterton Lakes, H. Frank Lawrence, described the Mexican as "a remarkable ranch hand" who had "few equals in the country ... "[11] He added:

On the drive south we moved slowly, not averaging ten miles a day. We divided into two parties; the first rode out of camp to herd from sundown to midnight, slowly bunching up the herd as they settled for the night. At midnight one rode into the camp and roused the relief; they in their turn now held the cattle until dawn when they would be relieved by those who had breakfasted and the herd was again set drifting and grazing.

The Walrond Ranch, one of the largest spreads in western Canada, was financed by British interests and staffed mostly by American cowboys. This is a view of the upper ranch buildings about 1893. *Glenbow Archives/NA–237–11*

Little Bow Ranch Company).

The trail drives that brought many of the American cowboys into Canada followed a pattern. In 1885, a writer visited one of their camps at breakfast and described what he saw:

The chuckwagon travelled ahead of the drive, the cook being accompanied by a rider who drove the extra saddle horses to the new camp. By the time the other crews arrived, the cook had his tent pitched and a meal ready.

The drive went smoothly, but Lawrence noted that the cowboys did not appreciate taking orders from a Mexican and shortly after they got to the new range, he was replaced by an experienced American named Jim Dunlap. Disgusted, Ca Sous returned to Montana, settling for a while on the Blackfeet Reservation with his wife's family.

While the Cochrane Ranch experienced its settling-in pains, other companies were adjusting to the western frontier during the same period. In 1882 a group of British investors formed the Oxley Ranch. It selected a lease northwest of Fort Macleod and picked up its foundation herd just across the border in Dupuyer, Montana. The Walrond Ranch also had British backing, with Sir John Walrond-Walrond being the leading investor. It found the cattle it needed in the Judith Basin, south of Fort Benton. Like the Bar U, these companies upgraded their herds with the addition of quality bulls from Chicago, eastern Canada, and Great Britain. Other early outfits included the Stewart Ranch, Alberta Ranch, Glengarry, and the CC (or

A picturesque hardy lot of fellows, these wild cowboys, as they sit on the ground by the fire, each man with his can of coffee, his fragrant slice of fried bacon on the point of his knife blade or sandwiched in between two great hunks of bread, rapidly disappearing before the onslaughts of appetites made keen by the pure invigorating breezes of these high plains.[12]

One of the cowboys had shoulder-length hair, piercing grey eyes, and a weathered face. He wore a flannel shirt, broad-brimmed hat, leather chaps, and "great spurs, tinkling at every stride."[13] Finishing his meal, the cowboy saddled his horse and rode off to take his appointed place on the flank of the herd. The observer continued:

The others soon follow, camp is broken, and wagons securely packed ready for the road and the work of the day commences. The cattle seem to know what is coming. On the edges of their scattered masses the steers lift their heads and gaze half stupidly, half frightened at the flying horsemen; as the flanks are turned they begin closing in toward one another, moving up in little groups to a common centre. As they "close in masses," they are gently urged onward by the drivers in the rear, until the whole herd is slowly moving forward, feeding as they go, in a loose wide column.[14]

When the Military Colonization Company, or MCC, was established, it encouraged young Englishmen to buy into the firm and homestead land adjacent to the lease.[15] One of those who responded was Bob Newbolt, a young man from a military family who decided he wanted to be a cowboy. Before leaving England he bought a complete riding outfit, perfect for the English countryside but completely unsuited to the Canadian West. Early in 1884, he travelled by steamship, railway, and stagecoach to Lemhi, Idaho, where MCC officers were buying three thousand head of cattle. Newbolt met Tom Lynch, who was in charge of the drive, and was told that he would be a night herder—one of the least likely places an inexperienced cowboy could get into trouble.

Almost from the outset, the green Englishman was the butt of cowboy humour. The first trick was to make him think that the night hawks stayed with the cattle from sunset to sunrise. While the other herders were relieved every two hours throughout the night, Newbolt was left by himself until dawn. Even when he met other cowboys in the darkness, he was not able to distinguish one from the other, and it was several days before he realized he had been tricked.

But Newbolt got his revenge. One night he found Tom Lynch's nephew sleeping on the job, so he quietly took the man's horse and led it back to camp. When young Lynch awoke, he had to carry his saddle two miles to the rendezvous. As Newbolt later recalled, when Lynch "found his horse tied to the wagon, he was fairly in a rage. When he learned how it had got there, he was going to murder 'that bloody Englishman.'"[16] For the rest of the drive, Newbolt was confined to camp whenever Lynch was on night duty to prevent any retaliation.

Newbolt also began adjusting to the western lifestyle:

So far, on this trail and night herding, I was dressed in my English clothing, flannels, puttees, bowler hat and all. These garments were far from suitable for such use so I outfitted myself at Deer Lodge with a complete western cowboy outfit, excepting only a "six shooter," something I never did carry or use. I put my beloved bowler in the wagon where I thought it would be safe, but the riders found it and soon riddled it with bullets.

After the cattle had been on the trail for several days, the foreman decided that Newbolt should graduate from his quiet old mare to something more befitting a cowboy. So the men saddled a bronc for him, which promptly threw Newbolt three times. Finally, a Mexican quietly showed him

Englishman Bob Newbolt stopped in Montreal to be photographed while on his way to become a cowboy and rancher in western Canada. Later, American cowboys used his hat for a target and filled it full of holes. *Glenbow Archives/NA-1046-5*

Billy Hyde, one of the first cowboys in Canada, started this spread on Willow Creek, a few miles northwest of Fort Macleod. It was called the Trefoil Ranch. *Glenbow Archives/NA-237-24*

how to hobble his stirrups and keep one rein tighter than the other to make the horse go in a circle. He then rode the bronc to a standstill and gained the grudging respect of the seasoned veterans. "I was developing into a pretty fair cowhand," he recalled, "and the boys were beginning to treat me with a good deal more respect than was the case at the first of the trip."

The next adventure occurred when the herders camped for the night near a small Montana town. Most of the cowboys descended upon the local saloon and when some differences of opinion occurred, they began to shoot up the place. Newbolt took refuge under a billiard table but joined his drunken companions when they rode out of town. Next morning, the sheriff placed them all under arrest and would not allow the herd to move until the damages had been covered. Newbolt was carrying the payroll for the MCC so he reluctantly paid out twenty-five dollars for each man who had been

at the saloon, "myself included, disregarding the fact that I had taken refuge under the billiard table during the shooting."

Under Tom Lynch's expert guidance, the MCC herd moved slowly across Montana, then stopped at Fort Macleod where Mounted Police officers, acting as customs agents, counted the stock and collected the duty. By the time the trail drive reached the MCC range on the Bow River, Newbolt had become an experienced cowman. He then spent the next couple of years working for the MCC, trailing in another herd of cattle, assisting on roundups, and performing the usual chores of the cowboy. In 1886, when his mother and two sisters decided to come to Canada, he established the Bowchase Ranch adjacent to the MCC, registered his DIO brand, and became an independent rancher. He stayed in the district for the rest of his life but always remained very much an Englishman, both in dress and in habits.

Many cowboys who came on the cattle drives did not stay. Their biggest complaint was the lack of saloons, for prohibition was rigidly enforced in the Canadian West. For example, it has been said that one of the reasons cowboy artist Charlie Russell and B.J. "Long Green" Stillwell stayed in the High River area for only a few months in 1888 was a shortage of liquor. Other cowboys left the country because they were too nomadic, never staying in one place long enough to put down roots.

The first prairie ranches were located along the foothills from the Bow River to the American border. The region offered excellent winter grazing, while the streams flowing from the mountains provided ample supplies of water. Sheep Creek, Little Bow, Mosquito Creek, the Oldman, and other watercourses became synonymous with the early years of ranching. The foothills also were close to the Mounted Police headquarters at Fort Macleod, providing a limited market for their beef and the protection ranchers believed necessary on the frontier.

Besides the huge ranching companies, many small operators and ex-Mounties took up land in the region. Some called themselves ranchers but in fact did the work of cowboys, spending much of their time in the saddle and performing all the duties of the crews they couldn't afford to hire.

Billy Hyde had a small ranch along Willow Creek, while Jim Dunbar started ranching in 1882 near the Porcupine Hills.

Once the range was opened, the industry grew rapidly. By 1884, there were forty-seven cattle and horse ranches in the region, all leasing land from the government. Some of the larger companies had acquired the maximum one hundred thousand acres. These included the Cochrane, Walrond, Oxley, Bar U, and Halifax Ranches, and the Jonas Jones/F.C. Inderwick partnership. A few of the operators were ex-whisky traders, such as Orris S. "Hod" Main, "Dutch Fred" Watchter, and Dave Akers, while others leased only a few acres for their small herds. For example, Alex Begg had fourteen hundred acres on the Highwood, Lord Boyle had five thousand acres at Pincher Creek, and Jim Bell had five thousand acres at Slideout.

With the construction of the Canadian Pacific Railway in 1882-83, and its completion late in 1885, markets in eastern Canada and abroad opened up. The railway also offered ranchers the opportunity to spread into the trackless lands all the way from Wood Mountain to the Cypress Hills and Pakowki Lake. These tended to be smaller spreads, where Ontario influences were almost as strong as those of Montana and Texas.

Englishman F.C. Inderwick had a ranch on the North Fork of the Oldman River, seen here in 1884. This is where he brought his wife, Mary, who admired the skill and good manners of the local cowboys. *Glenbow Archives/NA-811-4*

The first big spread in the area was the Medicine Hat Ranching Company, launched in 1883 with 150 head of cattle from Ontario. Four years later, Mitchell Brothers located a ranch at Elkwater Lake, while others were seeking out the grasslands south of Maple Creek. American ranching interests also began to take advantage of the Canadian grasslands when the Circle Ranch acquired a large lease near Medicine Hat and later moved to the Little Bow. By 1890, ranching activities had also crept out from the Alberta foothills, so that a few small spreads were found north along the Red Deer and east of Lethbridge. But the majority of stock remained near the foothills, with seventy-five thousand cattle between the International Boundary and Pincher Creek, and another forty-three thousand north of them to the Little Red Deer River.

A number of ranchers specialized in horses, importing stallions from Britain and eastern Canada. Probably the most famous of these was the Quorn Ranch, formed by the Quorn Hunt Club of Leichestershire, England. Their plan was to raise remounts for the British cavalry and horses for fox hunting and other gentlemanly pursuits. Other early horse outfits included the Bow River Horse Ranch and the High River Horse Ranch. In addition, sheep raising was gaining a foothold, particularly in the Medicine Hat region. Near Cardston, a number of Mormon settlers also put to good use the expertise they had gained in sheep ranching in Utah.

As the years passed, the Canadian cowboys became a mixture of American westerners, Ontario farm boys, English immigrants, and boys born on the western frontier. They included Anglos, blacks, Mexicans, Indians, halfbreeds, and men from every social class on the continent. But their teachers and their role models were the cowboys who had learned their trade in Texas, Wyoming, and other centres of America's ranching West.

They had the American "savvy" when it came to handling cattle but they also learned to cope with unique situations such as blizzards at calving time, and with clothing and horse gear adapted to meet Canadian conditions. If they wandered beyond the cattle ranges, they often went to Vancouver or Winnipeg—rather than Seattle and Chicago—and became accustomed to their friends going "home" to England, sometimes on a cattle boat. They watched polo being played at gymkhanas, saw red-coated Mounted Police enforcing the law, and tried to keep up with the West's changing but always conservative liquor laws. They were cowboys through and through, but they were Canadian cowboys.

THE GALICIAN AND THE COWBOY

IN THE EARLY 1900S, CALGARY JOURNALIST L.V. KELLY
WROTE A SERIES OF STORIES ENTITLED "THE MAN FROM THE EAST,"
TELLING ABOUT EASTERN GREENHORNS WHO HAD AMUSING EXPERIENCES
IN THE WEST. THIS ACCOUNT APPEARED IN THE 17 NOVEMBER 1906 ISSUE OF
THE CALGARY HERALD.

The Man from the East yawned with ennui. The weather was just snappy enough to make one's blood jump and he longed for action. Lighting a cigar he strolled down Eighth Avenue watching closely for items of interest which might lead to interesting disclosures. Just in front of him walked two men. One was a young fellow dressed in the regulation Stetson, with sweater, high-heeled boots, and canvas clothing. A few paces in advance of him walked, or rather slouched, another young fellow. His face was brown, even the corners of his mouth and two fingers of his left hand. He wore a battered soft hat, strenuously used, overalls, and a heavy sheepskin coat thrown open in front and showing a hard-used flannel shirt.

A hearty hand lighted on the shoulder of the Man from the East. And put it about two inches out of true. A heartier voice saluted him and the Man from the East turned to meet a rancher acquaintance.

"What you doing?" said the hearty voice.

"Sizing up pedestrians," said the Man from the East. "I have just managed to place those two fellows in front."

"Who are they?" asked the acquaintance, glancing over the two in question.

"One is a cowboy in town for a holiday, and the fellow in the sheepskin coat is a Galician [Ukrainian] or some other outlander," elucidated the Man from the East complacently. "You can't fool me."

"Very clever deduction," smiled the curious western man. "Say, come to my place this afternoon. I'm going to have some horses broke."

The Man from the East accepted with alacrity and the western man became curious again. "How could you place those fellows so accurately?" he asked, with a quizzical look at his companion.

"Oh," said the Man from the East carelessly, "that's easy for me. The cowboy had his Sunday clothes on. New riding boots, new clothes and fringed gauntlets. His face was tanned and his shoulders had a slight stoop brought on by long, tiresome riding. The other fellow was easier—full hardened hands, soiled and dilapidated hat, sheepskin coat. All pointed to a laborer, and he looked foreign so I called him Galician."

"That's good work," said the western man admiringly. "Don't miss the broncho show at my place."

The Man from the East waited feverishly for the time to come when he could see some real riding. Dinner was bolted and he rushed to a livery to hire a rig. In an hour he was at the ranche and looking at the collection of wild-eyed ponies and horses in the circular enclosure, next to the big pasture. A few men strolled aimlessly around, or sat listlessly on the top bars of the corral.

Finally one said it would be a good idea to

rope the outlaw horse and have it ready when the "buster" arrived. A man jumped from the rail and strode into the middle of the corral. The horses crowded away and stood watching with high heads and steady eyes. Every movement of the lone man brought a corresponding move from the horses.

"Is the big bay the one?" called the rope artist, and he was told it was. The man slowly swung the rope and the horses started with increasing speed to run around the edge of the enclosure. With almost human intelligence, the big horse hugged the fence, seeming to know he was wanted, and the other horses crowded between the roper and his quarry. At the psychological moment the coils straightened and the noose dropped square on the bay's neck.

Silently the great horse reared and struck blindly in hopes of landing on the horrible thing that was choking his life out. Other men ran and seized the rope; it was put around a post and every inch of slack was taken advantage of until the horse's head was tight against the edge of the corral and he swayed dizzily on his feet. A saddle was quickly but cautiously thrown on the captive's back. He dazedly allowed the profanation, and then the "buster" appeared.

The Man from the East, who had been exuberantly hugging a corral post in the excess of his pleasurable excitement, gasped with surprise and then furtively looked for his friend the rancher.

The broncho buster was his "Galician" of the forenoon.

Stepping quickly to the horse, the rider swung himself on as the animal plunged and attempted to rear. The rope was immediately loosened and the frantic horse, bawling with rage, reared and struck and plunged, and finally settled down to some whirlwind bucking. High in the air he went, head down and four flint-like feet bunched together. He hit the ground "sixty times a second," as a cowboy stated, with all the weight of his rigid body and the added jolt of the drop. Plunging, "sun-fishing," "swapping ends," and straight bucking seemed to the green on-looker to be more than human endurance could stand, but the rider stayed firmly in the saddle and with one careless spur raked the fighting horse's neck while the other heel aggravatingly rasped the animal's hip.

"What do you think of my 'Galician?'" asked a voice, and the Man from the East knew his time had come.

"Who was the other fellow?" he meekly countered.

"Bank clerk from up north," said the rancher. "He got the riding stoop from pushing a pen."

LIFE ON THE RANGE

THE TYPICAL COWBOY

MANY EARLY RANCHES NEEDED THE EXPERTISE THAT ONLY A SKILLED COWBOY
COULD PROVIDE. SOME WERE EMPLOYED TO BRING HERDS FROM MONTANA
WHILE OTHERS CARRIED OUT THE ROUTINE DUTIES OF THE RANCH.
A FEW SETTLED DOWN TO LONG-TERM EMPLOYMENT AT A SINGLE RANCH,
EVENTUALLY OWNING THEIR OWN SPREADS, WHILE OTHERS
COULD NEVER STAY IN ONE PLACE FOR LONG.

For them, ranches in Texas, Nebraska, Wyoming, or Canada were all the same. If they could perform their duties from the back of a horse, it didn't matter where they were.

Their titles varied. Some were called cowboys, cowpunchers, or cowhands, while others were buckaroos (a corruption of the Spanish term *vaquero*). Bronc riders were known as horse breakers, peelers, bronc busters, or twisters, while crews included cooks, wranglers (from the Mexican term *caverango*), hoodlum drivers (the men on roundups who drove the wagons containing wood, water, branding irons, etc.), as well as foremen, the wagon bosses, and their assistants, known as straw bosses.

In 1888, Henry Norman, a visitor to the West, was fascinated by cowboys. He saw them everywhere on the streets of Calgary, and day or night a half-dozen could be found lounging in the Royal Hotel. "He is an odd, but on the whole, thoroughly pleasing figure," commented Norman, "especially on horse-back, always loping or cantering smoothly along, an enormous wide brimmed felt hat with an ornamented leather hat band on his head."[1]

He said the typical dress of the cowboy was a "blue flannel shirt, his legs encased in enormous leather trousers called 'chaparejos' (everything the cowboy wears is called by a Mexican name) or more commonly 'chaps,' his stirrups covered by great flopping 'trappaderos,' his reata or lasso coiled at his saddle bow, with thin, single-rein hackamore or plaited bridle held delicately between his thumb and finger, and contrasting oddly with his enormous spurs, big enough to disembowel his small steed." Norman observed that the average cowboy usually had a cartridge belt round his waist and that while in the saddle he carried a revolver in a pocket of his chaps. "It is only when on foot," he noted, "that the cowboy carried his shooting iron on his hip."

Over the years, the basic dress of the cowboy

Although travellers and journalists seemed to think that all cowboys wore chaps, sombreros, and revolvers, early photographs show that wasn't true. The cowboys in this group near Jumping Pound in the late 1880s are wearing a variety of clothing and hats, and there isn't a revolver in sight. *(Left to right, front row)*: W. McPherson, W.W. Stuart, B. Alford, R. Alford, Mr. Ricks, and Percy Johnson; *(back row)*: John Bateman *(extreme left)* and Howard Sibbald *(extreme right)*. *Glenbow Archives/NA–1939–2*

remained unchanged. He had a flannel shirt of any colour, usually blue but sometimes striped or checked. He wore denim or corduroy britches covered with leather or angora chaps, a neckerchief, sombrero, leather riding boots with high heels, and spurs. In winter a buffalo coat and in summer a buckskin or cloth jacket topped his ensemble. A long slicker was carried in a roll behind his saddle.

But not everyone dressed that way. Johnny Franklin, a noted bronc buster, usually wore a jacket, vest, and cloth cap. In fact, vests were quite popular. Others liked stiff-brimmed hats similar to what the Mounted Police wore or even ordinary narrow-brimmed hats. And many eschewed the use of revolvers and cartridge belts, except when they were on the range, where a gun might be needed to shoot a wolf, kill an injured steer, or bring home

wild meat for supper. But it is interesting how often a cowboy ran into some trouble on the range and had no firearm of any kind. Some didn't even own guns, while others found them to be too cumbersome on routine rides. More often, they took guns if there was some chance of killing birds or big game for food, or if wolves had been seen in the area and their hides were bringing a good price.

A visitor to a roundup camp near Lethbridge in 1907 noted that every part of a cowboy's outfit was designed for a specific use.

The broad-brimmed hat is far more efficient in protecting the eyes from the sun than is a straw hat. The black silk handkerchief protects the neck from sunburn, and the chaps are comfortable for riding and keeping the legs warm in a way which nothing else would. The heels of the

A.T. Inskip, a cowboy at the Bow River Horse Ranch near Cochrane, poses astride his horse in the 1890s. *Glenbow Archives/NA-2084-48*

top boots are made very high in order to prevent the feet slipping through the large Western stirrups, for the cowboy does not ride with merely the toe in the stirrup, and if by any chance they should be thrown it is a matter of life or death to have the feet free, as otherwise they might be dragged for miles.[2]

Spurs were essential. And these were not useless little ornaments but huge plated spurs with gigantic rowels. In 1881, when journalist W.H. Williams walked into a

Fort Macleod restaurant full of cowboys, he saw that "nearly all wore heavy Mexican spurs, which clanked and jingled as they walked about in a manner that would have made a blind man think he was in the company of a lot of convicts in transit."[3]

Almost from the time the first American cowboy arrived, there were "greenhorns" who tried to emulate him in dress and mannerisms. The real cowboys scorned these "dudes." In 1885, Charles Wood, editor of the *Macleod Gazette*, commented that "every man who lives or works on a cow ranch, wears chaps and a big hat, and flourishes a six shooter, is not necessarily or probably a cowboy. The general cowboy, who attends to his work and does it well, has not the time to parade around the country showing off."[4] Ten years later, a cowboy at the Little Bow roundup camp also complained about the fakes who were giving real cowboys a bad name. He said they drank lemonade, acted drunk, and made the girls believe they were dangerous outlaws. They "dress themselves up in the garb of cowboys, spurs the size of small cart wheels, hat cut with a scissors and covered with mud to look old and tough."[5] They were, he concluded, "too lazy to plough and too shiftless to own cattle." Some people derisively called them "T. Eaton cowboys"—a forerunner of the later term "drug store cowboys."

The "dude" was often a lazy useless youth who affected the dress of a real cowboy to impress others. If he ever worked on a ranch, it was probably in some menial task in the barn, and was of

Vests were obviously very popular amongst this Willow Creek roundup crew in 1895. *(Left to right)* Ben McDonald, George Winder, Charlie Millar, Charlie Vaile, Mike Herman, Charlie Haines, Jim Johnson, George McDonald, captain of the roundup Duncan McIntosh, rancher George Lane, Walter Wake, and two unknown. *Glenbow Archives/NA-118-3*

(Left): Charles Inderwick, newly arrived from England, is seen here *circa* 1884 in the best fashion of a western cowboy, right down to the whip and six-shooter. He was owner of the North Fork Ranch. *Glenbow Archives/NA-1365-1*

(Right): Gordon Forster, whose family had a ranch in the Cessford area of eastcentral Alberta, donned full cowboy dress for this photograph in 1907. *Glenbow Archives/NA-101-12*

short duration. He had a tendency to be boastful and arrogant, swaggering through streets and into bars as if he were a tough gunfighter. Yet he was careful not to play his role when real cowboys were in town.

These phonies should not be confused with the immigrant lads who dressed as cowboys to have their photographs taken for the folks back in the Old Country. It was quite common for young Britishers to bedeck themselves in all the finery of a western cowman and distribute the resulting photographs far and wide. In 1906, a reporter noted that "the English fellows around Calgary have a way, doncherknow, of having their photographs taken a la broncho buster and sending it home to the old folks just to let them see how the son is doing in the wild and wooly west."[6] In one instance, a young man dressed entirely in western gear and with his horse by his side had his photo taken in front of the Calgary City Hall. The resulting picture

was then sent to England. "In five or six weeks an acknowledgement came, the folks at home congratulating him on his smart appearance, and also on the tidy and well kept appearance of his horse stable."

Even experienced rancher Fred Stimson could not resist posturing when he went to Chicago in 1881. While there, he outfitted himself in a fringed buckskin shirt, brand new leather chaps, and stiff-brimmed hat. Then, leaning on a tooled leather saddle and with a long quirt elegantly dangling from his wrist, he posed for a studio photograph.

The cowboy's most important possessions were his horse and saddle. His horse was sometimes referred to as a cow pony or cayuse and was usually the best the cowboy could afford. It was often valued more for its stamina than its appearance. A man needed a reliable pony that worked with its master on the range, travelling long distances across open country, and coping with summer storms and winter blizzards. On roundups, a cowboy usually rode his own horse only when moving camp. The rest of the time, he had access to the ranch's remuda, sometimes wearing out two or three horses a day during the difficult task of locating cattle and bringing them to the main herd.

In order to impress or amuse the folks back home, some Englishmen at the British American Ranch in the late 1880s posed for a tableau they entitled, "A Fallen Villain." *Glenbow Archives/NA-239-3*

Cowboys often bragged about the intelligence of their horses. One man claimed that once he had designated a cow or calf in a herd, he could turn his horse loose without a saddle or bridle and it would bring the critter to the branding fire. Of course, no one had actually seen him do it. But there was no question that a well-trained horse was the cowboy's best ally. It kept a rope tight after an animal had been roped, allowed itself to be guided by knee pressure when cutting out a cow from a herd, and generally made life easier for its owner.

The cowboy's ability to control his horse often amazed visitors. In 1884, a newly arrived settler from Winnipeg commented that "there is a trick in riding a keose [cayuse] which requires a severe and dangerous apprenticeship before one can be said to have mastered it. The way a horse will go scampering over a prairie punctured with badger holes is only exceeded by the way in which he will try to throw you when he is not running full tilt."[7]

Many of the early saddles used by Canadian cowboys were American made, adapted from styles originating in Texas, California, and Oregon. While all had a common origin in the conquistadors, over the years regional saddlers introduced modifications that they believed resulted in more efficient and comfortable saddles than those made by their competitors. It was all a matter of personal choice. By 1884, there were two saddlery shops in Calgary and one in Fort Macleod, all of which usually copied American styles. The early models tended to have high pummels and cantles. For example, an Oregon-type saddle of the 1890s had round skirts, a short tree, a horn that was high and fully sloped, and a high, straight cantle. The Texas saddle of the same period had a long tree, narrow fork, and straight cantle, with the seat and side jockeys being made in one piece. The fenders and stirrup leathers were wide, and the skirts long and deep. The long tree gave the rider room to shift from one side to the other to ease the numbness in the seat of his pants.

The saddle used in breaking horses was specially designed for that purpose. It had a very high

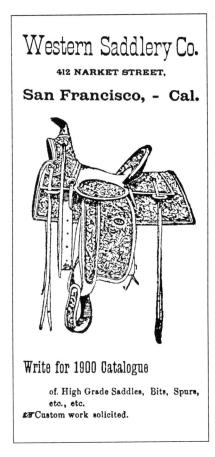

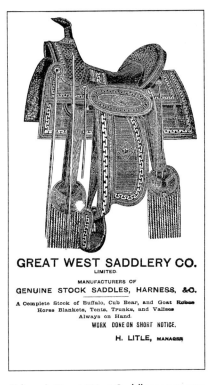

(Left): This advertisement for a California stock saddle appeared in the *Macleod Gazette* during the winter of 1900–01.

(Above): Great West Saddlery was one of the largest firms of its kind in western Canada. This saddle was advertised in the *Macleod Gazette,* 18 January 1901.

in 1890 saw a number of horses being broken to saddle. According to what he was told, an animal would be driven into a corral, roped by the front feet, and brought down. Another cowboy would run up and sit on its head while a hackamore was put in place. The horse would then be led or dragged around the corral until it was "halter broke." Then the horse would be saddled and the bronc buster would take over. The bronc would rear and buck, but the cowboy would stay in the saddle and ride it to a standstill. After two or three such rides the horse would be considered broken.

But it didn't always work that way. While the visitor at the Begg Ranch watched, he learned that there was no professional bronc rider among the crew. The horse had been thrown and halter broke, but who was going to ride? He explained:

It then turns out that nearly everybody has something the matter with him. It is at times like this that one finds out what fearful and noxious diseases your friends are suffering from … At last some benighted idiot volunteers to ride and climbs on. The bronco bucks backward, forward, sideways, and round in a circle, his back arched and his head sticking out between his hind legs, while the poor devil on his back clings to the horn of the saddle and looks as if he would give all he possessed and a darned sight more to be sitting peacefully on the prairie.

cantle and sloped back. The forks also were high and sloped in front, the horn being high enough so that the rider's hand could hook around it when climbing aboard. No wonder the saddle seat was called the "hurricane deck." When riding a bronc, the cowboy sat erect in the saddle, ready to shift his weight depending upon the movement of the beast.

There were two kinds of bucking horses the bronc rider had to deal with. One was the ordinary range horse that had never been ridden and needed to be broken to the saddle. The other was the outlaw, a wild thrashing beast that refused to be tamed. The range horse—unless it turned out to be an outlaw—was handled in a routine fashion, a good bronc buster being able to break seven or eight in a day's work.

A visitor to Alex Begg's ranch near High River

This cowboy is ready to pick out a horse for breaking at a ranch in the Milk River area. *Glenbow Archives/NA–777-1*

We stand around and grin and shout, "Stay with him." "Hang to him." "Stick your spurs In," and other remarks of the same kind to him.

At last the broncho, getting tired of bucking, starts to run, and he and the herder, who is also mounted, and who is supposed to follow and see that the bronco does not run over a cut bank or get into trouble, disappear across the prairie.[8]

The visitor himself tried to ride one of the broncs and said it was an experience he'd never forget. "After you have been on a few minutes you don't know which is your head and which your heels, or what your name is, or how old you are. All you feel is an indistinct impression that one end of your spine is sticking out about four inches and bumping against the saddle, and that the other is sticking about the same distance into your brain and is working about in there."[9]

Breaking an outlaw horse was a different matter. In later years, some became famous as rodeo horses because they would never willingly submit to the saddle. As a cowboy once said, "An outlaw is often conquered but never subdued."[10]

Wilfred Helmer had a rough ride while breaking a horse at the Forster Ranch in 1909. *Glenbow Archives/NA–101-42*

When western novelist Luke Allan visited a ranch in the Medicine Hat district, he watched attempts to break an outlaw. It was thrown, blindfolded by having a coat thrown over its head, and saddled. When the cowboy was astride the horse, he signalled for the hobbles and blindfold to be removed. As the horse leapt to its feet, the bronc buster slipped his feet into the stirrups and prepared for the ride. As the intention was to break the horse, not simply control it, the rider gave the outlaw its way for the first few seconds before tightening the reins. His next task was to predict the movements of the thundering, snorting beast. It suddenly lowered its head to its front knees, arched its back and pitched straight into the air, landing on the hard earth with a jarring thud. From there it spun into a rapid turn, "sunfishing" or twisting its body at the same time. It next moved forward in long jumps, landing with stiffened front legs, then kicking out its hind legs. Each time, the rider shifted his weight, maintained his balance, and prepared for the next onslaught.

The horse, failing to unseat the rider, went into a frenzy of snorting and snapping, making a blind

dash against a fence as though willing to sacrifice its own life rather than lose its freedom. Finally, after many attempts to throw the rider, the outlaw recognized it had met its match and stopped stock still, its head lowered. Once he was sure it was not a ruse, the bronc buster dismounted and left the tired, lathered beast for the other cowboys to turn loose from the corral. But this horse was a real outlaw; it had lost a battle, not the war. The next time the bronc buster, or anyone else, tried to mount it, the whole process would be repeated. In the end, such an outlaw was either turned loose on the ranch, destroyed, or—after the days of professional fairs—sold to a supplier of rodeo stock.

The cowboy had several other accoutrements besides his saddle. One was the lariat (taken from the Spanish term *la reata*), which usually was suspended from the right side of the saddle horn. Before the introduction of hemp rope, these were generally made of braided rawhide. A cowboy often passed the time during the long winter months by braiding a rope that was so perfect in width, weave, and size that it could be thrown with

amazing accuracy. Shorter ropes from twenty to twenty-five feet long were preferred for corral work, while ropes up to sixty feet in length were used on the range, particularly when bringing in wild stock.

In southern Alberta, cowboys often used the dally style of roping. Dallying (from the Spanish *da la vuelta* or wrapping) meant that the cowboy roped a critter before wrapping the other end around the saddle horn. The alternate method was to tie the rope securely to the horn before throwing the loop. As one old cowman remarked, "The advantage of the dally was that if the roper got into trouble—tangled in the brush, horse pulled down, or charged by the enraged critter—he could get rid of the rope and get loose. If the rope was tied, there was no way to get free in a hurry, and if the cinch broke, he lost his saddle as well as his rope."[11]

A good hemp rope had to be broken in before it could be properly used. It was stretched, sometimes held over a fire to singe off the "whiskers" and ultimately worked so smooth in the cowboy's hands that it slipped easily through its loop while singing through the air. Such a rope was put to use from the

Good ropes were needed when working in the branding corral. In this 1901 view, calves are roped and branded by an experienced crew of cowboys. *Glenbow Archives/NA-748-44*

time its owner arose in the morning. On the range it could be employed to pull a cow out of a bog, rescue a man in trouble at a river crossing, help drag a chuckwagon out of a mudhole, or be a source of fun when roping a wolf or coyote on the dead run. A rope could also serve as a temporary corral, as a bull whip to move lagging cattle, and even to haul a load of firewood into camp. In the corral, the cowboy might use it to drag the cows and calves to the branding fire, rope a bronc for breaking, or bring a fractious horse to a snubbing post for saddling.

Horsehair was also used for making ropes, as well as for hackamores and halters, the most attractive being braided with alternate hanks of black and white hair in a "salt and pepper" design. Hair ropes were seldom used in the corral, as they kinked too easily and were too light to throw, but served well as tie ropes. Some cowboys became known for their skill in braiding hair taken from manes and tails. Their craftsmanship was always in demand.

The other equipment of the working cowboy included his horse gear (quirt, saddlebags, bridle, etc.) and his personal possessions, which, while travelling, were kept in his "war bag." Behind his saddle was his bedroll, sometimes called his "shakedown." The itinerant cowboy could carry all his earthly possessions on his body and his horse. At night, his bedroll was laid out beside a campfire and his saddle became his pillow.

The larger ranches employed about ten cowboys in summer and half that number in the winter. And, contrary to their name, many were not "boys." A visitor to a cow camp near Lethbridge in 1907 noted that the crew ranged in age from twenty to sixty. That included cowboys, wranglers, the foreman, and cook. A small ranch might employ only one "hired hand" but take on more during a roundup or cattle drive. Often, a man starting his own spread with twenty or thirty cattle became rancher, cowboy, cook, and wrangler, all rolled into one.

During the winter months, some cowboys were kept on at ranches, where they worked for their room and board. No salaries were paid until the

Each cowboy had his "war bag" in which he kept his personal possessions. This man, working on the Milk River roundup, delves into his gear for tools for his morning shave. *Glenbow Archives/NA-777-21*

spring work started. And they were glad to have the lodgings, for many of them were as broke as when they arrived. Others might be lucky enough to find winter work in places like butcher shops or livery stables, but more often, several batched together in some isolated cabin and managed to survive on short rations until spring.

But while they were on the job, their main concern was the cattle herds. While the ranches started with Texas longhorns and rangy mixes of Shorthorns and Durhams, the owners of the big spreads began to upgrade the quality of the stock almost immediately. Purebred bulls had a dramatic impact on ranches where owners kept their stock segregated within their lease. For example, shortly after completion of the CPR, the Cochrane Ranch was able to export cattle that found immediate markets because of their quality. Yet one of the frustrations of the large-scale ranchers was that outfits with only a few head of cattle usually had scrubby bulls, and on the open range they often mated with the upgraded stock. In fact, one owner swore that his well-bred cattle seemed to prefer the runty scrubs over the purebred imports. The only solution was to keep their cattle close herded and to drive alien stock off their lease. But this was easier said than done, considering the large numbers of small leaseholders scattered through the country.

In 1889, ranchers tried a new approach and imported yearling and two-year-old Ontario and Manitoba cattle with a view to fattening them on the succulent prairie grass and then selling them. The Quorn Ranch brought in the first two thousand from Ontario, and within a few years other ranches were doing the same. In 1895, for example, the Walrond Ranch imported five hundred head from Ontario, buying them for $10 to $20 and hoping to make a good profit. In 1902, a rancher estimated a trainload of four-year-old stockers would fetch $58.50 apiece at the market.

These cattle were known as "dogies." This term had a variety of meanings; as one old rancher explained, "If you came from the East and didn't know much and tried to put up more or less of a front, the cow-punchers would call you a 'dogie.' It's something like a tenderfoot, only all tenderfeet ain't 'dogies.'"[12]

Many veteran cowboys hated dogies; they thought they were stupid. Unlike western range cattle, they had trouble foraging for themselves and were constantly causing problems. One cowboy said they were always getting stuck in mudholes, drowning in streams, falling over cutbanks, chewing up someone's saddle, or breaking into settlers' gardens. He also complained:

> Drive 'em off on to the range; do they bunch together like ord'nary civilized cattle? No sir, they jist saunters off in ones, twos and threes, like kids at a picnic, only they keep saunterin' and if you don't head 'em off, next time you want 'em they'll probably be somewheres down atween Milk River and the Gulf of Mexico.[13]

But there were profits to be made on dogies, even if their mortality rate was much higher than prairie-bred cattle. As a result, cowboys had to spend more time on the range, keeping the "pilgrim" cattle from wandering away or killing themselves. One cowboy was convinced that after a dogie had caused all the trouble possible, it would just "find a warm corner and lie down an' die. Why do they die? Just pure cussedness, an' that's the truth."[14]

Yet the cowboy did his job well, whether it was coping with the ruggedness of a Texas longhorn or the stupidity of a dogie. His lifestyle was summed up by a journalist in 1907 in the following manner:

> The cowpuncher is accustomed to risking life and limb. He is continually in danger from badger holes, cattle, horses or rattlesnakes. He is probably also one of the hardest worked beings on the face of the earth, and his life is spent in solitude, without the luxuries of civilization. Much of his work is not merely physically hard, but it wears on the nerves, and is extremely monotonous. But in spite of the long hours, the hard work, the inclement weather, ranging from a hundred degrees in the shade (and no shade within miles) to fifty below zero; in spite of the danger, the solitude; in spite of all these discomforts, men are fascinated by the life. They are free from the conventionality of civilization. They respect no man save for his worth.[15]

This description is similar to the modern romantic image of the cowboy, who is seen as the epitome of honesty, freedom, and hard work. According to a "Code of the Range" circulated in recent years, a cowboy is said to be one who always helps his neighbour, feeds a stranger and his horse, and maintains his free and independent spirit.[16] The 1907 journalistic view of the cowboy seems to be a forerunner of the mystique that later engulfed the cowboy all across North America.

FAR FROM HOME

A favourite western story concerns a Lethbridge doctor who treated a very ill cowboy. When the man was being released, he learned that the doctor intended to visit Europe.

"Then you must call on some friends of mine who will see you pleasantly entertained," said the cowboy. He sat and wrote a letter of introduction to the Marquis of Maitland at a castle in England.

"You know the gentleman, I hope?"

"Rather," said the cowboy, "that gentleman happens to be my father."[1]

Not all cowboys were landed gentry, nor were they British. They came from everywhere. Wanderlust drew some of them to the frontier, or the romance of cowboy stories in dime novels. Others were attracted by the potential of a new land, where a working cowboy might become a prosperous rancher. Many simply drifted into ranching after working in logging camps or mines, where the main qualification was physical strength. And still others had known no other life but the open range. In the bunkhouse there might be a man with a Texas drawl, another with a French accent, a halfbreed from the area, and someone who was decidedly English. Nicknames like "Tennessee," "Irish," "Colorado," and "Frenchy" were common although these did not always denote origins. For example, a young cowboy fresh out from Ireland was nicknamed "Missouri" because he had to be shown how to do everything. Another was called "Dutch" when he was really a German.

Initially, most cowboys were from the American West, but they were soon joined by "pilgrims" from other parts of the world who ultimately developed into seasoned cowhands. Besides Americans, the largest numbers came from Britain and eastern Canada, or were born and raised on the western Canadian prairies. When the Dominion census was taken in 1891, the enumerators often did not distin-

guish between ranchers, cowboys, and foremen, but they did show that the population was diverse. On a couple of ranches near High River, of those listed as "cowboys," eight were American, three English, two Scottish, and one each was from Ireland, Ontario, and France. At Maple Creek, there was no occupation listed as "cowboy"; the closest was "cattle herder" or "cow herder." Of these, nine were from Britain, four from Quebec, three from the United States, three from Ontario, and one each from Norway and France.

A notable American expatriate was Everett C. Johnson, a veteran cowboy by the time he arrived in Canada. Ebb (as he was called) was born in Virginia in 1860 and was raised in Minnesota. When

Everett C. Johnson was a veteran American cowboy who became foreman of the 76 Ranch in 1889. His experiences may have been the basis for Owen Wister's classic novel *The Virginian. Glenbow Archives/NA-2924-2*

he was fifteen, he started driving a stagecoach in the Black Hills and in 1876 he became a cowboy in Wyoming, where he rode with Buffalo Bill Cody and Portugee Phillips. He became foreman of the Powder River Cattle Company and was captain of the Johnson County roundup at nineteen. He also was friends with the Sundance Kid and with some of the men who took part in the Johnson County War. According to Johnson's son, "He became a friend and hunting companion of Owen Wister, who used my father's character and some of his adventures in the book *The Virginian*."[2]

In 1886, Johnson was sent by the Powder River Cattle Company to Canada to scout out a possible location for a new ranch. He chose a lease along Mosquito Creek near the present town of Nanton. Because of its brand, this ranch became famous as the 76. When it was sold in 1889, Johnson took over as foreman of the Bar U but left there to marry the niece of a local rancher; the Sundance Kid was his best man. Some time later, Johnson established his own spread, the Two Bar Ranch, near Cochrane.

A typical American cowboy was Ed McPherson, who was born in Missouri and "might almost say I was born on a hoss."[3] At age fourteen, he became a drover with a trail herd bound for Abilene, Kansas, and the next year he was on the Chisholm Trail, taking cattle from Jesse Chisholm's ranch on the North Canadian River to the railhead at Wichita, Kansas. The next few years saw him in Dodge City ("at Boot Hill there were only three gravestones marked out of the 32 there"), the Daggett Ranch in Texas, along the Pecos, and then down into Mexico. From there he drifted back to Texas, north to Indian Territory, then to Billings, Montana. He recalled:

I heard that Crystal [Cresswell] and Day were starting a ranch in Canada. I hired on with them to work on the Turkey Track with the headquarters 25 miles southeast of Swift Current. I came up in 1904 and we had two good years. Then came the hard winter of 1906. That smashed the Turkey Track. They lost 18,000 head.

McPherson decided to move on, so he settled near Wood Mountain, where he leased land and ran cattle on Horse Creek until going bust during the Depression. He struggled alone at the ranch to make ends meet and died broke at the age of seventy-two—"a cowboy in the truest sense."

Another cowboy from the American "Wild West" was David Crocket Cantwell, who was born in Kentucky and glorified in the title of "Major." During the Civil War, he was a member of Quantrell's guerilla band and rode with Jesse James and the Younger brothers. He claimed to have left them before they became involved in bank and train robberies, but he was arrested on suspicion of being part of the James Gang. After his release, he moved to Texas where he was known as "Handsome Dave." There he went into partnership with two other cowboys but is said to have killed both of them when they cheated him out of his property. Some time later, he "was one of the principals in an elopement which resulted in the Major being confined for a time, although he was afterward acquitted."[4] His next move took him to Chihuahua, Mexico, where he worked on the ranch of De Laval Beresford, a British nobleman.

Cantwell might have remained in Mexico had a scandal not occurred at the ranch in 1902 when Beresford fell in love with Flora Wolfe, a black woman. Because of this relationship, his neighbours shunned him, and Beresford decided to look for lands elsewhere. At this time, Canadian ranchers were experimenting with Mexican cattle, bringing them north by rail, fattening them over the summer, and then selling them. Beresford sent Cantwell to scout the area to see if such a program would be feasible for his outfit and, if so, to select a lease. His choice became the Mexico Ranch on the Red Deer River.

Six thousand head of Mexican cattle arrived by rail that year, and the U Bar C brand was registered in Beresford's name. Cantwell brought several thousand more cattle from Mexico in the next couple of years and was planning to marry his childhood sweetheart when he died suddenly in Medicine Hat in 1906. He was described as a man "well known across the border in the great free range cattle days of Texas and Kansas."[5] Interestingly, Beresford was killed in a train wreck a few weeks later when returning south from his Alberta ranch. The Circle Ranch then acquired the lease, while the buildings became part of a homestead taken over by Hansel "Happy Jack" Jackson, who had been the local foreman since the first cattle had been shipped from Mexico. Over the years, Jackson

Hansel "Happy Jack" Jackson came north from Mexico to the Red Deer River about 1902 with cattle belonging to De Laval Beresford, a British nobleman. When the owner was killed in a train accident, the eccentric Jackson acquired the land and became a recluse. *Glenbow Archives/NA-78-1*

became a virtual recluse at the ranch and was remembered as one of the most eccentric settlers in the district.[6]

By coincidence, when Beresford's common-law wife lived near the Red Deer River, she was only a few miles away from Canada's most famous black cowboy, John Ware. Born a slave about 1845 in Texas, Ware became a cowboy after the Civil War. He came to Canada with the Bar U trail drive in 1882 and worked as a bronc rider and cowhand there until 1884. He then moved to the Quorn Ranch, where he took charge of the horse herd. At the 1885 roundup Charlie Wood noted, "The horse is not running on the prairie which John cannot ride."[7]

Three years later, Ware started his own ranch on Sheep Creek and married the daughter of a black cabinetmaker. When homesteaders settled on grazing lands around his ranch, Ware moved to the Red Deer River in 1902 and ranched there until he was killed in a riding accident in 1905.

During his lifetime, Ware experienced some of the discrimination levelled at all blacks, but his skill and personality tempered the hostility. According to historian David Breen, "The stories that have contributed to his emergence as a regional folk hero centre upon his remarkable horsemanship, his prodigious strength, his good-natured humour and general kindness, and his loyalty to friends and neighbours, as well as his willingness to take novice cowhands under his guidance."[8]

Not all blacks were treated so kindly. One day when a black stranger walked into a Medicine Hat hotel bar, Tony Day, a Texan, "removed his foot from the rail and drawled, 'Niggah! Pfft'" and the man left.[9]

Although they were not often mentioned in newspapers and literature of the day, black cowboys were fairly common in Canada. For example, Tom Rengald was considered one of the top hands at the Chipman Ranch at the turn of the century, while Felix Luttrell (nicknamed "Big Enough" because of his size) was an experienced rider in the Little Bow Pool. One of the best-known blacks was Green Walters, who came north with Tom Lynch's trail drive in 1883. A cook and cowhand for several

John Ware was one of the most famous bronc riders and cowboys in western Canada. He owned a ranch near Sheep Creek and later moved to the Red Deer River. He was killed in a riding accident in 1905. Ware is seen here about 1896 with his wife and children, Robert and Nettie. *Glenbow Archives/NA-263-1*

outfits, including the Oxley, Bar U, and the CC, Walters took part in the roundups and slowly developed his own herd, registering the Ox Yoke brand.

Walters was remembered for his excellent singing voice and sense of humour. When Englishman J.L. Douglas visited the CC Ranch in 1886 he described him as "a sort of general servant, who is about the most original specimen I have ever come across; he is a very little fellow and built in the most extraordinary way imaginable; he sang plantation and other minstrel songs all the time and kept us in roars of laughter and the more we laughed the funnier he became; he would be worth a small

fortune to anyone who could transplant him home as a music hall artiste."[10]

About 1890, just as he was ready to move to his own ranch on the Highwood River, Walters froze his feet and lost most of his toes. Crippled, he was forced to quit ranching and moved to Kansas.

Other black cowboys gained attention when some noteworthy incident occurred. In 1908, for example, lightning struck and killed Jim Whitford at the Hyssop Ranch near Chin Coulee. He had been gathering horses with four other cowboys when a lightning bolt picked him from the five during a thunderstorm. "The unfortunate fellow had been around Lethbridge for seven or eight years," commented a reporter, "and had worked for several different horse and cattle outfits . . . On the ranch he was always a favorite; he was a hard working fellow and consistently steady in his habits; everybody had a good word for 'Nigger Jim' as he was universally known."[11]

Ranchers also had a good word for an unnamed black cowboy who participated in a Calgary rodeo soon after the turn of the century. When a steer broke loose during the bulldogging event, endangering the crowd, the cowboy "caught a horn, threw his body across the neck, grabbed a nostril and brought him down. He held him 'til men on horses came up to drive him out."[12] Later in the show, a bucking bronc threw its rider and the same black cowboy galloped alongside the outlaw, grabbed the horn, vaulted into the saddle, and rode the horse in. "There was no need for him to do

John Ware's brand was advertised in the *Calgary Tribune*, 12 December 1892. Originally called the four nines, or the four canes, it was later reduced to three.

this," commented Fred Ings, "but it was a very spectacular trick and brought loud applause from the onlookers."[13]

Even rarer than black cowboys were female cowboys. Most of the women involved with range life were either wives or daughters of ranch owners. Some were accomplished riders who helped around the corrals and at branding time, but seldom, if ever, were they included in the general roundups or the gruelling work of breaking horses.

A woman described simply as Jane was one exception. She had been living with her abusive husband on a Montana ranch when about 1906 she finally pointed a gun at him and told him to get out. She sent her two daughters away to school, gathered up six hundred head of cattle, and left for Canada. After she crossed the line near Breed Creek, she dug a cave into the side of a coulee and pitched a tent in front of it. She remained there, squatting on land leased by the Milk River Cattle Company, until one day two lessees told her to leave.

"You're on our land," they said, "and we're going to push you off."

She drew herself up to her full height. "Oh, no," she said quietly. "You used the wrong word there, gentlemen. No one is going to push me off anything. If you ask me nicely, I'll go, but no one has ever pushed me anywhere. Before you push me, I'll go into that tent, I'll bring out a .45 and I'll fill you full of lead."[14] When they changed their demand to a request, she rounded up her herd and, with a hired cowhand, went north to the Medicine Hat area. However, misfortune followed her, for she arrived at the new range late in the year, just before the terrible winter of 1906–07. As a result, her entire herd perished, and she was obliged to return to Big Timber, Montana.

She wasn't the only woman who was handy with guns. In 1900, a man insulted the daughter of rancher when she walked down a street in Cardston. She immediately returned home, armed herself with a revolver, and forced her detractor to fall on his knees on main street and make a public apology. The woman paid a ten-dollar fine and costs for her performance.

There were few women residing on ranches in the early days, so many cowboys and ranchers did their own domestic chores. Here, a man at the Wineglass Ranch near Fort Macleod catches up on his laundry. *Glenbow Archives/NA–4035-191*

Although women on the frontier seldom participated in cowboy life, they were excellent observers. Three notable examples are Agnes Skrine, Mary Inderwick, and Evelyn Springett.

Agnes Skrine was the wife of Walter Skrine, a successful English rancher in the High River district. She later became famous as an Irish poetess, writing under the name of Moira O'Neill. In 1898, when she wrote "A Lady's Life on a Ranche" for the distinguished *Blackwood's Edinburgh Magazine,* she waxed eloquent about the mountains and wild flowers but said little about the day-to-day ranching activities. Like other wives of well-to-do ranchers, her interests centred on her home and her social life. Her only reference to the outdoors was the pleasure of shooting, fishing, and hunting; her singular comment about cowboys was to complain

about breakfast being late "because the Chinaman had taken a knife to one of the 'boys,' and the boy is holding him down on a chair in the kitchen."[15]

Mary Inderwick was different. She was from Ontario and married an Englishman in 1884 at his North Fork Ranch near Pincher Creek. Rather than being aloof like Agnes Skrine, she was a gregarious woman who did not feel bound by social barriers. In fact, she found many of her husband's effete English friends to be snobs, and preferred the company of cowboys. "They are a nice lot of men," she commented. "I love their attempts to help me appear civilized. Though they ride in flannel shirts they never come to the table in shirt sleeves. They have a black alpaca coat hanging in the shack attached to the house and each one struggles into it to live up to the new regime which began with a bride at the ranche. This is done so enthusiastically and with such good will that I have no qualms of conscience that I am a nuisance."[16]

Instead of staying in the ranch house and confining herself to household duties, Mary took every occasion to accompany her husband out on the range. One day when helping him move cattle from one range to another she had a close run in with three old bulls. They trapped her in a narrow coulee, and only the timely arrival of her husband saved her horse from being gored. "I hardly ever blunder into such difficulties," she commented, "and generally can drive a few cattle all right."[17]

Evelyn Springett was the daughter of Alexander Tilloch Galt, one of the Fathers of Confederation. She married Arthur Springett in 1893 and spent the next ten years at the Oxley Ranch, where her husband was manager. Although busy raising a family, she often rode with her husband to kill a beef for the ranch or to accompany visitors to inspect the cattle. She got along well with the cowboys and even started her own small herd, registering the Circle Arrow brand. She recalled she used to sit "on the top bar of the high corral fence and watch the men at work. Johnnie Franklyn and Billy Stewart were famous 'broncho-busters' in their day, and it was really a wonderful sight to see them ride."[18]

Perhaps the most unusual woman involved with Canadian ranching was Lady Ernestine Hunt, the eldest daughter of the Marquis of Allesbury. A free spirit, she had wandered the globe from South Africa to Australia and by 1903 was training steeplechasers in Ireland. In 1906 she came to western Canada "with the vague idea of starting a ranch" and leased forty thousand acres southwest of Calgary. Her sole interest was in horses, and by the fall of that year she had selected seventeen animals from her herd to be trained in Ireland for the steeplechase. When a reporter met her in Montreal she was personally supervising their loading.

"She is a dark complexioned young woman about 28 years of age," he wrote, "and wore a sombrero hat, black waist, khaki colored skirt reaching to the knees, leather leggings and shoes. Her hair was cut short."[19]

Although the animals were half-wild and the deck hands would not come near them, Lady Ernestine

> had the most absolute confidence in her ability to handle the animals in proper shape. Indeed, she had already succeeded in winning the confidence of the animals as evidenced by the fact that she could handle them just about as she pleased.[20]

Although some women—particularly the wives of foremen—fulfilled the duties of cooks, this position was often taken by Chinese. Some were newly arrived from China and spoke little English but ruled their kitchens like emperors. They often were the butt of jokes, usually crude ones, and were universally referred to as "John." Yet their skill as cooks made them valuable members of the ranch crew. Some, such as Sung Lung at the A7 Ranch and Mow at the CC, remained with a family for years. According to one pioneer,

> Most of these men still wore hair in pigtails and some wore oriental clothing. Some were good horsemen and added to their prestige by their ability to "skin" a four-horse team and a chuckwagon from camp to camp at roundup time.[21]

Louie Hong was a well-known cook who came to Canada shortly after the turn of the century. He found a few odd jobs around Calgary then became a cook for the Pat Burns outfit. He immediately gravitated to the Blackfoot cowboys in the crew—perhaps because they were all "outsiders"—and learned his English from them. On the roundups, the fare was plain to the extreme. He recalled, "The main food was sow belly and prunes, while tea and coffee were made from slough water."[22] Hong later opened a store in Cluny and became one of the leading merchants in the town.

Many of Canada's foothills ranch owners were from England, a few from titled families, and, as a result, a number of younger sons and others came to the West seeking work. Others unrelated to

Mary Inderwick, an Ontario woman, married an English rancher in 1884 and found the western cowboys to be "a nice lot of men." She took every opportunity to accompany her husband out on the range. *Glenbow Archives/NA-1365-2*

nobility also gravitated to ranches in search of employment. Many were well educated and remained in the districts for the rest of their lives, leaving behind a record of their experiences. By comparison, many American cowboys were nomadic to the extreme, only semi-literate, and had no interest in writing about their exploits. The result is that numerous sources exist recording the presence and activities of British-born cowboys.

Claude Gardiner is a good example. When he considered buying a ranch in Canada, a friend suggested he work as a cowboy for a year to see if the kind of life suited him. Accordingly, in 1894 Jim Bell, of Slideout, hired him on at Bellevue Ranch. An accomplished rider, Gardiner was immediately pressed into service for the fall roundup, looking after the remuda and moving the horse herd to each new camp. One of the first people he met was Percy Kennard, son of an English doctor, who had been a cowboy for the Cochrane Ranch for five years. Kennard later started his own ranch near Elkwater Lake. Gardiner immediately took to cowboy life. He wrote home:

> You eat everything off the same plate, a tin one. I was told we did not live as well as some of the other outfits but still we did not do so badly. It was fun to see the bucking horses; there were some every day and it was as good a show as Buffalo Bill's. The men here ride very well; it will be some time before I can tackle a bucking horse.[23]

In late summer, Gardiner moved to the upper range, near the Rocky Mountains, to look after the Bell cattle. He was to spend the next nine months in a line cabin, a log building about fifteen feet square with an adjacent corral. His entire food

Mow was a cook at the CC Ranch near Mosquito Creek. He is seen here working in the ranch kitchen about 1905. Note the pages from old magazines that paper the walls.
Glenbow Archives/NA-2307-49

supply consisted of flour, bacon, dried beans, dried apples, tea, sugar, baking powder, pepper, salt, and tins of tomatoes and corn. Fresh meat was supplied during winter; meanwhile, he supplemented his fare by shooting ducks and prairie chickens. He learned to cook, but not without trouble. On one occasion he wrote: "My beastly oven won't bake at the bottom so my loaves are done beautifully on top and raw on the bottom. I took them out just now and stood them on top of the stove but that does not answer well."

Before leaving the greenhorn Englishman, Bell set out a number of tasks for him, including haying, fence mending, and trail cutting. Over the next several weeks, Gardiner made only periodic trips to Fort Macleod and was back at the upper range for the roundup in the fall. During the winter of 1894–95, he remained in the line cabin, usually alone, looking after the cattle. He built a corral for the calves and was always busy feeding the cattle, keeping a watering hole open for them, and worrying about the wolves prowling around the herd. ("I have to ride about them nearly every day for 4 or 5 hours," he commented.) In mid-winter, his clothing differed from the usual cowboy attire of the period. He wrote:

> I do not find the cold knocks me up at all. Of course, I wrap up for it. I always wear 2 pair of trousers. When I ride and it is a cold day I put on 2 pair of the German socks, a pair of rubber overshoes, 2 overcoats, cap over my ears, woollen comforter, and a pair of woolen mitts with a pair of buckskin ones over them. You can only see my eyes.

The life was harsh but Gardiner loved it. The following summer, he bought the Wineglass Ranch near the Porcupine Hills, married the daughter of an Indian Department doctor, and stayed in the hills until 1921, when his wife inherited a small fortune and they moved to Victoria.

Gardiner may have been a successful cowboy, but like a number of other Englishmen of means, he soon became a rancher on his own. Another

Englishmen, William Ogle, started the same way, but his life took a different direction. He arrived in western Canada late in 1888 "in search of adventure" and was hired by a rancher from the Wood Mountain area. When he was paid off in the fall, he moved in with a local settler and spent the winter poisoning foxes and coyotes and selling their hides in Moose Jaw. He added to the family's larder by killing prairie chickens.

That winter, Ogle, who had ridden since the age of three, learned he had a facility for breaking horses. As he recalled:

> Fred caught up a buckskin, saddled him up good and tight with my brand new $75 California saddle. He held his hand over the horse's eyes while I got on and he hit the pony on the rump. I pulled leather for all I was worth and I managed to stay on. When I got him in the open I turned him into the deep snow and kept him going for an hour and got the best of him.
>
> Afterward Fred told me that the horse had killed a man so they were able to buy it cheap.[24]

In the spring of 1889, Ogle blew all his earnings in Regina during a month of festivities, including dinners "and other enjoyments not quite so innocent." Broke, he headed back to Wood Mountain and followed some fellow cowboys to Montana to pick up a herd of unbroken horses. These were delivered to the Maclean Ranch, where Ogle learned the finer points of horse breaking. The next winter he spent alone in a shack in northern Montana and worked from time to time for the N Bar N Ranch. In the spring he took part in the roundup, then drifted farther south to the Powder River Ranch in Wyoming, where he joined a trail drive bringing cattle from Texas to Montana. This time, he saved his money and returned to the Wood Mountain area, where he married a Sioux woman and started his own ranch.

Ogle moved freely between Montana and Saskatchewan and over the years became so respected as a rancher and cowboy that he was asked to judge the riding events at the Calgary Stampede in 1912 and at Winnipeg a year later. He served overseas during World War One, and when he returned to Canada he decided to give up ranching. He sold his outfit, including 1,000 horses and more than 650 cattle, and returned to Britain, where he spent his declining years. In this, he was the exception, for most English immigrants who had tasted cowboy life on the prairies were never content to return to the Old Country, except for occasional visits.

Both Gardiner and Ogle were successful English cowboys. But this was not always the case. In fact, Claude Gardiner was disgusted with the English ranchers and cowboys in the Pincher Creek district. He mentioned the son of a clergyman who "is one of the usual English sort who does nothing but play polo and drink and play the fool generally . . . Nearly all the Englishmen out here go on in the same way, pony racing, etc., and are the laughing stock of all the Americans."[25]

An American reporter noted the unpopularity of the British and wrote the following narrative, supposedly told by a foolish Englishman in 1907 to friends in a Calgary hotel:

> "No sooner was I on a 'raunch,' don't you know," he said, "than I decided I must go astride of a good broncho. But," he shook his head, "that horse was a 'buster,' don't you know. No sooner was I astride than up he went hooty-tooty, first on his front legs, hooty-tooty; and then on his hind legs, hooty-tooty; and then down, hooty-tooty; until, don't you know, I really didn' know whether I was a-foot or horseback, doncher know."[26]

But, as indicated by the 1891 census, the British Isles were well represented in the cowboy community. In fact, the Irish were often as prevalent as the English. With the Irish love of horses and the mass emigration from the Emerald Isle in the nineteenth century, this should not be surprising. In fact, "Irish" was a fairly common nickname on the western frontier.

While all these British, American, and European cowboys were making their mark in the

Many Indians became skilled cowboys, some working for local ranchers while others had their own herds. These two Blackfoot cowboys are seen at the Indian Department corrals about 1902. *Glenbow Archives/ NC-5-6*

Canadian West, so were its Native inhabitants. Indians had been expert horsemen generations before the days of ranching and naturally gravitated to that work. Almost from the beginning, ranchers hired Indians or Metis on their roundup crews and in the branding corrals. As one cowboy commented, their "skill, resourcefulness, and endurance" was greatly respected.[27] At the turn of the century, for example, a Blackfoot Indian nicknamed "Cupi" was so skilled in guiding cattle across rivers that his services were sought by ranchers when fording the Bow. C.J. Christianson recalled his performance when a herd of Circle steers needed to be crossed near Stobart. He said the Indian, mounted on a roan cayuse, slipped into the water downstream with the first steers to cross. Whenever the animals tried to mill or turn, Cupi slapped the water with a willow whip and forced them back on course. In this way, he went back and forth through the deep water until all the animals had safely forded the stream.

During the 1880s, the government established band herds in fulfilment of its treaty obligations and hired Indians to look after the stock. Soon, many of them switched to cowboy attire or combined the two cultures. It was not uncommon to see an Indian with the usual western gear but wearing long braids. Many had only a smattering of English

but enough to carry out their duties. In the 1890s, some Indians began to raise their own cattle and became ranchers as well as cowboys. And as young men graduated from boarding schools, they dressed and talked like other western cowmen.

A typical example was Joe Red Blanket, a Blackfoot, who was hired by one of the big outfits in the 1890s as a night herder on the roundup crew. However, a few years later he broke his leg while on the job and spent the rest of his career as a cook's helper. Another Blackfoot cowman was Daniel Little Axe. He started as a cowboy but was so ambitious that by 1900 he had the largest herd of cattle on the reserve. He established the Teepee Ranch, where for many years he hired other Indians to put up his winter feed, build shelters, and round up stock.

On the Blood Reserve, men like Bobtail Chief, Heavy Head, and Bottle were experienced cowboys by the turn of the century. Later, such school graduates as Cecil Tallow and Chris Shade started as cowboys and became successful ranchers. Similarly, many Metis from Wood Mountain, Pincher Creek, and Maple Creek spent a lifetime in the saddle. In most cases, their fellow Anglo cowboys considered them to be Natives first and cowboys second, seldom accepting them as equals. Only the most exceptional men surmounted the colour bar. One such cowboy was Belknap "Ballie" Buck, a half–Gros Ventre Indian who became manager of the Circle Ranch and was admired by everyone for his skill and leadership.

Alex Gladstone and Dan Nault, two Metis from Pincher Creek, were experienced cowboys. Both worked on roundups and for ranches in the district. They are pictured here about 1900. *Glenbow Archives/NA-102-5*

But regardless of where they originated, after their experience in the saddle, Americans, Englishmen, Indians, and others all shared the Spanish/American heritage that came north with the first cattle drives. Certain stereotypes existed among the newcomers, both negative and positive. Some English cowboys were at first considered inept and subject to ridicule because of their accents and their mode of speech; Americans were sometimes looked upon as being callous and too ready to fight; and Indians were saddled with frontier discrimination that portrayed them as unreliable and untrustworthy. On the positive side, Englishmen often were recognized for their education; Americans as skilful at their job; and Indians as natural horsemen. But like any stereotypes, they were neither completely true nor all inclusive.

In most cases, a man had to prove himself and if he did so, then national differences were of less importance. This happened when John Ware showed his ability to ride a bronc and when Englishman Bob Newbolt turned his cow pony into a jumper while on a cattle drive. Similarly, when a green Irishman nicknamed "Missouri" became the butt of a practical joke, he was a good sport about it and was accepted by his fellow workers. A cowboy mentioned that Missouri became "as good a cowman as you would wish to see, being young and strong, always willing to learn, and ready to take a joke."[28]

Sometimes the transformation from greenhorn to veteran cowboy was so complete that there was little to distinguish between American cowboys and those from other lands. The Marquis of Maitland's son, for example, was described as "a particularly tough-looking specimen of the breed."[29] At the same time, some American cowboys, who had the reputation of being quick with the gun, became peaceful fellows in Canada.

At a glance, the differences between Canadian and American cowboys did not seem to be great. Both tended cattle and horses, took part in round-ups, and performed chores that were identical whether on the Canadian or northern American plains. Their differences were more in the realm of their political surroundings than in their day-to-day activities. The American attitude of individual free-dom and the right to bear arms contrasted with Canada's preoccupation with law and order. As a result, American cowboys had more gunfights, more lynchings, and more disputes with Indians than their counterparts in Canada. Also, the exis-tence of prohibition in western Canada until 1891 meant there were no saloons, and even the brothels or "disorderly houses" tended to be orderly.

Other factors in Canada, such as strong ties with Victorian England, ownership of ranches by British and eastern capitalists, heavy emphasis on exports of live cattle to Britain, a small population of original settlers, and peaceful relations with Indians, all offered a more regulated society than that of Texas or Wyoming.

As a result, while the cowboys on both sides of the border shared a common work ethic, their attitudes and actions differed according to the conditions of the country. The similarity between the cowboys in the two countries was summed up by Tom Whitney when he moved to Maple Creek from his home in Montana in 1905. He was sur-prised to find Canadians "used the same language and wore store clothes"[30] but noted that most of the settlers were from Britain. "Should you holler 'Scotty' on the street," he said, "you'd see half the people . . . stop to see if you were speaking to them." For the next few years, Whitney moved back and forth across the border, experiencing the com-mon bond offered by ranching yet remaining aware of the contrasts.

When a Scottish friend accompanied him to Montana, Whitney introduced him to some of these differences. In Great Falls, they visited a cafe where the menu included "anything that crawls, creeps or climbs." From there they went to the Klondyke House where a female orchestra was performing and women were serving drinks. In the gambling room another woman was singing to the accompaniment of a "piano thumper." They also visited a free picture show where "percentage girls" were selling drinks. Finally, they ended up at a dance hall where the Scot picked up "a palomino filly with a roached mane" and had a wild time for the rest of the night. Most of these amenities were noticeably absent in Canada.

RANCH AND TOWN LIFE

The cowboy's life may have centred upon cattle but there was more involved than roping and riding. Between the spring and fall roundups, there were chores to be performed and duties to be fulfilled. Similarly, from fall to spring—if the cowboys were lucky enough to be kept on the payroll—there were many tasks to be completed to assure the safety of the cattle and the success of the ranch.

The amount of ranch work often depended upon the size of the operation and number of horses and cattle. On a small spread, one hired hand would be kept busy as a jack-of-all-trades, while on a larger spread the ranch hands might have the opportunity to specialize. Either way, there was always plenty to do.

Following the spring roundup and branding of the new calf crop, there were usually numerous chores around the ranch headquarters. These in-cluded mending fences, fixing sheds or building new ones, feeding and watering the horses, clean-ing the stables, cutting and bringing in firewood, and looking after any stock being kept in the corrals or stables. During this period, the usual tools of the cowboy were wire cutters and ham-mers rather than lariats and branding irons. Many ranches also cultivated several acres of land, grow-ing oats for winter feed, and if the ranch owner had a family, there might be a large garden and a field of potatoes to tend.

Branding often took place in the ranch corral. Here, crews are at work at Jumping Pound Ranch in the 1890s. *Glenbow Archives/NA-1939-3*

If the cattle were kept near the ranch instead of on the open range, the branding would take place in the corral. One of two methods was usually followed. The most sophisticated involved driving the cattle through a chute and into a squeeze gate where the animal was rendered immobile while the brand was applied. The other was to drive the animals into a corral where a calf or steer was "heeled," i.e., roped by the hind legs and dragged to the campfire. There it was held down and branded. The animal might also have a piece of skin sliced from its cheek and left hanging as a "wattle." Another option was to slit or cut a piece of the ear to leave a distinctive mark. These methods were used to distinguish an animal in winter when hair obscured the brand or when dust during a roundup made identification difficult.

Work on a horse ranch was similar, except the stock could wander farther, forage easier, and was tempting prey for the rustler. Because the large horse ranches were intent on improving the breed, they imported stallions, which required constant attention and were never turned loose on the prai-

rie. On small spreads, the horses were rounded up and brought to the corrals every evening.

"Five o'clock is the general hour for getting up," said a visitor who observed the morning chores being performed at a ranch near Medicine Hat in 1905, "and while the cook is preparing breakfast, the other men feed and water the horses that are kept in the stables, the cows are milked, and any other animals requiring attendance are looked after. As a rule, by six o'clock work is all over."[1]

In the early years, before the big blizzard of 1886–87, haying was not a major enterprise. Some hay was put up for the calves and any stock kept in the corrals over the winter, but many stockmen had a blind faith in the chinook winds and the ability of stock to forage for themselves on the open plains. But after the bitter lesson of 1886–87, haying became one of the most important tasks of the ranching crew, and some cowboys worked steadily all summer between roundups to assure an adequate supply for the winter.

Haying began as soon as the spring repairs were finished. At daybreak, the crews were out with the mowers, hoping that the rain would stay away until the grass could be cut, raked, and piled into stacks. An old cowboy recalls the process:

> Two mowers would cut for a day or two; then the hay would be raked into windrows; a sweep, usually a long squared log with a team on each end, would drive down the windrow and gather a good load, which was bucked in to form a bottom; then a slide would be placed against it and the next sweep load would be slid up over the top by means of side pulleys and ropes to which these teams would be hooked. In this way a stack would be built up to the required height and the slide moved out a bit so that the process could be repeated.[2]

Of course, the routine ranch duties still remained. The cattle had to be checked daily, herded onto new ranges when needed, and kept within the lease or at least within reasonable distance of the ranch. Sometimes, if the weather was fine, the haying season ran into the fall roundup. In 1906, for example, the White Mud roundup in southern Saskatchewan had to cover the same territory as in the spring roundup, but with far fewer men because many ranches were still haying.

The fall roundup was also the time to cut out any cattle destined for market. This might result in a trail drive to the nearest stockyards, perhaps several days away. Such a drive was done in a leisurely fashion so that the stock arrived at the buyers' corrals in top condition.

Large ranches used squeeze gates for branding and handling cattle. A chute led from a corral to a narrow passage where the animal was confined until the work was done. This is a view on the Springfield Ranch near Beynon, Alberta, about 1890.
Glenbow Archives/NC–43–22

Cowboys preferred to be in the saddle, but this wasn't always possible. After the bad winter of 1886-87, putting up a plentiful supply of hay became an essential part of ranch work. These men are working at the Walrond Ranch in 1893. *Glenbow Archives/NA-232-14*

Before the cold weather set in, cattle on large ranches had to be herded to their winter range. In southwestern Alberta, foothills offered better protection from the icy blasts of winter and cattle often wintered there. A line cabin might be located nearby, which cowboys used as a base camp while looking after the herd. Big ranches sent two or three men to these winter quarters while others often rotated a single cowboy to prevent any one man from getting "cabin fever" as a result of being isolated for too long.

A ranch visitor in 1905 noted that winter was an easy time on the ranch, even though it was by no means a period of idleness. On a large ranch there were a considerable number of animals to feed, calves to be kept under shelter, and weak animals to round up and care for.[3]

Even as early as the 1880s, some viewed the cowboy's life as romantic and exciting. A young Englishman writing home in 1889 called it "an awfully jolly life," but by his description, he probably had very little responsibility (and talent).[4] His main task during the summer when everyone else was haying involved driving a herd of two hundred horses onto the prairie each morning and staying with them until their return at nightfall. In late summer he helped to cut and sack oats, and in October worked in the branding corral. Even with these innocuous tasks he managed to get bucked off a horse and dragged with one foot in the stirrup and to get lost in a blizzard for four hours.

A British newspaper, giving advice to prospective candidates for ranch life, was frank about its lack of glamour. "If a man can't stand monotony," it said, "he had better not try ranching. His [present] daily life may be wearisome in its sameness, but it is quite likely one of wild excitement by the side of ranche life."[5] Yet many young men ignored this advice, visualizing ranching as an endless round of outdoor living, hunting, and having complete freedom from the drudgery of business life.

On small ranches, particularly those run by

Cowboys and ranch hands building a stable in the Drumheller area about 1912. *Glenbow Archives/NA-2612-24*

end to end. At one end were the living quarters for the manager and his family; next was a combined kitchen and dining room; and at the far end, under lock and key, was the food storeroom. Unbleached cotton lined the walls and ceiling, and a few pictures, some cut out of British magazines, were on the walls.

bachelors, a cowboy might live in the main house. Larger ranches had bunkhouses, and the cowboys either ate there or in the dining room of the house. Bunkhouses were often low log buildings, a few built specially for the purpose but others being the original homes of ranchers that were abandoned as soon as they could afford something better.

In 1886, a man from Fort Macleod described a typical bunkhouse. He said it was usually a log cabin with a big stove that could be used either for heating or cooking. There were bunks for the men although some preferred to sleep in their bedrolls on the floor. As for washing or cleaning up, they performed "their brief toilets out of doors, where there is plenty of room in this country."[6] The bunkhouse walls were decorated with deer antlers, pictures from pictorial newspapers, fancy advertising cards, and other knickknacks. In general, he concluded, "on most of the ranches the cow-boys have most comfortable quarters."

The Oxley Ranch on Willow Creek near the turn of the century was typical. The manager had a substantial frame house set apart from the rest of the ranch buildings; his family had its own governess and Chinese cook. The manager lived in a long house, which was actually three buildings placed

The bunkhouse stood nearby. It was described as "a low flat-roofed log building, white-washed within and without. It was distinctively primitive and had no modern sanitary arrangements."[7] At meal time when the cook sounded a large triangle, the cowboys came running. "They seemed all to eat at an incredibly fast rate," noted a lodger, "after which they cut and rubbed pipefuls of plug tobacco and then lighted choking sulphur matches . . . Some did not smoke, relying instead on a fresh cud gnawed out of a black plug of Macdonald's chewing tobacco."[8]

A notable feature of the dining room, common to many ranch homes, was a "lazy Susan" table, made by mounting a wood-covered buggy wheel atop a round dining table. About fourteen inches smaller than the table itself, the upper platform sat about three inches off the table, contained the food, dishes, and other accessories, and could be rotated from one hungry cowboy to another. Fred Anderson, a cook at the Oxley Ranch, took credit for introducing the table and is said to have patented the idea.[9]

The Oxley Ranch at the turn of the century had a lady cook, wife of the manager, and because of its affluence the food was good and varied. There was plenty of meat, potatoes, and basic foods. Desserts were made from dried fruit, the apples being most preferred for pies and stewed fruit. Dried peaches and apricots were less popular, while prunes were at the bottom of the list. Tea came in lead-lined chests and green coffee beans arrived in large tins. About once every two weeks, the cook roasted a supply of coffee and then ground it in a coffee mill as needed. The cowboys were fond of both tea and coffee, consuming large amounts with Eagle Brand condensed milk.

Ranch cooks came in all sizes and forms. Many early ones were Chinese while others were simply recruited from the available crew. A few were women, particularly by the turn of the century, but many shared the same characteristics. "Techy as a cook" was a common expression in the Canadian West.[10] Even if they weren't the butt of good-natured humour, some cooks had a way of losing their tempers and sometimes chasing cowboys out of the kitchen with a meat cleaver or frying pan. On the other hand, cowboys had the reputation of stealing pies that were set out to cool.

At the L4L Ranch near Nanton, cooks seldom stayed for more than a season. They were hired in the spring, cooked for the crews until after the fall roundup, and then were let go with the rest of the hands who weren't needed for the winter. But while they were there, the cooks had complete charge of the kitchen and the supplies. They seldom strayed far from the kitchen, so whenever a cowboy or anyone else was going to town, he

was given a list of groceries to buy. If he forgot—perhaps because he was nursing a hangover—he became the most unpopular man on the ranch as everyone went on short rations.

In their bunkhouses, the cowboys slept, played mouth organs or mouth harps, sang songs, and otherwise entertained themselves. Some men were well read, having their own books or borrowing British newspapers from the main house. Others were virtually illiterate and had trouble writing even a short note. Liquor was generally forbidden in the bunkhouse, although a cowboy returning from town sometimes slipped a bottle in with him. Being caught with liquor could be a firing offence.

Cowboys developed their own unique expressions and phrases that became indicative of their way of life. As a visitor to a roundup camp noted in 1907, "The cowpunchers have little respect for the English grammar or the English language. They have constructed a style peculiarly their own, which is far more descriptive, and which contains far more color than the language of the ordinary town-dweller."[11] In the 1890s, a Lethbridge druggist made a collection of some of the best. Among the personal nicknames he encountered were Bleary-eyed Bill, Tanglefoot Ben, Poker Brown, and Alberta Jim. Some of the aphorisms he recorded were:

The bunkhouse was the only home that many cowboys ever knew. This one, photographed in 1894 by S.A. Smyth ("The Ranchman's Photographer") was dubbed "Bachelor's Hall." *Glenbow Archives/NA-237-15*

The cook was essential to cowboy life, whether in camp or at the home ranch. This "grub tent" at the 1896 High River roundup was under the direction of Charlie Lehr, one of the most popular cooks in the region. *Glenbow Archives/NA-466-22*

"Long faced enough to eat oats out of a churn," "Thick as flies on a dead Indian," "Perky as a mile hoss at a quarter race," "Tough as the beef of a superannuated work bull," "That pony ain't as large as a bar of soap after a hard day's washing," and "Trousers so tight that they must have growed on him when he was young."[12]

While leisure time in the bunkhouse may have been appealing, particularly in bad weather, cowboys were outdoorsmen who often spent their free time in open-air pursuits. Impromptu rodeos were held on weekends, just for their own entertainment. Another never-ending source of enjoyment was to place a greenhorn visitor on a so-called "quiet" horse and then step back and watch the fun. Some of the classic western stories concern a quiet, plainly dressed cowboy who turned out to be a veteran bronc rider and turned the tables on the pranksters.

Hunting and fishing were popular, particularly for those in line cabins or on short rations. British cowboys brought sporting rifles and pistols with them and enjoyed hunting deer, ducks, and upland game. However, when Claude Gardiner arrived in 1894, he discovered he could not get cartridges for his English army revolver or rifle. He also told his father, "I don't think much of your six shooter. I blazed away at a skunk with it the other night; I hit it once but did not kill it and it got away . . . The boys out here use the Colt frontier pistols, those with a long barrel and .44 cal; they are much better to shoot with."[13]

One outdoor activity that combined work and sport was wolf hunting. The prairie wolf was the bane of ranch life and caused such havoc that the government placed bounties on their hides. During the summer of 1876, the Oxley Ranch alone killed fifty wolves. The foreman complained that the big grey beasts ran in packs of nine or ten and could bring down a full-grown cow.

Ranch hands or indigent cowboys trying to make a living during the winter poisoned the

The bunkhouse was often a log building, sometimes the rancher's former home, which was turned over to the cowboys when a new house was built. The substantial bunkhouse at McPherson's Ranch, seen here in the 1890s, was a good indication that the cowboys were well cared for. This later became the High River Horse Ranch. *Glenbow Archives/NA-466-16*

wolves for ranchers. A few ranch owners also imported hounds for both business and pleasure. Wolf hunting or coyote hunting became a Sunday sport to replace fox hunting for the British aristocrats. The hounds were usually a mix of Irish wolfhounds and Great Danes and were trained to work in teams to bring an animal to bay.

Some individual wolves were quite famous in their districts. One, known as the Big Hill King, had her den in the Longview district west of High River and became such a menace to local ranchers that a two-hundred-dollar reward was placed on her head. On one occasion, a cowboy pursued the grey beast for twenty miles but was unable to catch her. Then he sighted the wolf and her cubs along the steep banks of Tongue Creek and guessed her den must be near. He went back to his ranch, picked up a couple of dogs and a shovel, and descended upon the area. As the rider approached the creek, the male wolf attacked the dogs but was shot and killed. The cowboy located the den and two of the cubs were slain, but the Big Hill King and two other cubs escaped.

Over the next few months, raids by the three wolves continued. No amount of vigilance proved effective; the animals were seen but never caught.

Finally, the desperate ranchers imported a professional wolfer who spent the next summer exclusively on the trail of the King. When at last he trapped and killed her, he found she measured seven feet six inches from tip to tail. The skin was mounted and for years was displayed at the High River Horse Ranch.

The sport for a cowboy occurred when he sighted a wolf on the prairie and went after her with a lariat rather than a rifle. In 1891, two cowboys riding near Willow Creek saw an old wolf that had been terrorizing the herds for months. She was distinctive because she was almost pure white with only a small spot of colour at the root of her tail. The two cowhands immediately pursued at a full gallop, their ropes twirling above their heads. The old wolf wheeled and turned, but she was no match for the expert ropers. A loop skilfully dropped over her head brought the beast tumbling to earth. When the cowboys dismounted, they found she had strangled to death. Her coat was damaged but the boys collected their thirty-dollar reward and were able to sell the hide because of its colour. "She was a most prolific breeder," commented the *Macleod Gazette,* "and she and her offspring have

Prairie wolves were the bane of ranch life. Here a wolf feasts on a carcass on a western ranch. *National Archives of Canada/PA-187408*

This wolf thought it was smart. After cattle had gone through the dipping vats near Antelope Ranch in eastern Alberta in 1905, they were bewildered and confused. The wolf chose that time to attack and kill the weaker animals. Cowboys caught the marauder in the act and ran it down on horseback. Displaying their trophy are Harvey Davies at its head, and an unidentified man; on horses *(left to right)* are Houghton, Walter Davies, and Shantz. *Glenbow Archives/NA-2157-3*

probably done more damage to stock than any other dozen families of wolves in the district."[14]

There were other challenges for a good roper besides wolves. Coyotes and other critters provided just as much sport. A cowboy named Tom Murray, for example, roped a coyote on the range near Fort Macleod. A week later he caught a porcupine in the same fashion, and then came his real test when he roped a full-grown lynx. He was so proud of his last catch that he sent the skin into town to have it tanned and preserved.

A few cowboys could always be found hanging around Fort Macleod, Maple Creek, or other communities in the ranching areas. Some were out of work while others were in town to pick up supplies or attend to business. The big influx of cowboys usually took place after the spring and fall round-ups when they had money in their pockets, or when they passed a town during a trail drive taking cattle to market.

At the beginning of the ranching era, some of the towns were extremely primitive. In 1881, Fort Macleod consisted of one row of buildings, mostly sod-roofed and made of logs. Dwellings and businesses were intermingled, with no front yards, and buildings jammed against each other. They were whitewashed on the outside and dingy and smoky inside. When a Toronto reporter visited a restaurant, he found it full of cowboys waiting to be fed. As soon as the dining room doors were opened, the men crowded through and found seats on the long benches at the dining tables. The meal, though roughly served, featured excellent local beef. The speed at which the cowboys consumed the food amidst a steady hum of conversation amazed the reporter. "A great deal of slang pervaded," he noted, "and not a little profanity, but though there was some pretty rough joking all were extremely good humoured."[15] After the meal was cleared away, the men settled down to smoking and playing cards. Prohibition was in effect, but when the Mounted Police were off on other business, someone always managed to produce a bottle.

Many of these cowboys were fresh from the United States and not yet accustomed to Canadian laws. In 1883 the Mounted Police arrested a cowboy named Charlie Wilson in Maple Creek. But as the Mountie was taking Wilson to the police tent, he picked up a Winchester rifle, disarmed his keepers, and sent them on their way while he made a hasty retreat to the United States. "The cow-boy is a terror to those red coats in Her Majesty's service," observed a Manitoba newspaper.[16] During that year, some of the cowboys picked up for liquor or gambling offences were Muskrat Charlie, Alberta Jim, Dutchy, and the Virginia Kid.

But most cowboys were out for a good time, not for a confrontation with the law. Like so many other western Canadians, they abhorred the prohibition against liquor, and when they came to town they frequented the brothels and gambling joints where illegal booze could always be found. "About the only thing to do in those days . . . was to get drunk, fight, or go horse racing," recalled an old

cowman.[17] This was at Medicine Hat in 1884. Gabe Lavallie went to a horse race south of town where a man named Ed Rowe was selling whisky at fifty cents a cup. He had a keg with the head knocked in and dipped out a cup every time someone paid their money. By the time the races were over, some of the cowboys were too drunk to move.

The police tended to be lenient with the cowboys as long as they didn't cause trouble. Just after the turn of the century, when saloons had become legal, a constable named Jack Redmond earned the reputation of turning Maple Creek into an orderly town. When cowboys rode in after the fall roundup, he met them at the livery barns and relieved them of their guns. Redmond didn't mind fistfights but he didn't want any killings. As Tom Whitney recalled:

Cowboys from both sides of the Line were wont to get into free for all fights in the Maple Creek bars and it is whispered that the Mounted Police used to enjoy some of these fights hugely. And just as long as the fighting was kept within reasonable bounds the Police let the boys work off steam.[18]

Fort Macleod was one of the leading ranching towns in the West. This is a view of its main street in 1898. *City of Lethbridge Archives/P19780260001*

After the repeal of prohibition in the 1890s, bars became the home bases for many cowboys when in town. As a cowboy entered the bar, the bartender placed a bottle in front of him, and gambling for drinks usually followed. Sometimes the bartender kept a pair of dice and cylinder handy, while in other bars the men matched coins and played "odd man out." The cowboy had to do all his drinking while standing at the bar, where a brass rail served as a foot rest. If a cowboy got too drunk to stand, the bartender would haul him into a back room to sober up, or, if it was a mean-spirited place and the man was broke, he was tossed out on the street. While drinking, the men rolled cigarettes, smoked pipes, or made use of the handy cuspidor when chewing tobacco.

Veteran rancher Johnny Martin recalled a cowboy from Crawling Valley who got so drunk he had to be carried to his hotel room. When the manager looked in on him next morning, he was surprised to see the curtains had all been removed from the windows.

"Why?" asked the manager.

"There were no sheets on the bed."

"You're under the bed," said the manager.[19]

On another occasion, Bill Pender, who had worked for the Circle Ranch and then the Burns outfit, came into Bassano and joined his pals at the bar. When he passed out, a pal said, "My gawd, poor Bill's dead," and that gave them the idea of holding a funeral. Someone got a wooden casket and Bill was placed inside, hands folded across his chest. The town dray arrived, and after the box had been loaded aboard, a funeral procession headed to the cemetery, a long line of mourners following behind, many swaying in their saddles. "Fortunately," said an onlooker, "no one was steady enough to use a shovel so they just left him on top of the ground and returned to town to drown their sorrows."[20] Several hours later, Pender awoke and the shock of his situation sobered him up so quickly that he was on his horse and out of town within the hour.

Yet excessive drinking had its tragedies. In Pincher Creek, William Welch, better known as "Billy the Kid," made a drunken bet that he could cross the creek during a raging flood in the summer of 1902. His horse made it, but Billy was swept away by the current. Several days later, someone discovered his body, still clad in chaps, in a pile of driftwood below the town. The Kid was a well-known bronc rider and had competed in the first Territorial Exhibition in Regina in 1895. On a number of other occasions, drunken cowboys were drowned at river crossings or died of exposure on the prairies. And in 1898, Frank Lowe, an American cowboy at the CY Ranch, blew his brains out while suffering *delirium tremens*. He had smuggled some whisky back to the bunkhouse after having been on a three-day binge in Lethbridge.

William Welch, better known as Billy the Kid, drowned in Pincher Creek in 1902 as the result of a drunken bet. An experienced bronc rider and cowboy, he wagered that he could cross the creek during a raging flood. His horse made it, but he didn't. *Glenbow Archives/NA-2539-7*

But much of the drinking was simply a form of revelry and blowing off steam after being cooped up at the ranch. Sometimes the exuberant cowboys tried to shoot up the town or ride their horses into the local saloon, but a night in the lockup usually solved the problem. According to one old cowboy, "The boys came into Calgary once in six months and stayed one or two weeks until the wages were gone. One of their games was to get onto their cow ponies outside the Queen's Hotel and race up Stephen Ave. to the Royal, the last man in paying for the drinks."[21]

Besides drinking, gambling was a popular pastime with cowboys. On the ranch, the men were sometimes restricted to poker, and a few owners frowned on them playing for money. But in the larger towns, illegal joints had everything from cards to wheel games. Some were honest, but in others a cowboy could lose his summer earnings at the hands of a skilful card shark.

At the turn of the century, a young Englishman named "Two-Gun" Cohen was working on a ranch near Wapella, Saskatchewan, when he became friendly with a fellow rangeman named Bobby Clark. The cowboy showed the "pilgrim" how to find out if a pair of dice were loaded (drop them in a glass of water to see if the same side always comes up). Then he taught him how to cheat:

> Supposing you want to throw a seven, you pick the bones up and hold them in your hand with the three and four uppermost. You pretend to shake them, but really hold them steady and make the rattling noise by knocking your cuff buttons against the buttons on your coat. Then you throw them on the table with a twist so that they spin around but don't turn over.[22]

He also taught the Englishman how to deal from the bottom of a deck, how to "deal seconds" (taking the second card from the top), and how to "bring in a cooler" (switch a pack for a stacked deck). After that, the neophyte learned how to use a confederate with a mirror or wear a mirrored signet ring to read the cards while dealing. He learned his lessons well, for in later years, while a bodyguard in China, he supplemented his living through professional gambling.

Other popular gathering places for cowboys were dance halls and brothels. In the early 1880s, most available women were Metis and Indians, some of whom had never been to a "white" dance before. The cowboys called them "bronchos" who had to be "broke" to perform quadrilles, waltzes, and other forms of dancing. A visitor who attended a cowboy dance in Fort Macleod felt sorry for such a woman. He commented:

> The broncho's lot is not a happy one, and she has not sufficient of her white sister's art to pretend that she in the least enjoys a dance. While her wild and woolly partner turns a hand spring in front of her, kicks over her head two or three times, and performs various other graceful feats, she hangs her head on one side,

A couple of cowboys provide entertainment for their fellows near Cochrane in the early 1900s. Alex McKay *(left)* takes the part of a preacher reading the Bible while Ed Townend ignores him and carries on with his drinking. *Glenbow Archives/NA–1130-15*

stands first on one foot and then on the other (her shoes hurt her), and looks on with stolid indifference.[23]

And because of the liquor associated with such events, fights were common. A lively melee occurred at a dance near Maple Creek in 1885 when a cowboy named "Mexican Jack" and his crew arrived in town after bringing in a herd of cattle from Montana. During the dance, a Metis got into a dispute with one of the cowboys, and the two groups took sides. The Metis were in the majority but according to an observer, "The cowboys had their shooting irons with them and gave an exhibition of how close they could shoot to a man's head without harming him."[24] Cooler heads prevailed and peace was restored, but later in the evening when Mexican Jack took up a collection for the musician, he used his six-shooter to convince the dancers to "Put in half a dollar, stranger."

In later years, when there were more women in the neighbourhood, dances were held at settlers' homes or at ranch houses. An old timer recalled being invited to a dance at a rancher's home where cowboys came from thirty miles away. "Cowpunchers," he said, "who usually look as good as dead and buried . . . give you the surprise of your life when they get on the floor to the turn of 'Deitcher's Dog,' or something akin."[25] There were no dress rules, but many cowboys wore kerchiefs for neckties and had their high-heeled boots with the spurs attached. These spurs, commented a visitor, were too valuable to be left lying around.

Square dancing predominated, although there were a few waltzes and two-steps. The music that evening was provided by a fiddle, mouth organ, hair comb, a couple of cow ribs, and a one-string mandolin. The unvarnished floor was covered with a sprinkling of rolled oats to keep the dust down. When lunch was served, the cowboys, who were accustomed to plain food, dove into the layer and angel cakes, then continued to dance until daylight.

The shortage of women during the early period on the frontier meant that brothels were an essential part of cowboy life. Virtually every town in ranching country had one or more houses that served the local population of townsfolk, cowboys, settlers, and anyone else seeking the enjoyment of female company. An old-time cowhand who had visited houses from Maple Creek to Fort Macleod believed that cowboys differed from other clients such as coal miners and loggers. He noted,

> After weeks or even months of nothing but cows, horses and other riders for company, they wanted to enjoy the pleasure of female companionship, to sit and relax and have a drink and listen to talk. Most of all they wanted to take their time doing everything, to string out the enjoyment of whatever they were doing.[26]

Because they were generous with their money, the cowboys were welcome visitors, and when the roundup crews came to town, the houses were busy day and night. By the turn of the century, Calgary had a dozen brothels, some consisting of two- and three-storey houses along Nose Creek or at South Coulee, including ones that featured Oriental prostitutes; the town of Fort Macleod had three houses, Medicine Hat two, while Pincher Creek had a row of shacks where the "girls" plied their trade across the street from Fred Kanouse's hotel, a dive noted for dealing in bootleg whisky. Maple Creek, Moose Jaw, Gleichen—all had their establishments, which were well known to almost every cowboy on the range.

One of the most wide-open towns was Lethbridge. By the 1890s, it had a half-dozen brothels operating at "The Point." The most famous bordello in town was run by Carrie McLean, known to everyone as "Cowboy Jack." She began working as a prostitute in Montana when the first cattle drives arrived and ultimately opened her own establishment. She had an imposing two-storey house with a horse trough in front where drunken cowboys frequently dumped their frolicking pals.

Calgary also was lenient when dealing with its "soiled doves." A reporter in 1906 observed that at Nose Creek "things are going at a tremendous clip

Lethbridge was one of the most famous wide-open towns in cowboy country. By the 1890s, several brothels were operating at "The Point," just west of town. The notorious houses can be seen in the background in this 1909 view. *City of Lethbridge Archives/P19851150000*

and new houses are opening weekly. In one establishment there are 12 white girls and between two others are divided 25 Japanese women, recent arrivals. In all these houses the 'professors' beat out ragtime unhindered . . ."[27] In a raid on one of the houses, those arrested included, "Mrs. Sexton, a buxom wench in stylish attire . . . Mrs. Northcote, of comely figure, flowing golden locks and rosy cheeks . . . and Miss M. Brown, of more ample proportions."[28] Not until well after the turn of the century were the houses closed, or at least moved to less visible locations.

When they returned to their bunkhouses, many young and carefree cowboys were hungover, broke, and happy. Unless they had aspirations of buying their own spreads, they did not bother with bank accounts or property. They had their horses,

bedrolls, war sacks, and freedom of the open range. They worked hard at the ranch, took pride in their profession, and played just as hard when they went to town. It was all part of a cowboy's life.

══════

ROUNDUP

The way old timers tell it, there were at least three "first roundups" and three "last roundups" during the golden age of the Canadian cowboy. Actually, it was all a question of definition and perspective; everyone likes to take part in some important historical event.

What were roundups? Well, they changed over

the years. At first, a few ranchers in a small area rounded up their cattle in the spring to brand the calves and take the herds back to their ranches. Later, roundups were also held in the fall to cut out any stock destined for market. As the ranching areas and numbers of cattle increased, roundups were held in different regions and included not only local ranchers but anyone who believed some of their stock may have drifted onto another range. They sent a cowboy representative, or "rep," to look for their brand and bring their cattle back home.

The first roundup of record took place in 1879 near Fort Macleod and involved a handful of ranchers. In June, Tom Lynch had trailed in most of these cattle from Montana; by mid-summer the ranchers knew they had launched their businesses prematurely. The land was barely free of buffalo, the cattle were unaccustomed to the region, and starving Indians were wandering the countryside. When the government declined to buy the stock, the ranchers decided to have a roundup in early August and take their cattle to Montana until conditions improved. Sixteen ranch owners got together and elected William F. Parker, an ex-Mountie, as captain. The rest of the outfit con-

sisted of ex-policemen Jim Bell, Bob Patterson, and Edward Maunsell; police officers William Winder and Albert Shurtliff; and J.B. Smith, Fred Kanouse, "French Sam" Brouard, Jack Miller, Joe McFarland, Dug Allison, Henry Olson, Billy Hyde, Tom Lee, and O.H. Morgan. Only two or three were experienced cattlemen.

They found only about 600 head of cattle. Maunsell's herd had shrunk from 103 to 56 in a couple of months; Parker's herd was virtually wiped out; and all the others showed losses of some kind. A short time later, the animals were driven to Montana and were not returned until two years later.

The second roundup (but called the "first regularly organized round-up" by the *Fort Macleod Gazette*) took place in the spring of 1882.[1] It covered a vast area from the confluence of the Oldman and Belly Rivers to the foothills. The crews split into three parties, each rounding up cattle along the Waterton, Belly, and Oldman Rivers. South of the Peigan Reserve they fanned out, searching to the south fork of Pincher Creek. By the time they were finished, they had several thousand head, which were then split into three herds near Mill Creek for branding. Some ranchers, like

Cowboys relax during a roundup in the Maple Creek area in the 1880s. Notice the rope corral at right for holding the horses.
Glenbow Archives/NA-1508-5

North Bow Cattle Round Up.

The above Round Up will start from the C.P.R. iron bridge, east of Calgary, on June 12th. Anyone wishing strays gathered wil kindly send brands to the Secretary at P.O. Cochrane

WM. BREALEY,

11-w2i   Secretary.

Horse Round-Up

The horse round up north of the Bow will commence on April 24, '99. Parties can have their horses gathered and taken care of for $2 a head.
Send applications to

ADAM DALGLEISH.

Captain.

Calgary, March 22, 1899.

m24-w1m

ROUND UP NOTICE

The Jumping Pond cattle round up will be gin on Thursday, June 15th. Parties wishing stock gathered should notify the secretary on or before the above date.
Rates $2.00 per head up to five head.

W. W. STEWART,

1 9-5w   Secretary.

By the turn of the century, roundups were occurring in many areas of Saskatchewan and Alberta. These notices in *The Calgary Herald*, 15 June 1899, contain offers to look after cattle or horses for ranchers with no reps at the roundups. Stray, unbranded cattle were sold to pay the expenses of crews.

Tom Lee, cut out their cattle from the main herd and drove them back to their ranches for branding. Two other outfits, Andrew Shurtliff and Ives & Sharp, removed their cattle from the main herds. The other eight outfits involved in the roundup counted their stock, branded the calves, and turned the cattle loose again on the prairie. One of the smaller ranchers, Tony Lachappelle, sold his entire herd to Muirhead & Co. for thirty-five dollars a head.

The ranchers were pleased with the roundup. "We are informed that the Pincher Creek cattle are in splendid condition," commented the *Gazette*, "and we can easily believe this, as that country can hold its own with any of these parts, all of which are hard to beat."

Farther north, the Cochrane Ranch held its own roundup, with orders from Montreal to brand everything found on the range. By implication, this included the stock of any small operators whose animals may have drifted onto the Cochrane lease. When a cowboy named Tex recognized a cow and calf in the holding corrals as pets of a nearby family, he protested that these should not receive the "Big C" brand, but the manager overruled him. When small ranchers who had been helping with the roundup learned of this, they immediately quit and checked the losses in their own herds. Realizing that anything unbranded might end up in the Cochrane domain, they began searching isolated coulees for small pockets of unbranded cows and calves. By the time they were finished applying their own brands, they had more than replenished their herds and had given the Cochrane folk a lesson in neighbourliness.

The third "first roundup" occurred in the spring of 1884.[2] This one was larger than either the first or the second, covering the Highwood, Pincher Creek, Fort Macleod, and Lethbridge districts; it was described by L.V. Kelly as "the greatest round-up that ever took place in the history of Alberta."[3] It included one hundred men, fifteen chuckwagons, and five hundred saddle horses, all under the direction of Jim Dunlap, foreman of the Cochrane Ranch. Many big-name ranchers were there—Fred Stimson, John Quirk, George Lane, John Ware, and Frank Strong. The crews swept the area from Whiskey Gap north to the mouth of the Little Bow, to the Highwood, west to Mosquito Creek, and along the foothills to Willow Creek. There the crew split, Dunlap leading one outfit to

STRAY HORSES

Taken Up on the North Bow Round Up the Following Animals.

1 White Pinto Mare no brand.

1 Half Bred Clyde Mare, Bay, Blotch brand on left rump—

1 Dark Grey Mare, brand on right shoulder—

1 Brown Mare, LT right shoulder and yearling no brand.

1 Brown Mare and colt brand on left shoulder—

1 Bay Mare, brand on left shoulder—

1 Bay Mare and colt, brand on left shoulder—

Also brand on right shoulder—

1 Brown Mare, brand on left shoulder—

1 Brown Mare and colt, brand on left hip—

and vented on right shoulder with brand—

1 Bay Gelding 4 years old brand 2 on left shoulder.

Owners can have same on application to
ADAM DALGLEISH, Captain, or
HUGH LEE, Secretary,
j14w3   North Bow Round Up.

A number of branded horses were found during the North Bow roundup in 1899. Owners could claim them by paying a fee. *The Calgary Herald, 22 June 1899*

the Pincher Creek area and George Lane taking the other along Willow Creek.

Two months later, they had covered virtually all of southwestern Alberta and had rounded up more than sixty thousand head of cattle. But the task proved to be so cumbersome that the ranchers decided never to do it again. Instead, they would adopt the American practice of having local round-ups, with reps coming from ranches in other dis-

tricts. This became the norm over the next several years. In order to organize their activities more effectively, they formed the South-West Stock Association the following year.

Another major roundup occurred in 1887, after a particularly severe winter had killed large numbers of cattle and caused others to wander far from their home ranges. The general roundup was divided into a number of smaller roundups, each covering a specific range. The overall responsibility for coordinating the work fell under the direction of Howell Harris, foreman of the Circle Ranch. He was also captain of the local roundup in his own district, and joined with other ranchers when they worked the ranges leased by the Walrond, Oxley, and other big outfits.

Early in May, Highwood River ranchers called a meeting to plan their part of the roundup. They elected Alfred Ernest Cross as captain, and chose six men to represent the Mosquito Creek and Highwood ranchers at the roundups to be held on the southern leases. To prepare for the Highwood roundup, plans were made to move the branding corrals from Tongue Creek (where their roundup had met in 1886) to a location near the Bar U. Another set of corrals would be built at the forks of Mosquito Creek. The ranchers also decided "to prosecute to the fullest extent of the law any settlers who are caught dogging, running, or otherwise worrying cattle."[4]

On 10 June, the roundup crews assembled at the frontier town of High River and were divided into the Mosquito Creek Pool, under Tom Lynch, and the Highwood Pool, with George Lane as wagon boss. Bar U and Sheep Creek ranches dominated the latter pool.

The Mosquito Creek outfit, with over one hundred riding horses, travelled east from High River to the mouth of the Bow, gathering cattle in a strip forty miles wide. Many of the cowboys were inexperienced, and the horses young and wild. After travelling about seventy-five miles, the outfit seemed to be making progress and had a bunch of cattle gazing peacefully near the camp. The cowboys were settling down for supper when the day

Howell Harris, foreman of the Circle Ranch, was a leading figure among Canadian ranchers. He is seen here *(left)* at his outfit's roundup camp near Lethbridge in the 1890s. *Glenbow Archives/NA-118-1*

wrangler, Jimmy Johnson of the Oxley, arrived and picketed his horse. But something frightened the animal, and it broke loose, dashing into the remaining horses and causing them to stampede.

The cowboys immediately ran to head them off, but the horses took off across the plains. About a dozen cowboys pursued them on foot until the herd finally stopped; then a newly arriving cowboy caused them to take off again when he threw a bad loop that missed. At this point, two veteran cowboys–Hunter Powell, "a beautiful roper and one of the best cow hands that ever came to the country,"[5] and Henry Minesinger–told the greenhorns to go back to their camp. The two men set out after the herd and quietly returned with them after dark.

The horse stampede also caused the cattle to disappear, so next morning Ernest Cross, Dan Riley, and another rider headed out to bring them back. After hours of riding in wet, cloudy weather, the three men became lost and ended up at the confluence of the Bow and Oldman Rivers. They had eaten nothing since breakfast but hoped to meet the wagon crew somewhere along the river. Luckily, the wagons also had become lost, travelling in a complete circle and returning to the place where they had stopped for lunch. This is where the hungry riders found them. As for the cattle, they had crossed the river onto the range being swept by the Circle Pool.

Altogether, the roundups covered the entire area from the Bow to the Montana border with cowboys there from the Bar U, Walrond, Oxley, 76, Circle, and other big outfits. Ernest Cross was a rep at the Circle, Oxley, and Walrond roundups for the High River Pool and for his own A7 Ranch. Each ranch sent about fifteen cowboys, a cook, night herder, and horse wrangler. In some instances two or three smaller ranches worked off the same chuckwagon.

Each morning on the Circle roundup, Howell Harris designated which cowboys were to search various parts of the range and where to assemble the cattle. Later, they divided the herd into three large groups for branding. According to Cross,

> The bunches were kept well apart to permit comfortable working. The calves and cows were separated and when the cows had been cut out they were driven to a suitable grazing and watering place where their particular outfit was camped. This started the herd, which was moved and added to each day as the roundup moved on. The herd reached about 2,000 and an outfit was sent to drive them onto their range.[6]

After clearing the Circle range, Cross and the other cowboys in his group moved to the Walrond range where G.W. "Doc" Fields was the captain. Starting from the mouth of Willow Creek, they worked west along the Oldman River

The High River roundup crew, shown here in 1895, consisted of several outfits that worked together to amass the thousands of cattle on the range west of the town. Each outfit cut out its stock, branded the calves, kept those destined for market, and turned the others loose again. *Glenbow Archives/NA-118-5*

to the Porcupine Hills. On Willow Creek, each ranch cut out and branded its own stock and then moved north to the Oxley, where the same process was repeated. Jim "Pat" Patterson, a former Texan, was captain of this roundup and covered the area from Willow Creek east to the Little Bow.

The entire roundup took almost two months. Because of the effects of the winter storms, cattle were scattered all over the range; some had even drifted into Montana. Those animals were rounded up and sold in Chicago, with the money being sent to the respective owners.

Ranchers followed the pattern established by the 1887 roundup for the next two decades. As the ranching areas expanded, the number of local roundups increased. The opening of eastern and British markets via the CPR in the late 1880s meant fall roundups became more common. This not only gave the ranchers a chance to brand any stock missed in the spring and to count their numbers, but also to cut out the animals destined for market. In this roundup, instead of separating the calves and cows, it was the steers and dry cows that were cut out from the herds. If they were ready for

market, they were driven to the nearest railway loading chutes.

Over the years, the roundup became associated with the romantic image of the cowboy. Journalists could gather at the camps and witness all the excitement of men cutting out cattle, branding, and seeing thousands of head of stock in one place. In later years, the most vivid memories of old-time cowboys were the fun and adventures experienced as part of a roundup crew.

Fred Ings, once a cowboy and later a ranch owner, waxed eloquent about his roundup days. "In looking back now I can see it! Hear it! Live it again! A roundup day! From the first call to roll out in the dawn, till we stamped out the last coals of our fire and turned in, a little stiff and weary, to sleep the dreamless sleep of youth."[7]

In preparation for a roundup, each cowboy brought six to eight horses (his "string"), bedroll, clothes, and slicker. The bedroll often consisted of a canvas tarp, thin mattress, and blankets or sleeping bag. Clothing and any personal items were wrapped inside the bedroll when moving camp. The gear was tossed into the bed wagon, and if the ranch didn't provide a tent, the men had to sleep under the stars. As they assembled, the cowboys would meet old friends from other ranches and catch up on the news and gossip. A journalist who visited a roundup camp in 1894 described the gathering of the crews.

> A cloud of dust is faintly visible on top of the divide nearly three miles to the east; and watching it a few minutes with our glasses we see that it is being raised by a jolly band of five cowboys, who are riding like mad, each leading four or five horses. Looking away to the north, we see a mess wagon, or "chuck outfit," approaching, drawn by four horses, and well laden with supplies. Behind this two riders are driving 10 loose horses. And similar small detachments continue to arrive from every direction all the forenoon, until, when all the ranches along the river have furnished their quota, the force numbers 135 men and about 1,200 horses.[8]

The next day, the captain instructed the riders to set out, while the cook and wrangler packed up the two wagons—a chuckwagon (or "mess wagon") and bed wagon—and headed for the noon camp. All the other ranches at the roundup did the same. They were led by a man on a horse, the "pilot," who knew the country well and could take them to the best campsite. In the rear, riders herded along the dozens of horses (the "remuda") to be used later by the cowboys. The chuckwagon contained all the food for meals, as well as an iron stove, cook tent, tin plates, and cutlery. It had a mess box bolted at the back; the door was hinged at the bottom and had a leg so when lowered it made a table for the cook. The bed wagon held all the cowboys' bedrolls, rope for the rope corral, horse shoes, branding irons, harness leather, saddles, anvil, extra rope, and—if needed—a load of firewood.

At the end of the first day, the wagons reached their designated encampment, hopefully near wood and water. Each outfit set up camp and made a corral for the horses by stretching a rope from the wheels of the bed wagon in a diamond-shaped pattern, held about three feet off the ground by strategically placed stakes. In each camp, the cook and his helper immediately set to work on the evening meal, and by the time the hungry riders came in from the range, everything was ready. The cattle collected during the day were put into a single herd, and riders circled them all night. After some time on the trail, the roundup camp might stop for several days so that the cowboys could work from a central location.

Just before dawn each day, the clanging of a triangle summoned the cowboys to breakfast, and soon they were seated by the chuckwagon devouring

Chuckwagons usually went ahead of the roundup to the next camping place and had a meal ready when the tired cowboys came off the range. This is the wagon from the Bar UM outfit near Arrowwood, Alberta.
Glenbow Archives/NA-692-21

The roundup cook had to be sure the crew was well fed and happy. This unidentified cook has just baked some pies and has a meal ready for the cowboys. The table he is leaning on is actually the back door of the chuckwagon. *Glenbow Archives/NA-2307-54*

have keen eyesight; and for roping, the horse had to be strong, intelligent, and capable of being trained.

Once they had their orders, the cowboys set off in twos or fours to their appointed rounds. "These men present a decidedly picturesque, not to say brigandish appearance," commented a journalist, "as they dash across the prairie, with their red, blue, and gray flannel shirts, canvas trousers, leather chaparejos, broad sombreros, colored silk handkerchiefs knotted around their necks, well-filled cartridge belts from which hang their six shooters, their high-topped cowhide boots and large Mexican spurs."[11]

By sunset, these men might have replaced their mounts two or three times, tiring each one by rigorous riding through coulees and across the open country, searching, prodding, and herding. Cowboys returned in time for lunch, and while some of the men watched the cattle, the rest went to camp to eat. When they finished, the others took their turn. Riders usually made two circuits during a day, one before noon and the other after, covering some sixty to seventy-five miles.

In this way, the roundup moved across the range, gathering up everything in its path. Bulls not needed for breeding (which was most of them) were roped, thrown, and castrated so they could be sold as steers in the fall. Each day the herd grew larger and had to be watched around the clock to keep it from drifting or splitting up. Regardless of the weather—rain, sleet, or blizzard—the wranglers had to stay with the cattle.

Sometimes, while still on the open range, the cattle were divided according to their brands, each outfit taking its stock some distance away and applying their brands to the calves. In most instances, particularly when the roundup consisted of several large ranches, they preferred to take their stock to their home ranch for branding. This would be done after the entire range had been scoured and the herd of several thousand cattle divided according to their brands. Reps from other ranges also cut out their stock and prepared for the long ride home.

their grub and steaming cups of black coffee. A visiting journalist commented on the quality of the food. For breakfast, he said, the cowboys had steaks, buns, jam, and coffee; for lunch and dinner, beef, canned tomatoes or corn, rice pudding, prunes, pie, bread, butter, jam, coffee, and tea. "Pork and beans," he concluded, "is not the staple article of diet."[9] According to one of the cooks, his job was "to keep the belly wrinkles out of the crew."[10]

After breakfast, the captain gave his orders for the day and the night herder arrived with the saddle horses, which had been grazing all night on the prairie. They were driven into the rope corral, where each man lassoed the horse he planned to ride. Under ideal conditions, a cowboy had different horses for different jobs. For working the range, he needed one with strong legs and good wind; for night herding it had to be sure-footed and

After a roundup in the Alberta foothills in 1893, cattle destined for market were driven to the corrals at the home ranch. From there they were taken to the nearest railway shipping point. *Glenbow Archives/NA-237-16*

In 1891, a British journalist, possibly reflecting his readers' attitudes about the treatment of dumb animals, described the branding scene from the calf's viewpoint:

He had cantered trustfully in by his mother's side, along with a great company of cows and calves; he had soon become aware that he was being shadowed through that restless, bellowing mob by a mounted man, from whom there presently sprang a whirling rope, in which the poor victim's legs became entangled, and by which he was dragged through the dust into the clutches of three fiends in human shape, one of whom knelt on his neck, while another held his hind legs, and the third slit his ears, slashed his dewlap, and otherwise mutilated him; while a fourth had indelibly burnt the occasion on his memory, and the owner's initial on his hide, with a red-hot, hissing branding-iron.[12]

While bringing the cattle back off the range, the cowboys had to deal with many problems. In addition to the threat of stampedes and bad weather, they often had to cross swollen rivers. This would be hard enough under normal conditions, but with many newborn calves in the herd the cowboys had to show patience and skill. Some of the calves would dash away from the rushing water and have to be roped and dragged across. If they were too little, they were put into one of the wagons or carried over by cowboys.

Once they were back home, or at an agreed location, the fires were built and the calves branded. If several ranches still had their stock together at this point, they would be taken one at a time, starting usually with the largest outfit. Their cattle would be cut out of the herd, and the calves roped by the hind legs and dragged to the fire for branding. Two "rasslers" flopped the calf over, one pulling a hind leg straight out while the other knelt on the neck and held the front legs as the brand was applied. When they were done, they turned the stock loose on the prairie, where they were left to graze until the fall roundup, when the same process was repeated. In later years, any young calves around at the fall roundup were taken to corrals at the home ranch and fed over the winter.

There were variations, of course, depending on the range, size of ranches, and economic conditions. After a particularly bad winter, ranchers might be just as interested in counting numbers as in branding calves. Also, the arrival of trainloads of dogies meant that a special fall roundup might be necessary.

In the spring of 1904, the Matador Ranch imported twenty-two hundred head of Herefords from Texas for fattening. When the arrival date was announced, the chuckwagon and equipment were overhauled, saddle horses rounded up, and the party set out for Waldeck, a short distance east of Swift Current. The trains arrived at dusk and Texas cowboys accompanying the stock began the unloading. "These cattle were weak," commented one of the Canadian cowboys, "all horns and bones, after their long haul from the Texas Panhandle."[13] They were driven slowly northward for fifty-five

miles, grazing along the way, in a trip that took almost a week.

When the dogies arrived at the South Saskatchewan River, the water was low and they lost only three head. "That was a wonderful sight. Twenty-two hundred red and white animals swimming ten abreast."[14] They were pushed another ten miles beyond the river and then turned loose on the prairie.

In the fall, the roundup began. The Matador joined with the 3 Bar 3 and Triangle Ranches to cover the vast open area north of the river. As soon as some of the steers had been collected, they were brought to the wagons and close herded while other cowboys continued the search. One night, during a violent thunderstorm, the herders worked in two-hour shifts, huddling in their slickers against the driving rain. Luckily, the cattle were confined to a narrow defile, and in spite of the thunder and lightning, they did not stampede.

When they were all assembled, the Texas dogies were moved slowly towards the CPR railway line. "These steers which were in such poor shape when they arrived in the spring," said the cowhand, "had effected a wonderful transformation. They were fat and blocky and ready for shipment to

Branding cattle on the open range required expertise with a lariat. A cowboy roped an animal around the head while another caught it by the heels. While the animal was stretched out on the ground, the men quickly applied the brand. This view, showing cowboy Bob Rutherford on the right, was taken near Medicine Hat in the late 1890s. *Glenbow Archives/NA-631-2*

Chicago."[15] The animals were allowed to amble at their own speed so that none of their weight was lost during the trek. When they arrived at the Waldeck loading chutes, they were prime for market.

There were few things a cowboy on the range feared more than a stampede. Once a herd started running and scattering, it might take weeks to gather it up. Stories about stampedes and their related adventures abound. For example, in 1898 a roundup near Calgary on the Two Bar range was disrupted by two stampedes. The first happened one evening after the cattle had been settled down and the riding horses turned out to graze. As the crews were waiting for supper, a couple of ducks flew over the camp and landed in a nearby pothole. Without thinking, Angus Sparrow picked up his

shotgun and fired at them. The noise stampeded both the horses and cattle, and it took the cowboys four days to gather them again. Perhaps it was an understatement to say that the men "were a bit upset around the camp" at the Calgary ranchman.[16]

The second stampede happened when a horse being ridden by a night hawk, Jack McDonald, stumbled, throwing his rider. He landed on some sleeping cows, which immediately jumped up in fright and stampeded the whole herd.

On a roundup on the Little Bow, about four thousand cattle had been gathered in one spot when an old cow came prowling around the camp. She found a four-gallon garbage can with a few potato peelings at the bottom but when she tried to get at them, her head got stuck. As Bert Warren recalled,

A number of Bar U cowboys rest in the grub tent during the 1901 roundup. (*Left to right, lying in front*): Charlie McKinnon, unknown, F.R. Pike, unknown, and Hudson; *(back row)*: a Mountie, Fitch, Herbert, Hudson *(in profile)*, unknown, cook Charlie Lehr, and Milt Thorne. *Glenbow Archives/NA–1035–6*

Now that the cow was scared as well as blinded she started to run in the direction of the wild herd. This scared them and they all started to run with clattering hoofs. The noise soon became deafening . . . a wild stampede was on.[17]

The experienced cowboys quickly divided the herd and managed to get each bunch under control, but it took them another three or four days to round them all up again.

At a fall roundup camp south of Gleichen, two tents were pitched at Indian Lake—one for the cook and the other a sleeping tent for the men. "Slim" Marsden and Bob "Rosie" Rose had finished their two-hour stint at night herding so the latter returned to camp to wake up the next two men. He lit a candle that was placed on a shingle attached to the centre pole, roused the two, then crawled into his blankets. However, the two men went back to sleep and when the candle burned down, it toppled onto the grassy floor of the tent.

Marsden wondered why the relief team hadn't appeared, so he finally rode over to the tents. When he smelled the smoke, he galloped into camp, yelling at the men to wake up. "In the excitement," he recalled, "my horse struck the tongue of one of the wagons and I took a wildcat to terra firm, and a hard bump, landing up immediately between the two tents."[18] There was pandemonium as the tent floor became a sheet of flame. Cowboys tumbled out of their sleeping bags and tried to save their personal belongings while others used hats, war bags, and tarps to stamp out the fire.

Meanwhile, the smoke drifted over to the herd, and they were off on a stampede. The horses in the rope corral also broke free but ran to the main horse herd, where they were quieted by wrangler E.J. "Bud" Cotton. Next morning the cowboys surveyed the damage. One of the men had suffered smoke inhalation, war bags and bedrolls were destroyed, and one cowboy lost a brand new pair of Texas-made riding boots. In addition, it took them an entire week of hard work to gather the herd again and take the steers to the shipping point at Stobart.

Practical jokes were common at the roundup camps; a classic was to send a greenhorn on an all-night bird-hunting expedition. On one occasion, a roundup crew was camped near Verdigris Lake when the cook innocently remarked, "A mess of snipe for breakfast would be the clear ticket."[19] The cowboys immediately entered the spirit of the ruse and talked about the necessary preparations for a snipe hunt—whips, old tin cans, gunny sacks, and so on. A greenhorn fresh out from Ireland was not invited to go until he begged to be included.

When it was pitch dark, the cowboys started for the site of the hunt. On the way, two men entered into a noisy argument as to who should hold the sack. At length, a third cowhand suggested the greenhorn should have the honour since he didn't know anything about driving snipe. Most of the cowboys didn't like the idea but when the greenhorn promised to do his best, all parties eventually agreed. When they reached a small coulee about half a mile from camp, they lit a fire of small sticks. They explained to the greenhorn that the men would startle the snipe with the noise of the cans and drive them from all directions down into the coulee. Once this was done, they would follow them very quietly for the final roundup. His job was to keep the fire burning brightly and to stand with the sack held open so the birds could flock into it. When he had taken about three dozen birds, he was to close the sack and tie it.

The greenhorn, of course, did as he was told, and waited. Meanwhile, after a few minutes of noise, the cowboys returned to the camp and went to bed. An hour or so later, a shower of rain deluged the area and the greenhorn finally realized he had been the butt of a practical joke. He returned wet and tired but was a good sport and said nothing about it the next morning.

Sometimes these practical jokes backfired. At a roundup camp north of Lethbridge, someone suggested to a new hand that they needed fresh beef. Normally, a good two-year-old heifer would be chosen, but in this instance the young cowboy was told to bring in a Texas longhorn. One of the jokesters commented, "This animal was the poorest

One of the last big roundups along the foothills took place west of Calgary in 1908. This is a view of the herds near Cochrane Lake. *Glenbow Archives/NA-381-1*

beef type one could imagine, being about a foot and a half across where it should be widest, and five feet across the horns. In fact, the most likely-looking place to cut steak would be right behind the ears of the critter."[20]

Although the cowboy was green, he successfully cut the steer out of the herd and chased it into the rope corral, where he expected it would be brought down and killed. Instead, the wild steer broke through the end of the corral, ripped into the guide wires of the cook tent, and brought the whole thing down on the tricksters. When the cowboys fought their way out of the canvas, the longhorn chased them onto the chuckwagon, where they were stranded until help came.

The dipping vat also offered a chance for humorous experiences. On one occasion, the Bar U, Circle, and Pool outfits were running a dip near Twelve Mile Coulee when a young lady came with friends to witness the spectacle. One of the night herders offered her a quiet horse and persuaded her to accompany him on a tour. When they arrived at the dipping vat another cowboy, who considered himself a lady's man, tried to move in on the couple by proclaiming his vast knowledge of the dipping process. No cattle were in the drip pen, so he climbed inside to point out certain features of the operation. Just as he started, however, a big wet steer rushed from the vat and took after him. The cowboy made a wild dash for the fence but slipped on the treacherous ground and slithered into the noxious mixture. He wasn't hurt, but a cowhand noted that even his mother wouldn't have recognized him after his unexpected bath. Needless to say, he didn't get the girl.

The first of the "last roundups" occurred in the spring of 1907 after a terrible winter that had virtually destroyed many herds. Sensing the end of an era, journalists flocked to the camps, and in later years cowboys remembered those days. There was, of course, more than one roundup that season, but the largest was centred in the historic ranching district of southern Alberta. It covered the entire region from the foothills to the Cypress Hills, and from the Bow River to the Montana border.

On 28 May, eight large outfits—the Oxley, Circle, Maunsell, McGregor, and two each from the Bar U and the Little Bow Pool—assembled at Eight

Belknap "Ballie" Buck was one of the most respected cowboys in Canada. Part Gros Ventre Indian, he had worked for several big outfits in Montana before becoming foreman of the Circle Ranch near Lethbridge in 1901. *Courtesy Helen Parsons Neilson*

Some cowboys sent across the river rounded up a few cattle there and held them close to the river bank as a guide to the cattle crossing, while other riders cut out a bunch from the big herd on the south side and drove them to the river. These latter stepped in with eagerness to drink and, finding themselves crowded from behind by the mounted cowboys, were swept out into the current.[21]

As the cattle started to swim for the opposite bank, they were carried downstream. But the experienced cowmen had anticipated this and had chosen the landing place carefully. Once this first bunch was safely across, the others followed, until the entire Circle herd was on the north side. In the end, they had lost only one calf.

However, when another outfit lost seven cows and a couple of calves during the crossing, the rest of the ranchers decided to use the bridge at Lethbridge. This was done early in the morning before there was any traffic from town. A long line of cattle plodded down the steep embankment and onto the bridge. "There the steady thunder of their hoofs broke on the still morning air like the measured tread of a vast army."[22]

Mile Lake near Lethbridge, where they elected Belknap "Ballie" Buck as their captain. He was an old-time Montana cowboy and foreman of the Circle Ranch. The next day, the crews split, the Oxley and McGregor wagons going into the Pakowki Lake district for their own separate roundup while the other six worked three main coulees—Chin, Etzikom, and Verdigris.

Two weeks later, these six assembled at Tyrrell Lake near New Dayton with some six thousand to nine thousand cattle. These were driven north to Lethbridge, where the Circle riders undertook the task of getting their herds across the flooded river. According to author Katherine Hughes:

This concluded only the first part of the roundup, but because they were close to town the cowboys were given a couple of days' holiday to cut loose. Then it was back in the saddle again, working the area south and west through Magrath and Cardston, and north along the foothills to the Porcupine Hills. From there, the roundup moved north through the Little Bow country and eastward toward Brooks. J.J. Young, publisher of *The Calgary Herald*, missed the southern part of the roundup but caught up with it at George Lane's spread twenty miles from Brooks in early August. By that time, the area had been swept and a thousand cattle were being moved through the dipping vat. "It was hot and dry," he noted, "and the galloping horses flanking the slowly moving mass of beef stirred up the dust like an army going into battle."[23]

The second "last big roundup" occurred in 1911. Mange was still a problem, so in that year the Alberta government appointed a mange inspector to combat the problem in the area northeast of Three Hills. In May, ranchers and cowboys gathered at the Cornish Ranch and elected Ted Gardiner, foreman of the Imperial Ranch, as captain. Over the next six weeks, the cowboys scoured a vast area east of the Red Deer River, bringing thirty thousand cattle to the dipping vats at Snake Lake. All the cattle were put through the treatment, then close herded in Big Valley for two weeks before going through the whole process again.

And the third "last" roundup? That occurred in 1921 when the Matador Ranch closed down and the stock moved to Montana. When the work was done, so was the "last" roundup.[24]

RANGE ETIQUETTE

WHEN A STRANGER RODE INTO A COW CAMP,
HE WAS INVITED TO "PULL HIS SADDLE OFF AND COME AN' EAT,"
BUT HE WAS NEVER ASKED HIS NAME OR WHERE HE CAME FROM.
RANGE ETIQUETTE DID NOT ALLOW IT.

If he was given a job he was simply asked, "What are we to call you?" He was taken at face value and later judged by his actions. It was considered a person's own business what his name was and what his past life had been.

If a hand found it necessary to make a fast getaway on a ranch horse, he was honour bound to return that horse at the first opportunity. Loyalty to the brand for which he worked was one of the outstanding characteristics of the old time cowboys. Men were known to starve, freeze, fight and die for the outfit that employed them.

When working the range, no one was supposed to ride ahead of the man leading the circle. Everyone followed the boss until told, or motioned with a jerk of the thumb what to do. On riding into camp, everyone was careful to approach downwind from the fire and cooking pots. The space between the mess wagon and the fire was sacred ground—the cook's private domain.

Leaves from the Medicine Tree, 1960, 279

RISKY BUSINESS

DANGERS AND DISASTERS

BEING A COWBOY WAS A RISKY BUSINESS.
NOT ONLY WERE THERE BADGER HOLES TO TRIP AN UNWARY HORSE,
RATTLESNAKES TO SLITHER INSIDE A BEDROLL, AND SKITTISH HORSES
TO THROW A MAN WHEN HE LEAST EXPECTED IT, BUT THE ELEMENTS OF NATURE
—BLIZZARDS, PRAIRIE FIRES, LIGHTNING STORMS, AND BLAZING SUN—
COULD WREAK TERRIBLE HAVOC AS WELL.

Blizzards, in particular, were no man's friend. A cowboy caught on the open range faced imminent death if he could not find shelter. Blinded by swirling snow, he had to rely on his own instincts for self-preservation and sometimes had no option but to hope that his horse would lead him to safety.

His horse may have been his closest companion, but at the same time, it presented his greatest danger. No matter how well trained, it could react violently to a flapping saddle blanket or a sudden dust devil, rearing up and unseating its owner. Or it could catch a foot in a hole and tumble to the ground, crushing the rider under its weight. Even the famous horse breaker John Ware was not immune to such an accident. In 1905, he died of a broken neck when his horse stepped in a badger hole and threw him.

Another cowboy, P.L. Pineo, had twenty accident-free years as a cowboy, but when his horse hit a badger hole he might as well have been a greenhorn. Pineo was working for the Alexander Ranch at the 1891 spring roundup, gathering in a herd of cattle near the forks of the Oldman and Belly Rivers, when his horse stumbled. Before he could get out of the saddle, the horse fell on him, crushing his right leg. Other members of the crew sent for help, but the injured cowboy lay on the prairie for seven hours before a wagon arrived. He then endured an agonizing seventy-mile journey across the open prairie to a Lethbridge hospital. Fortunately, the doctors were able to save his badly swollen leg.

Then there was a young English cowboy named F. Yate-Lee who was herding horses near Calgary in 1899 when his horse threw him; one foot caught in the stirrup and he was dragged to death. When found, he was still holding the rope around the horse's neck, but it was twenty feet long and he had been unable to shorten the line to control the horse before falling unconscious.

This eighteen-year-old cowboy, Tom Graham, has his lariat on his saddle in readiness for any task or emergency. He was photographed at Crawling Valley, in central Alberta, about 1893. *Glenbow Archives/NA-237-20*

Something similar happened to Chris Christianson, a well-known horse breaker for the Circle outfit. He was returning to camp one evening when his horse stepped in a badger hole, stumbled, and rolled over. Christianson had no time to recover before his horse got up; the cowboy was left hanging upside down, his head and shoulders touching the ground. His right foot was caught firmly in the stirrup, and the left stirrup had flipped over to the right side of the horse.

Had the animal stampeded, Christianson would have died, but luckily he was surrounded by three experienced cowboys. They stood stock still while Christianson slowly reached up and grasped the buckle on the latigo, which held the saddle in place. Suddenly he gave a swift twist, jerked the buckle open, and the saddle slipped off just as the horse bucked and galloped away. Christianson's foot was still stuck in the stirrup, but the saddle was now safely on the ground.

When busting a bronc, a cowboy always risked permanent injury or death. In 1891, Charlie Morton was breaking horses near Regina when one of them reared back and fell on him, crush-

ing his ankle. By the time he reached the hospital, his foot was in such bad shape the doctors couldn't save it, and later the whole leg had to be amputated. Four years later, another cowboy breaking horses near Lethbridge inadvertently walked behind one of the broncs and was kicked in the stomach. He suffered fractured ribs, a punctured lung, and a broken collar bone. He recovered but gave up horse breaking.

River crossings were especially hazardous for cowboys. Rushing currents, especially in the spring, and other perils such as quicksand and unexpected snags in the stream required skill and composure. Although a cowboy preferred to stay in the saddle when crossing, if the water was too deep, it was safer to slip into the water on the upstream side and hold the saddle horn until reaching shallow water. Some caught the horse by the tail, but, in doing so, risked being kicked.

A river filled with thrashing, bawling stock during a cattle drive only increased the danger. Some cattle panicked in deep water and tried to turn back; others floated helplessly with the current and had to be rescued. During the crossing, the cowboys were busy plunging through the water, trying to prevent any drownings. If a horse lost its footing, the cowboy had to hold on for dear life for fear of being pulled under his horse or washed away in the current. Interestingly, most cowboys did not know how to swim.

In 1902, three cowboys from the Truchot Ranch were crossing a bunch of horses a mile upstream from Medicine Hat when they ran into trouble. A horse ridden by J.L. Ingram slipped and fell, tossing the rider into the South Saskatchewan, where the current promptly carried him away. He likely had been kicked during the fall, for he made no attempt to save himself. Four years later, another cowboy drowned in the same area. Joe Hawkins had been helping to drive a herd of ninety horses across the river at Police Point. He was in the lead, but when his horse reached deep water it suddenly reared back and fell on its rider. The incident stampeded the herd and the frightened animals rushed back to the shore. Four other cowboys tried to control

Crossing a river was always a dangerous enterprise. A cowboy could be knocked from his horse, get caught in quicksand, or drown in a raging torrent. This herd has made a safe crossing of the Red Deer River near Morrin about 1900. *Glenbow Archives/NA-2612-14*

them, but they too were unseated and were rescued only with great difficulty. And when they looked around, Joe Hawkins was gone. Earlier, when they were riding down towards the river, the young cowboy admitted he couldn't swim. When asked what he would do if his mount tried to throw him, he said he would "stick to the horse."[1] He didn't.

Cowboys could also expect trouble from wild range cattle. Texas longhorns were reputed to be tough fighters, but even a Shorthorn or Hereford could be dangerous on the open range, and a cow could be mean if anyone interfered with her calf. A cowboy never, but never, approached range stock on foot. The animals seemed to ignore men on horseback, but became immediately curious, often aggressive, towards anyone afoot.

If a cowboy became unseated on the range, the first thing he did was check for range cattle. If they were far enough away, his next problem was catching his horse. Cowboys usually had extremely long lines on their horses to make recapture much easier. While a horse that was free might not allow the cowboy to come right up to it, neither did it necessarily stampede out of sight. With the long rope

trailing behind, the cowboy could recapture it before the animal sensed the danger. If the horse did take off, the cowboy had several worries—wild cattle, being lost on the prairie, and lack of food.

Just after the turn of the century, a Lethbridge cowboy named Bert Warren had a near brush with death when he was unseated. He had gone in search of some missing horses and had run his own horse about ten miles before finding them near Coaldale. Seeing the fresh horses take off at a gallop, the cowboy's mount grew agitated and began to prance around and throw his head back in excitement. As the cowboy recalled,

Suddenly he stumbled and fell, took what the cowmen called a real "wildcat somersault," and the last I remember I was on my back and the horse's rump end coming straight at me. When I woke up, I was sitting on the river bank opposite [a] ranch-house, with an old axe handle in my hand. Where I got the axe handle I did not know—I do not know yet—but as I had to walk through a lot of range cattle I must have picked it up for self-defence.[2]

He had absolutely no recollection of anything after the fall, yet he had walked for several miles through prairie country that was cluttered with stray herds of wild cattle. His axe handle would have been useless against an enraged bull. The ranch owner found him on the river bank and took him home. Next morning he was transported by buggy to Lethbridge, where the doctors said he had a broken collarbone and cracked ribs. Later, when the rancher rounded up Warren's horse, he found that the saddle horn was broken off and the cantle damaged.

If the saddle had hit me with such great force I would surely have been killed, so Buck must have struck me with his own body. As it was I was laid up about a month.[3]

A cowboy fording a deep river sometimes had to slip from the saddle and hold the saddle horn as the horse carried him to safety. In this view, a rider is fording the Milk River near the American border. *Glenbow Archives/NA-777-18*

Even in a corral, livestock could be a threat. One time a cowboy was trying to rope a calf from a mixed herd. He had just about succeeded when the mother came after him. Without hesitation, the cowboy dropped the rope and fled to the fence. A veteran cowman watching the performance bawled him out and told him he should have stood his ground and looked the cow straight in the eye. Recalled the cowboy:

Without a word I passed him the rope. He went to rope the calf again, and the mother immediately charged. He stood his ground for a very short while and endeavored to look the old cow in the eye, but this didn't help matters a bit. Deciding at length that discretion was the better part of valor he made for the fence. He had barely climbed out of her reach when she came smack against the poles with all her force, just missing him by about a split second.[4]

Runaway teams could also pose problems. If the team wasn't brought under control, it might smash the wagon or upset the occupants during flight. This is what happened to rancher A.S. Stronach. He was returning from Irvine in his democrat when the team bolted and he was thrown out. The cowboys knew something was wrong when the horses arrived back at nightfall with only their harness clinging to them.

Next morning, more than fifty cowboys scoured the area for the missing man. Two days later they found him in the badlands, wandering about in a delirious state. When thrown from the buggy, he had landed on his head, and was in pitiful shape. "His complete recovery is regarded as extremely problematical," commented a Medicine Hat newspaper.[5]

Two of nature's most serious efforts to make life miserable for the cowboy were blizzards and prairie fires. But these hazards of the frontier had existed long before the establishment of the cattle industry. Hunters froze to death in blizzards, and prairie fires destroyed entire Indian camps. One of the first casualties of the North-West Mounted Police was a young constable who became lost in a blizzard.

In 1879, Edward Maunsell set out from his ranch on the Oldman River to complete some business in Fort Benton, Montana. He and his two companions, Tony Lachappelle and an Indian named Patsy, encountered blizzard conditions shortly after leaving the St. Mary's River and were unable to reach Milk River that night. Instead, they had to camp on the open prairie and use buffalo

Cattle could be dangerous on the open prairie. A cowboy had to avoid being unseated among wild stock, and to watch for angry cows while their calves were being branded. Here, cattle are being cut out for branding on the Willow Creek range in 1898. *Glenbow Archives/NA–365–1*

chips for fuel. When they had exhausted the supply in the immediate vicinity of the camp, Maunsell wandered farther afield and promptly got lost. Only when he discovered signs of his old footprints was he able to find his way back to the campfire. The next day, the trio travelled through Whiskey Gap, and on the other side they ran into another blizzard. Here Lachappelle got lost when hunting up the horses, which had wandered away. He found the camp when Maunsell threw some fat in the fire and caused a flareup of light, but now they were without horses. The trio turned back and finally made it to a trader's cabin on Lee's Creek; from there Maunsell was taken to Fort Macleod with badly frozen feet.

A year later, Maunsell learned that some of his cattle had drifted down to Lee's Creek so he went to round them up. He found them near the St. Mary's River and camped beside them. It snowed heavily that night and next morning dawned bright and clear. Slowly Maunsell trailed his cattle northward, but the intense glare of the sun on the snow began to affect his eyes. Finally, he was in so much pain that he closed his eyes completely, confident

that he would reach Standoff, a few miles north. After travelling for some time, a Blood Indian stopped him. When the cowboy tried to look at him, he found he was snow blind.

The Indian explained that Maunsell wasn't travelling north. "He was heading straight for the Rockies where there was not a solitary settler," said his biographer. "He would, in all probability, have died a lingering death."[6] The Indian gathered up Maunsell and the cattle and took them to Standoff. There the local trader, "Dutch Fred" Watchter, applied a poultice of tea leaves to Maunsell's eyes and had him taken home to his ranch. Several weeks passed before the rancher recovered his sight, and during that time his eyes caused him excruciating pain.

This was not a unique experience. An old-time cowboy from the Matador Ranch explained that the most dangerous time for snow blindness was immediately after a storm, when cowboys were out rounding up the scattered herds.

As the sun came out the reflection on that vast expanse of snow was dazzling and many cases of snow blindness were recorded. The pain is excruciating and as one is temporarily without sight it is necessary to stay in a dark room for about three days with a bandage over the eyes to keep all light out. Even then, if one is not careful, it may leave the eyes a little weakened.[7]

The ranching industry suffered through a terrible winter in 1886–87. It began with heavy snows that melted and formed a crust; then for three months the prairies were plunged into a deep freeze as one storm followed another. Horses could manage to paw through the crust, but the cattle were helpless and soon began to starve. Canada was only four or five years into the ranching industry, and ranchers believed optimistically that the chinooks would always allow the cattle winter access to the prairie grass. As a result, there was no general move to put up winter hay, and crops of oats and tame hay were virtually unknown in the region.

Dogies, or stocker cattle, which had been imported with a view of fattening them on the luxuriant prairie grass, only added to the problem. They were entirely unaccustomed to western winters and died by the thousands. At one point in mid-winter, there were some forty thousand starving cattle within a short distance of Fort Macleod. Cattle drifted with the storms in this unfenced country, hoping to find grazing farther south. According to L.V. Kelly:

> Clustering in the coulees or huddling in the open, the animals suffered and died in enormous numbers. Some, breast-high in packed and crusted banks, died as they stood; some who were sheltered somewhat by bluffs or coulees starved pitifully, ravenously searching for food until the frost had reached their vitals. The bodies of great steers were found in the spring, heaps of them, with their throats and stomachs punctured and torn by sharp splinters from dried and frozen branches and chunks of wood which they had swallowed in their anguish.[8]

The cowboys were out on the range for most of the winter but there was little they could do. Rancher John Quirk even dragged some of the half-frozen beasts into his yard, where he attempted to revive them, but without success. By the spring of 1887, the losses were enormous. Medicine Hat and Highwood River district ranchers had lost about half their herds, while the Calgary and

Many cattle died during the West's harsh winters. Those that survived were often too weak to recover when warm weather finally returned. *Glenbow Archives/NC-43-32*

The wide open prairie sometimes had few landmarks to help a cowboy if he became lost, or was caught in a blizzard, hailstorm, or prairie fire. This is a view of cowboys trailing cattle for the Bar UM ranch near Arrowwood, Alberta. *Glenbow Archives/NA-692-22*

Pincher Creek owners suffered about a 25 percent loss. Some typical losses were: Glengarry Ranch, six hundred head; Quorn Ranch, just about all its "pilgrim" cattle; A.E. Cross, three hundred; Tom Lynch, over two hundred; and the N Bar N, in the Wood Mountain district, four thousand. The latter American outfit pulled out of Canada in discouragement.

Cowboys, of course, preferred to stay in the bunkhouses during blizzards, but this wasn't always possible. Sometimes they were caught on the trail; even the spring or fall roundups were subject to unseasonable storms. When these happened, cowboys often stayed with the herds, keeping them from scattering and drifting off the range. When the large herd of Cochrane cattle arrived in 1882, for example, they were just in time for an early fall blizzard. This was followed by a thaw and then bitterly cold weather, which caused a thick crust to form on the snow. The orders from Montreal were to keep the cattle on the Cochrane range so the cowboys were out all winter, in all kinds of conditions, driving the starving stock back onto the home range.

In the early 1890s, Fred Ings was almost lost in a blizzard as he drove a herd of beef cattle for the Mosquito Creek outfit. He was on the night shift when the storm struck and was kept busy trying to keep the stock from drifting. "I was riding a surefooted, thick-set, little gray horse," he recalled, "but I had a dozen falls that stormy night."[9] Soon he lost all sense of direction. Luckily, his partner, who had been riding at the front of the herd, came back and said he was heading for the camp. Following the lead of his companion, Ings finally reached safety. His partner was Harry Longabaugh, the Sundance Kid. The storm was so severe that the foreman would not send out another crew to replace them. Instead, they waited for the blizzard to pass and then set to work rounding up the cattle again.

In October 1905, three cowboys and a foreman were rounding up cattle north of the Oldman River along the Little Bow when they ran into a storm. They had a small outfit, only a tent and a couple of extra saddle horses. The weather was beautiful when they arrived at the Sundial Ranch lease, so the foreman and one of the hands went ahead to look for more cattle while the others rounded up those found in Snake Valley. That evening, they pitched their tent, picketed the horses, cooked their grub, and went to bed early. Recalled one of the cowboys:

During the night one of us awoke and wakened the other, to see what an awful blizzard was raging outside, and it surely was a bad one. When morning came it was worse if anything. We could not see thirty feet from the tent.[10]

They managed to hobble the horses and turn them loose but there was no way they could make a fire; it was too stormy outside and the tent filled with smoke when they tried to make one inside. For breakfast, they ended up eating a couple of bannocks left over from the evening meal. Without a fire, the tent was so cold that there was nothing for the cowboys to do except crawl back into their bedrolls.

They stayed cooped up without food for two days, all the while worrying about the foreman and other cowboy, who did not even have a tent. Finally, the third morning dawned bright and clear, and the two cowboys were able to recover their horses and make their way to the Sundial Ranch. There they were relieved to learn that their companions had found shelter and were none the worse for the experience.

Some people weren't so lucky. Jim Dunlap, foreman of the Cochrane Ranch and captain of several roundups, died after he froze his feet during a storm in the fall of 1887. Another man named George was a night herder for the Circle Ranch when he became lost in a blizzard. He was out in the storm for thirty hours and when he was found both feet were frozen and he had become deranged. The doctors saved his feet and most of his toes, but he was never quite the same again. Like others who were injured on the job, he was made a roundup cook, but finally returned to his native Kentucky.

Prairie fires may not have been as hazardous to the individual cowboy as blizzards, but they certainly caused havoc among the stock and destroyed huge sections of the range. In the years before fences and settlers, there were no fireguards. Sometimes, natural obstructions such as rivers or lakes, or perhaps a fortuitous rainstorm, were all that could stop a raging prairie fire. Occasionally, careless settlers caused the fires, but more often the culprits were lightning storms or the sparks from wood-burning locomotives.

The fall of 1885 had been warm and dry in the Fort Macleod area. By late October, there were at least three fires burning out of control. The first started along the Belly River and swept towards Monarch and Lethbridge. The next one erupted in the Porcupine Hills. "It looked as if the whole south end of the hills was a mass of seething fire, extending on both sides and along the summit."[11] The third started on the outskirts of town and roared south towards the Waterton River.

Cowboys from the Walrond turned out to fight the fire in the Porcupine Hills while the Cochrane outfit tackled the others. During the Waterton blaze alone, cowboys laboured for thirty-six hours straight, beating out a line of fire twenty-five miles wide.

A year later, fire plagued the Cypress Hills country. Jules Quesnelle, a Wyoming cowboy, was riding the north slope of the hills with three others when he noticed flames in the distance. "The grass stood all over from two to three feet high," he recalled. "The top fire was jumping 15 feet in the air."[12] The men, recognizing the danger the strong wind posed, galloped to their noon camp and warned the others. Although they packed up as quickly as they could, the fire caught up with Quesnelle and his pals, so they had to turn back and ride through a narrow strip of flames. "We managed all right," he said, "but the horses were badly singed."

Others weren't so lucky. Gordon Quick had taken refuge in a bog, and, while it protected his body, he was later taken to hospital with severe burns to his hands and face. The fire also caught the foreman, John Anderson, who was driving a team. He turned the horses loose, wrapped himself in a blanket, and hid behind a wagon wheel until the fire passed. His assistant tried to ride one of the horses through the flames and was killed. "I never saw anything like it before or since," concluded Quesnelle.

One of the most graphic accounts of a prairie fire was written by Ralph Stock, correspondent for

A prairie fire was one of the most fearsome sights in ranching country. Thousands of acres of grazing land could be blackened and scores of cattle and horses killed before the conflagration ran its course. This is a view of a fire near Stettler, Alberta, in 1908. *Glenbow Archives/NA-1199-1*

Wide World, a British magazine. He was travelling across western Canada in 1902 when he stopped in Maple Creek to take in some "local colour." A friendly cowboy showed him to the hotel and afterwards they retired to the bar. Noted Stock:

> There were many faces in that bar-room, all weather-beaten and brown, and all bearing the unmistakable stamp of good nature. They belonged to a crowd of cowboys, "broncho-busters," and ranchmen from a hundred miles round, and a more jovial, rough-tongued, but thoroughly good-hearted community one could not meet.[13]

They were enjoying their beer when a man burst through the door and shouted, "Fire south of Piapot Creek! Wind rising; all turn out!" As the others got up to leave, the journalist stayed in his seat until the local fire guardian informed him that everyone had to fight the fire. He explained that no one got paid but anyone who refused faced a fifty-dollar fine.

Stock's new-found friend provided him with a horse, and within the hour they had joined a stream of wagons and riders heading for a red glow on the southern horizon. While they were riding, Stock asked the cowboy about the origins of prairie fires.

"Oh, lots of things," he replied. "The sparks from an engine, you know, ashes from a pipe, or a match thrown away while it is still glowing. Why, I've known even the sparks from a horse's shoe striking a stone to start a fire! But lightning starts more fires than anything else—not an ordinary storm, but just lightning and thunder without rain. We often get them out here."

As they approached Piapot Creek, they could see flames flickering through the huge billows of black smoke. "A faint crackling, too, could be heard, growing louder and louder till it merged into a dull roar, and soon we saw figures running hither and thither, silhouetted blackly against a blood-red back-ground."

When they arrived at the scene, Stock was sent to a "a little group of men with blackened and perspiring faces" at a supply wagon where he was given a slicker and a long stick with gunny sacks wrapped around it. He was then directed to a water barrel and told to soak the sacks whenever they needed it.

There were only twenty men fighting the fire when he arrived but the number soon increased to forty, all on foot and fighting what seemed to be a losing cause. He noted:

The fire spread like spilt quick silver. The thick prairie grass came to my knees in places, and the wind was rising steadily, fanning the flames in an alarming fashion. I beat and beat at the running lines of fire with my improvised mop till my arms felt like parting company with my body.

At one point, author Stock was almost run down by a pair of cowboys, one on each side of the line of fire, who were galloping along, dragging between them a wet cowhide weighted down with chains. They were followed by a line of beaters trying to catch any spots missed by the riders. Stock noted they were using anything and everything to stamp out the fire—slickers, mops, sacks, old saddle blankets, and hats.

They fought the fire all night. By morning the blaze had covered ten miles of prairie and was still ten miles wide. It roared through a coulee, reducing trees and brush to blackened stumps, then swept inexorably onto the open prairie again. It soon became apparent that if the wind didn't change, a nearby rancher would lose his house and buildings. The men ploughed a fire guard seven furrows wide but this did not ensure the safety of the ranch, for already the holocaust had jumped a well-worn trail that was twelve feet wide. Commented Stock,

I shall never forget with what frenzied energy the poor fellow fought to save his home, beating at the cruel flames like a man possessed. But, thank Heaven, the wind was decreasing— almost imperceptibly, it is true, but still enough to put fresh vigor into our aching bodies . . . Suddenly, as I worked, I felt something wet splash on my forehead. Of course, it must be a drop of water from the mop, I thought, and I continued my thrashing in the mechanical sort of way I had acquired during the last few hours. But another splash came, and another; then they came quickly, one after another. I had been too intent upon my work to take note of the sky before, but now I looked up and saw that it was black with clouds.

Stock glanced around and saw that everyone else had stopped working. In less than five minutes,

Men attempt to fight a prairie fire in the Ghost Pine Creek district of central Alberta in 1906. *Glenbow Archives/NA-1502-1*

Prairie fires sometimes caused stock to stampede far from their home range. This 11 January 1890 advertisement in *The Calgary Herald* seeks the return of horses that fled the Queenstown Ranch during a fire.

Reward for Strayed Horses

Stampeded from the Queenstown ranche during a prairie fire, 32 mares, 5 foals and one buckskin gelding, which stands about 16 hands. One of the mares has on a bell. A reward of $5 a head will be paid for the recovery of the same. They are branded with an O on left shoulder.
Apply to   w 3i

EDW'D. C. DAWSON,
Queenstown, Gleichen, N. W. T.

the rain was coming down in sheets and the fire was out. As the writer observed, "Nature had accomplished in that short space of time what the hand of man had failed to do in a night and half a day."

Two years later—1904—was another bad year for fires. Because of the hot, dry summer, the land was parched and the grass brittle and brown. One blaze started just east of Claresholm. There was a strong southwest wind blowing at the time, and ranchers far to the east could see the billowing smoke long before the fire itself. Evangline Warren, looking out of her window, saw the fire burst over Black Spring Ridge, forty miles from her ranch, as the flames travelled northeast "with the speed of an express train."[14] By noon, the fire had reached Sundial Butte and raced towards the Little Bow.

When Evangeline and her family reached the fire, they found cowboys there from most of the ranches in the district—Circle, Oliver, Mayer, Nolan, Coe, Hill, Nimmons, Link, Bulmer, and even the Hyssop Ranch, which was south of the Oldman River. She noted:

> They fought with walking ploughs, wagons, barrels of water and wet sacks, even in dragging green cowhides or split carcasses of animals . . . The women worked side by side with the men; hauling water, carrying wet sacks, bringing lunch, taking charge of saddle-ponies whose owners were beating out fire, and even at times giving a hand at the fire themselves.

The fighters stayed on the fringe of the blaze; to get in front of it would have been suicidal. The flames reached a height of fifteen to twenty feet and moved in a rolling motion, destroying everything in their path. Horses, cattle, antelope, coyotes, and other animals that could not get out of the way perished. The main fire had reached the Little Bow but then seemed to halt about eight miles north of Iron Springs. But, the following day, the wind changed to the north and the fires sprang up anew. Within five hours, the blaze had destroyed the grass as far east as Picture Butte Coulee, north of Lethbridge.

As soon as the wind shifted, the ranchers knew they were beaten, so they rounded up their horses and cattle and drove them south across the river, then set to work to plough fire guards around their buildings. Most were successful, with only the Circle Ranch losing its barns at the mouth of the Little Bow. When the fire finally ran its course, virtually the entire Little Bow range had been destroyed.

With the arrival of settlers, the danger of large fires decreased but smaller ones became more common. Farmers tended to plough fire guards as soon as they took up their homesteads so fires did not have a chance to take off. Also, there were more people in the immediate vicinity to halt the blaze before it got out of control. On the other hand, smaller fires became common as settlers tossed hot ashes outside, cleaned out their pipes while the tobacco was still glowing, or were careless while burning off grass within their fire guards. These fires were serious but they were nothing like the blazes known to the old-time cowboy, who saw the range ravished by fires that burned until nature put them out.

HORSE THIEVES

Even before the arrival of the North-West Mounted Police, the acquisition of other people's horses was a common practice on the frontier. In these instances, the raiders were Indians and so were their victims. In the finer points of the Blackfoot language, the taking of an enemy horse was considered to be a "capture" not a "theft." It was stealing only when you took something from your own people. Unfortunately, after the arrival of ranchers and settlers, the white people were viewed in the same light as enemy tribes, so the taking of a white man's horse was considered a noble feat, not a crime.

For several years the Mounted Police recognized this cultural trait and tended to go easy on so-called Indian horse thieves. Some of these raiders later went on to become important leaders of their tribes.

Two of the more audacious Indians to prey on ranchers' stock were Big Rib and The Dog, members of the Blood tribe. In 1887, they led a small war party on a raid against tribes in Montana, but bad weather and an unexpected fight with Crees caused them to turn northward to the Cypress Hills. Not far from the railway siding of Irvine they tried to take some horses from Abram Adsit's barn but were interrupted by the rancher's son, who shot wildly as the raiders dashed for cover. A short time later, The Dog returned, angrily firing two shots at the ranch house.

Next morning a Mounted Police patrol went in search of the raiders, and, in sheer bravado, Big Rib and The Dog showed themselves from a bushy knoll and fired several shots in the direction of the patrol. This resulted in a hasty retreat and the

formation of three more patrols to find the recalcitrant Bloods. Instead of going back to their reserve, the Indians next went to the outskirts of Medicine Hat, where they took two horses from Robert Watson's corral. As they were riding away, they encountered a lone Cree and took several shots at him before heading for Seven Persons Coulee.

Charlie Davis, a Blood Indian, was arrested in 1906 for stealing horses from ranches near his reserve, then selling them to settlers farther north. He served a term in the Edmonton penitentiary. *Glenbow Archives/NA–258–17*

The Bloods finally went back home, where they were apprehended and appeared in court to face horse-stealing charges. In the past, the judge had given only nominal sentences of two months in the guard house for such crimes, particularly when Indian horses had been involved. In this instance, however, he gave Big Rib and The Dog each five years in Manitoba's Stony Mountain Penitentiary.

But their adventure wasn't over. The two prisoners were taken by wagon to the railway station at Dunmore, but, despite their handcuffs and leg irons, they managed to escape. When they returned to their camp several days later, they were welcomed as heroes; even a fifty-dollar reward failed to bring them in. The raiders remained at large for the next three years, and not until Chief Red Crow made a deal with the Mounties did Big Rib and The Dog surrender. The original sentences were reimposed, but they were out in fourteen months with time off for good behaviour.

Indians continued to raid horses from local ranches well into the twentieth century, but the practice underwent some subtle changes. Whereas earlier raids had been undertaken to increase one's prestige, later ones were for profit and sometimes carried out with the connivance of unscrupulous whites. In 1905, police arrested seven Blood cowboys for stealing dozens of horses in southern Alberta, then running them through the Crowsnest Pass and selling them to a rancher named V.S. Chaput, who obviously was part of the scheme. The Indians got sentences of up to five years, but Chaput hired a lawyer and got off scot free, claiming he didn't know the horses were stolen. Said a disgusted Mountie:

> I could not understand how any intelligent white man could buy a big, strong horse for $10 or $15 and not suspect something to be wrong, particularly as some of those horses were brought to them early in the morning and showed signs of having been driven many miles.[1]

The following year another four Indian cowboys—Charlie Davis, Willie Crow Shoe, Philip Hoof, and Yellow Creek—began raiding ranches near the Blood Reserve, then driving the horses north to sell to new settlers. But like their compatriots, they were caught and given jail terms.

The first white horse thieves appeared in Canada almost as soon as there were ranchers. In 1876, an American cowboy named James "Slim Jim" Brooks stole thirty horses from three men—John Hughes, J.B. Miller, and J. Bastien—who had recently established small ranches along the Oldman

River. The Mounted Police received a report of the theft at midnight, so at daylight, Superintendent William Winder and three constables went in pursuit. They had no problem picking up the trail and saw the culprit as he was driving the herd across the Belly River. When Slim noticed the Mounties, he quickly roped one of the best horses in the bunch, changed saddles, and galloped off. After a chase of some fifteen miles, Cst. Ed Wilson got within a hundred yards of the horse thief, at which time Slim waved his rifle as if he planned to shoot. Wilson then opened fire. The first shot went wide, but the second one passed between Slim's arm and body. That was enough; the horse thief surrendered.

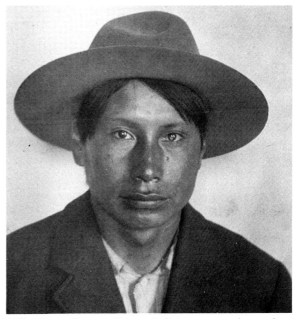

Willie Crow Shoe, a Peigan Indian, was caught stealing horses in 1906 and sent to prison. *Glenbow Archives/NA-258-7*

He was sentenced to five years in jail, but the closest penitentiary was at Stony Mountain, north of Winnipeg. Since there were no railroads, six policemen took the prisoner by wagon on the thousand-mile journey. Slim Jim already had a notorious reputation in Montana so the police did not want to take any chances of him escaping. The trip took a month, with Slim acting as cook and driving most of the way. He proved to be an excellent teamster and was "wonderful with the long four-in-hand whip."[2]

During the 1880s, as the cattle industry spread north from Montana, horse thieves moved with the herds. Canada's new ranching business produced an ideal situation for many law-breakers. Not only were there plenty of good horses to steal on both sides of the line, but as most ranches were a day-or-two ride from the border, it became common to procure horseflesh in one jurisdiction and dispose of it in the other. Some professional thieves blotted the brands or even forged bills of sale, while others found plenty of settlers willing to buy horses cheap with no questions asked. A brand on one side of the border meant nothing on the other.

$25 REWARD

—

The above reward will be paid for the recovery of three yearling colts, unbranded, One solid black filly, one solid brown entire colt, and one bay entire colt, with a little white on hind feet and white spot on forehead and snip on nose. The colts left their mothers in May last and can be identified by owner on sight

W. D. KERFOOT

s20tf   Grand Valley, Conhrane P. O.

When horses disappeared, the owners were often unsure if they had strayed or been stolen. This advertisement in the *Calgary Tribune* in 1892 makes it clear that the owner would recognize his colts if he saw them. *12 December 1892*

The two authorities—U.S. army and sheriffs on one side and North-West Mounted Police on the other—cooperated as much as possible, but vast distances, limited communication, and politics often made this difficult. To make matters worse, there were too few Mounties to cover such a vast territory. Every time a settler or rancher missed a horse, he assumed it had been stolen and reported the loss to the police. Half the time the animal had merely wandered away, and while the Mounties wasted valuable time searching for it, the real crooks played havoc elsewhere.

In 1884, Commissioner A.G. Irvine attempted to deal with the problem before it got out of hand.

First, he contacted U.S. authorities to see if they could set up some official joint procedures. The officer in charge at Fort Assiniboine, Montana Territory, wanted to cooperate, but word came from Washington that he was "not permitted by the authorities to enter into any negotiations on the subject."[3] Instead, they had to rely on keeping in touch by telegraph when a major theft occurred.

Inspector A.R. Macdonell commented to his superior that "the American 'Cowboy' . . . or horse thief, is a desperado of the worst description, who holds the life of a man as cheaply as that of an animal, being always well mounted and armed."[4] He said the United States was able to deal more effectively with the problem because ranchers were willing to take the law into their own hands. The U.S. officer told him that fifteen or twenty horse thieves had been lynched in Montana territory in the previous year alone.

Sgt. Major W.A. Douglas, of the Maple Creek detachment, encountered an example of this American justice when he went to Fort Maginnis, in eastern Montana, to recover four horses stolen from the Mounted Police. He was directed to the Stuart Kohr Ranch, where the foreman, a man named Anderson, rounded up the horses and let the Mountie pick his out of the herd. The commissioner reported:

> Mr. Anderson told him that the horses had been taken from thieves about 100 miles down the river from Rocky Point (south of the boundary line), where the thieves were surprised, and a complete outfit for defacing brands found in their camp. The cowmen on that occasion took about eighty head of horses from the thieves, and Sergt.-Major Douglas was told in reply to enquiries that, "that gang would not steal any more horses."[5]

The inference, of course, was that they had been lynched. The American authorities said they were part of a vast network of thieves that extended all the way to Mexico.

While Canadian ranchers did not resort to

lynching, there was at least one instance where the Americans obliged on their behalf. In 1885, two cowboys named Edward McDonald and Felix Constant stole a number of horses and mules from the Lethbridge area and crossed the line into Montana. There they went into a saloon at Dupuyer and tried to sell them, but when they couldn't produce bills of sale, local ranchers became suspicious. They were about to apprehend them when the two men rushed into a back room, barricaded the door, and threatened to kill anyone who tried to take them.

The ranchers placed a guard over the saloon, and by noon the next day some fifty cowboys and ranchers had assembled. Hopelessly outnumbered, the two men finally surrendered and were kept in the saloon overnight, with Charles Thomas and M.S. Rickard standing guard. They were unable to prevent what happened next.

> About 2 o'clock Thursday morning Rickard hearing a noise turned suddenly around and found himself facing a mob of between thirty and forty masked men . . . The crowd then went into the room, took the prisoners out, carried them about a half mile up the creek and hung them to a convenient tree.[6]

Both men were well known in Montana. McDonald had killed a man while stealing horses and also had been involved in a stagecoach holdup. Constant had murdered a man on the Musselshell River "and was known there as a horse thief and desperado."[7]

Another attempt to apprehend thieves who had taken Canadian horses into Montana probably would also have ended in a lynching had the opportunity

---

When the Mounted Police captured horse thieves, the officers sometimes had problems locating the owners of the stolen stock. In this notice, which appeared in the *Macleod Gazette* in 1883, only a few of the animals they found were branded. Some had been taken from horse thieves while others had been found near the Cypress Hills.

14 July 1883

Horses captured from Thieves, now in possession of N. W. M. Police, Fort Macleod.

1. Roan mare, aged, branded ;; on near shoulder, black points; with colt.

2. Light roan, 6 years old, no brand, four white feet, white face.

3. Buckskin, 6 years old, no brand, near hind foot white, star on forehead, black mane and tail.

4. Brown horse, 7 years old, no brand, off hind foot white, split ears, wall eye, blaze face.

5. Bay mare, 2 years old, brand diamond **B** on near shoulder, near hind foot white, star on forehead.

6. Black mare, 4 years old, branded diamond **B** on near shoulder.

7. Buckskin horse, no brand, four white feet, white face.

8. Bay mare, aged, branded **W** on near thigh, white hind feet, white face.

9. Buckskin mare, aged, branded diamond **B** on near shoulder, near fore and off hind feet white.

10. Sorrel mare, 3 years old, white mane and tail, blaze face, off hind foot white.

11. Buckshin horse, 6 years old, no brand, black points, two hind feet white.

12. Brown mare, 3 years old, no brand, split ears, light star on forehead, near hind foot white.

13. Chestnut mare, 6 years old, no brand, two near feet white, stripe on face.

14. Sorrell horse, 7 years old, branded diamond **B** on near shoulder, and heart above diamond on near thigh, white hind feet, stripe on face.

15. Sorrell colt, 18 months old, no brand, four white feet, white face.

16. Sorrel horse, near hind leg white, roached mane and banged tail, split ears, blazed face, branded with an Indian tepee (supposed to have been done by Indians).

17. Buckskin horse, branded small diamond on near hip, both hind legs white.

18. Brown mare, branded **A** on off shoulder, both hind legs white, blazed face.

Horses received from Peigan Indians, said to have been found beetween Milk river and Cypress.

One chestnut horse, blazed face, blind in the off eye, saddle marks.

One chestnut horse, white stripe on face, nigh hind leg white, branded **C** upside down.

Owners can obtain the same by proving property and paying expenses.

L. N. F. CROZIER,
Commanding Fort Macleod.

arisen. In 1881, two men named Frank Labrie and Peter Laprise stole 140 horses from J.D. Smith's ranch, west of Fort Macleod, and succeeded in making it across the Montana border. The telegraph carried the news to Fort Benton, and when the culprits were spotted northeast of town, a posse led by a soldier rode out and captured them on the Marias River. They were taking the thieves and horses to the army post at Fort Assiniboine when the posse split, some going to round up the horses and Jacob Wirtz, Ed Ranch, and Private Smith guarding the prisoners. According to reports:

> Wirtz put down his gun a moment to attend to some duty or other, when one of the thieves with one bound seized it and ordered Wirtz to throw up his hands. This Wirtz declined to do and reached for another gun near by. At the first move the thief shot him, the ball entering his body near the shoulder and passed clear through him. Ed Ranch next received attention with the order to throw up his hands. Instead of complying he went for his pistol and got it out, but not before he had received a shot which ploughed the fleshy part of his breast inflicting a severe wound.[8]

The thieves disarmed the soldier, mounted two horses, and rode off towards the Bears Paw Mountains with the warning, "Whoever follows us is a dead man." The posse surely would have lynched the two men had it caught them, but they were never apprehended.

That the men fled to the Bears Paws is significant, for it was one of Montana's hideouts for horse thieves. Livestock was stolen on both sides of the line, but geography and politics made certain areas more appealing than others. The Montana region south of Canada's foothills was never a major rallying point for horse thieves because of the Blackfeet Indian Reservation. This huge block of land bordered Canada from the Rocky Mountains to the Milk River country; it was well patrolled, and white intruders were discouraged. As a result, any horse thieves coming from the north either crossed the territory quickly or bypassed it by heading for the Sweetgrass Hills. The hills were a minor enclave for thieves, but because of local mining activity, the area was not isolated enough to serve the needs of the horse nabbers.

Farther east, the geography was ideal for those living outside the law. The Bears Paw Mountains began thirty miles south of the border, and southeast of them were the isolated badlands along the Missouri River. Immediately north of the line were the Cypress Hills and Wood Mountain, both with generous coverings of trees and adjacent to thriving ranching areas. The result over the years was that ranchers living west of the Cypress Hills tended to be bothered by individual horse thieves, sometimes from their own communities, while those east of the hills were subject to the harassment of organized gangs.

In 1887, Bill Graham, a clerk for the Indian Department, met a gang of eight thieves who were travelling north with about fifty head of stolen stock to sell to settlers in the Moosomin area. They arrived at his Moose Mountain agency in a driving rainstorm. Graham, not knowing who they were, let them use an empty log building.

> They were dressed like western cowboys and heavily armed . . . They had no wagons or vehicles of any kind; all their belongings were carried on pack horses and they had a lot of stuff, enough bedding and cooking outfit to fill a three tier wagon box.[9]

They made themselves right at home in the cabin. Someone produced a fiddle, and they spent the evening dancing hoe downs, singing songs, and generally having a merry time. Next morning they rounded up the horses and cut out those that were wild and unbroken. Their skills impressed Graham.

> I have never seen such horsemanship. These men were experts. They had no corrals. They lassoed the different horses when they were on the gallop, threw them, tied them up and then put a saddle on them. After twenty minutes or

so from the time they approached the animal with the saddle they could mount the beast, which would go off across the country, bucking, twisting and snorting, but the rider still stuck to the saddle. No sooner would one start off than another horse was thrown and saddled, and so on all morning and the greater part of the afternoon.[10]

The thieves told the naive clerk that they had bought the horses cheap and were breaking them to sell to settlers farther north. The work continued for the better part of a week until several of the animals were broken to saddle. Graham noticed that some horses had harness marks, indicating they had already been trained; these he was told would be sold for hauling. The clerk was so impressed with these "cowboys" that he bought a bay mare from them. Imagine his surprise two weeks later when he read that the horses had been stolen from the Wood Mountain area. The mare Graham bought belonged to an old priest, Father St. Germain, and was returned to him. This was the only animal ever recovered.

Graham learned that he had played host to a well-known gang of horse thieves who operated on both sides of the line near Wood Mountain. In this particular instance, they had stolen the horses from the Canadian side, driven them into the States to throw pursuers off the trail, then circled north to Moose Mountain. Later, the same gang was caught in Dakota Territory and two of them were lynched.

One of the most notorious gangs of horse thieves in the history of the Canadian West operated out of Wood Mountain at the turn of the century. Their leader was an American cowboy named Frank Jones, and an isolated part of the hills—just a couple of miles inside the Canadian border—served as their headquarters. There they were beyond the jurisdiction of the American sheriffs and could slip across the line whenever the Mounted Police tried to apprehend them. From this point they succeeded in terrorizing ranchers on both sides of the line for several years.

While their membership may have changed

Charles Winfield, alias "Kid Trailer," was one of the notorious Frank Jones/Dutch Henry Gang that terrorized the Saskatchewan/Montana border area at the turn of the century. He was only twenty years old when he was arrested in Montana in 1904 and sent to Deer Lodge Penitentiary. *Powell County Museum & Arts Foundation/1595*

from time to time, the gang included a Canadian, Charles "Red" Nelson (at one time it was called the Nelson and Jones Gang), Edward Shufelt, Tom Reed, Jim McNab, Andy Duffy, T.J. Birch, Charles Winfield (alias "Kid Trailer"), an ex-Mountie named Frank Carlyle, J.C. Brown (the Pigeon-toed Kid), and George "Bloody Knife" Zeglin.[11] Little is known about most of these men, except that McNab was a well-educated man from an old respected family in eastern Canada.

When the gang first started in the 1890s, it confined its raids to small ranches, where the owners could be easily frightened into silence. Then, as they became bolder, they hit larger spreads in both Montana and Saskatchewan. For example, ex-Mountie James Marshall "had his life made intolerable. His stock has been shot and run off."[12] As a result, he had to carry a rifle wherever he went. About this time, the gang encountered a rancher named "Cachot" McGillis on the plains and set him afoot. The family was terror-stricken that they would return.

In one instance, a rancher named Frank King laid information against Carlyle, but on his way home the gang intercepted him. Jones wanted to kill him on the spot but the others demurred. Instead, they held the rancher prisoner in their camp for more than two weeks. He was put to work building corrals and was "cuffed about and given a 'dog's life.'"[13] When they finally turned him loose King knew that Jones still wanted to kill him, so he did not take the main trail home. According to reports,

> As evening came on, he discovered Jones on horseback following him. He concealed himself in the bushes and watched Jones hunting for him for a long time. He eventually reached the police post, more dead than alive. His experiences in the outlaw camp were such, however, that he refused to institute proceedings and at once left the country.[14]

About 1900, a cowboy named "Dutch Henry" Ieuch (pronounced "youch") moved into the district, breaking horses for Fred Brown, Jack Stewart, and a number of other ranchers. Soon after, Pascal and Joseph Bonneau, who had a ranch near Willow Bunch, hired him. In 1903, Joseph bought 250 horses in Montana and left Dutch Henry to look after them over the winter. When he tried to collect them in the spring, however, the cowboy pulled a gun on him and ordered him off the range. The owner reported the matter to the Mounted Police, but as the incident had occurred in Montana there was nothing they could do. By the time the American authorities learned of it, Dutch Henry had taken the horses across the line to the secret camp of the Jones Gang. The next year, when U.S. officers killed Jones in a shootout, Ieuch became the new gang leader and its notoriety spread as the Dutch Henry Gang.

A year later, when Pascal Bonneau learned that some of the horses from his ranch had shown up near Moose Jaw, he identified them as the stolen ones. They were in the possession of Edward Shufelt, who was at that time running a saloon in Saco, Montana. Although the man produced a "bill of sale" from Dutch Henry, he was arrested and later tried in Regina. During the trial in 1905, a gang member, McNab, threatened one of the witnesses but fled across the line when the incident was reported to the police. In addition, Bonneau received several "anonymous and ill-spelt letters, threatening him with all manner of evil things if he persisted in his activities."[15] Instead of being intimidated, Bonneau was furious and felt gratified when Shufelt was convicted. The man threatened Bonneau as he left the courtroom, but he later died in prison.

George Zeglin was a horse thief, cattle rustler, and train robber. He was known in Canada by the alias "Bloody Knife" and was said to be part of the Dutch Henry Gang. When Zeglin decided to shoot up the town of Ambrose, North Dakota, about 1908, citizens there killed him. *Powell County Museum & Arts Foundation/1497*

The rest of the gang gradually broke up. Dutch Henry was said to have been shot and killed in Minnesota in 1906 when he got into an argument with a Canadian friend, Alexander McKenzie. Pigeon-toed Kid was shot by a deputy in 1908, while in the same year an irate citizen ended Bloody Knife's life as he was shooting up the town of

Ambrose, in the Dakotas. Ex-Mountie Carlyle was killed by two companions after he got drunk and failed to blow up a bridge during a train robbery. Birch was extradited to Canada and served four years in Edmonton Penitentiary, while Kid Trailer went to prison in North Dakota. Duffy and Reed fled, supposedly to Argentina, and McNab disappeared. Only Red Nelson decided to give up a life of crime. He began to use his real name, Sam Kelley, and homesteaded near Debden, Saskatchewan. He died at North Battleford in 1937.

The level of violence and lawlessness shown by the Dutch Henry Gang was unusual on the Canadian frontier. One cannot dismiss their activities as the antics of a bunch of American renegades; at least three of them were Canadians and one an ex-Mountie. It seems as though their isolation from the law at Wood Mountain and the fear they instilled in their victims caused them to be much more daring and overt in their actions than most Canadian horse thieves. In addition, the fact that Shufelt owned a bar at Saco and McNab had a ranch near Culbertson in Montana meant that they had semipermanent bases in the community, unlike other horse thieves who seldom stayed long in any one place.

The usual procedure for a horse thief operating alone was to ride into a district as a stranger, perhaps seeking work, and then disappear with local stock. Even better, he might enter a ranching area and leave without anyone knowing he had even been there. Once he had taken his loot, he could either hurry across the line or go to a different part of the Canadian West. He might be equipped with a running iron to obliterate or change the brand, or, if he had enough education, he might forge a bill of sale. Either way, if he sold the horses he often retired to a saloon in a safe area to drink up the profits until it was necessary to go out on another raid. In the meantime, he might join a roundup crew and receive wages while waiting for the right time to pick up another string of horses.

Shortly after the turn of the century, cowboys on the Bow River horse roundup were surprised

AFTER A BAD GANG.

A dispatch from Culbertson says: Constable Nicholas Moore and Sheriff Cosner, with a posse of 20 picked men and 12 mounted police from the Fort Peck reservation, are hot on the trail of the Jones gang of outlaws and robbers, on the headwaters of the Big Muddy, near the Canadian line. A posse of Canadian police has left Willow Bunch and will join the posse of the sheriff and Indians in an effort to capture the outlaws.

The posse is composed of a brave lot of men, well mounted and with provisions and ammunition sufficient for a long siege, and they are determined to rid the region once and for all of the desperate gang of thieves and robbers who have harassed and terrorized the ranchers of this section for years. The leader of the outlaws is a desperado of the most daring type, and it is certain that the gang will not surrender without a battle. It is not believed the officers will take any chances, but that they will get their men, dead or alive. Besides the reward of $500 offered by the governor, there is now a reward of $1,000 for Jones, the ringleader of the gang, and $800 for each of the others.

The activities of the Frank Jones/Dutch Henry Gang made the headlines throughout ranching country. *Lethbridge News, 25 February 1904.*

when a large number of the stock couldn't be found. Neither could one of the cowboys, a man named Milton Field. A few weeks later, Hughes, one of the ranch owners, learned that horses bearing his brand were being sold up north to farmers in the Didsbury area. A Mounted Police investigation soon revealed that a large number of horses with different brands from the Bow River range had been sold all along the line from Calgary north and that Field had disappeared again, this time permanently to the United States.

But border crossings were still the favourite way of getting rid of stolen animals. Two different countries with different laws and different brand registries offered a better chance of escaping detection. For example, when thirty horses were found on the plains near Mandan, Dakota Territory, the local sheriff suspected they were stolen but had a hard job proving it. All the horses bore one of three brands: Eight Bar, Flying U, or Circle Diamond. He checked with the registry offices in Montana, Dakota, and Wyoming but without success. At last he wrote to the Mounted Police, saying, "I think they come from across the line in your country, Canada. If any such stock is missing please inform me and also as to the reward."[16] The horses were found in March and the Mounted Police did not receive the letter until July; any likelihood of catching the thieves (if indeed the horses were Canadian) would have been remote indeed.

One of the most notorious horse thieves to ply his profession on both sides of the border was Sam "Kid" Larson, a former resident of the Medicine Hat district. By 1901 he was wanted in the United States for horse stealing, cattle rustling, forgery, resisting arrest, assault with intent to kill, and other offences that a Montana newspaper said could put him behind bars for 150 years. That summer, a stock inspector apprehended Larson in the Little Rockies, but while en route to jail, he stole a race horse, fired several shots at his captor, and escaped. A short time later near the Sweetgrass Hills, he opened fire on a number of cowboys whom he mistook for a posse.

From there he made his way into Canada with a herd of a dozen stolen horses and took refuge at the ranch of an old friend. However, his friend proved to be decidedly unfriendly, for he snitched to the authorities. The Mounted Police caught up with the wanted man near Seven Persons Coulee, set him afoot, and forced him to flee. Later they discovered where his pack horse was cached, but when they tried to ambush him, he opened fire and

escaped. The next day Larson was finally apprehended at Walton's Ranch.

He could have been arraigned for resisting arrest and other charges, but the police decided to bring him up on the relatively minor offence of illegally bringing horses into Canada. This would give the Americans time to have him extradited to Montana on more serious charges. As a result, Larson was fined fifty dollars or a month in the guard house. Though he chose the latter, the press began to refer derisively to him as the "Fifty Dollar Desperado."[17] Yet the police were sufficiently impressed by his reputation to keep him on a ball and chain at the Maple Creek lockup.

Extradition proceedings were initiated, but Larson didn't wait around to see what happened. His brother Henry came from across the line and bribed one of the guards, Cst. Henry Bowen, to help bust him out. Larson was freed of his ball and chain and hopped a freight train going west.

He was without boots, hat or coat. He took a cayuse at Irvine and rode south. At Hamilton's sheep camp he stole boots, coat and a blanket. At Jas. Wright's ranch on the Piegan, he stole the best saddle horse in the stables, a saddle blanket, bridle, and a new saddle. Well mounted, knowing the country, with apparently plenty of friends to help him, he had got clean away.[18]

But his career in crime was almost over. About three months later, a man identified as "Bud" Tyler stole a team of horses and retreated to a hideout near Giltedge in the Judith Mountains of Montana. When a deputy sheriff and two cowboys discovered the outlaw, he tried, unsuccessfully, to shoot his way out. Afterwards, the body was identified as the notorious "Kid" Larson.

In some instances the authorities recognized the difference between law and justice. This happened in 1889 when Bill Smith and John Dillon stole twenty-five horses from a rancher in Montana and were apprehended by the Mounted Police near Swift Current. They were charged with "having brought into

Mounted Policemen often visited roundup crews to settle disputes and look for cattle rustlers. Here, Cst. Riske joins riders from the Oxley and 44 Ranches in 1901. *(Left to right, top):* Wes Humberson, Randal McDonald; *(middle):* Bill Andrews, W.L. Watt (captain of the roundup and foreman of the Oxley), Cst. Riske, unknown, and Allan McDonald; *(front):* Jack Annear, Ed Leslie, Tom Boulton, Charlie Anderson, George McDonald, and Jim Ferguson. *Glenbow Archives/NA–365–3*

Canada property stolen in the United States of America."[19] The owner came to Canada and gave strong and convincing evidence against the horse thieves, but, to the surprise of almost everyone, the two men were acquitted. It turned out that the prosecuting attorney had offended the jury to such an extent that they let the men off just to spite him.

The judge had no recourse but to turn the men loose but then gave the surprising order that the horses were to be restored to the Montana rancher. He was saying, in effect, that "the jury found you innocent but you can't have the horses you stole."

As more settlers came into ranching country,

the days of cross-border raids came to an end. There were simply too many people around for a good horse thief to evade detection as he raced for the line. Instead, thievery became a more local affair, often undertaken by young kids who had none of the recklessness and flamboyance of the old-time outlaws. A ludicrous example occurred in 1915, when a seventeen-year-old boy, running away from the family homestead east of Medicine Hat, stole a rancher's horse and saddle. He was trying to reach the border but was headed off by the police and fled eastward. The Mounties found him five days later cowering near his brother's farm.

CATTLE RUSTLERS

There were two terms used for the purloiners of cattle on the Canadian frontier. One was the old familiar "cattle rustler," which referred to anyone who drove off someone else's steers, heifers, cows, bulls, or calves. The other was "cattle killer," a term in the 1880s and 1890s reserved almost exclusively for Indians. It referred to Natives who took a rancher's beef, killed it on the spot, and carried the meat back to their reserve. Both were "rustlers" in the strictest sense of the word, but the cattle killer's prize left the range on the back of a pack horse, rather than on its own four feet.

Certainly, the cattle killer was the initial concern of Canadian ranchers. Rightly or wrongly, the ranchers of the 1870s blamed starving Indians for the near destruction of their incipient industry and its curtailment for two years. The Mounted Police believed otherwise but there is no doubt that Indians, along with storms, wolves, prairie fires, and careless herding, combined to create heavy losses among the newly arrived cattle herds.

After the final destruction of the buffalo in 1880–81, the Plains Indians had no recourse but to return to their reserves to accept rations of beef and flour. The amount varied, depending on the way the political winds were blowing in Ottawa and the state of Canada's economy. When a recession struck in 1882, rations were reduced and cattle killing increased. In times of plenty (and these were few and far between) the slaughtering of ranchers' cattle decreased.

The disappearance of cattle was probably the most important cause of discord between Indians and cowboys. Whenever a beef went missing, ranchers were sure it had been slaughtered. Indians who abandoned their reserves to go hunting along the foothills faced particular animosity, both from ranchers and their cowboy crews.

The Stoney Indians, for example, often left their homes at Morley and wandered through the foothills as far south as the Montana border, hunting deer and other game. In February 1883, Charlie Harrison was checking his herd near Crowsnest Pass when he found a heifer and calf missing. The next day, with a Peigan cowboy, Running Wolf, they picked up the trail of two unshod horses that led them to a Stoney camp about twenty-five miles up the river. Because of the size of the encampment, Harrison did not confront the Indians but rode to the nearest Mounted Police detachment and swore out a complaint. Two Mounties together with Harrison and Running Wolf went to the campsite but found it deserted; in the snow they discovered a cache of beef. Running Wolf had no trouble following the trail, and later in the day they came upon a camp of six Stoney lodges.

When other ranchers heard about the killing,

These Stoney Indians were photographed at the OH Ranch near High River in 1891. Members of their tribe wandered the foothills in search of game and were sometimes accused of killing cattle. *Glenbow Archives/NA-466-10*

they formed a posse in Pincher Creek, consisting of two Mounties and three ranchers. They met at the Stoney camp and told the Indians they were under arrest.

> The sergeant . . . told his followers to go into the lodges and secure the firearms which they did. One Indian, noticing Const. Carroll coming out of the lodge with a rifle, gave a war whoop, which was echoed by the rest, and seized his rifle, whereupon Sergt. Ashe grasped the rifle with his hand and the other cocked his revolver and put it to the Indian's head, who seeing his determination, let go the rifle.[1]

The Stoneys were taken to Pincher Creek, where two men, John St. Joe and Jozippa, admitted killing the stock. They complained that they were starving and had been unable to find any game. The judge was unsympathetic. He rejected their plea of starvation and said, "The Government has given each band a reservation and feeds you on it, and the white men pay the Government for land to graze their cattle, and you have no right to destroy anything belonging to the whites."

The two men received jail terms of six months, while Running Wolf was praised for leading the ranchers to the Indian camp. When he accepted tea, sugar, tobacco, and five dollars, Running Wolf didn't bother to explain that the Stoneys were his people's traditional enemies and he would be glad to turn them in any time.

Farther north, a retired British general, T. Bland Strange, established his ranch adjacent to the Blackfoot Reserve. He was convinced that those Indians "were ever on the alert to kill a cow or a calf, although they were abundantly supplied with beef by Government."[2] In 1886 he lodged a complaint (one of many) with the local Indian agent but admitted he had given permission for Indians to butcher any cattle they found dead on the prairie as long as they brought him the hides. The evidence of cattle killing was so inconclusive that the charges were never proven. Strange was furious.

With all savages, leniency has no meaning but cowardice, and is followed by contempt. Cattle killing became common from impunity and the facility with which it could be managed among the vast herds scattered over wide tracts.[3]

On the Blood Reserve, grazing leases were issued to such companies as the Cochrane, with the result that hundreds of cattle were wandering under the very noses of hungry young Indians. As long as the beef ration remained at a pound a day per person, there was no trouble. However, as soon as it was reduced late in 1889, cattle started to disappear. During the ensuing winter, in one month alone a young man named Different Person killed a calf belonging to Jim Bell and was sent to the penitentiary for two years; White Top Knot butchered a Cochrane calf but escaped to Montana; and some Cochrane Ranch cowboys caught two Bloods trying to bury a live calf in the snow so that it would freeze to death and they could claim its carcass. When the cowboys tried to apprehend them, one of the Indians drew a revolver and they escaped. The authorities complained to Chief Red Crow. He sympathized but tried to explain the situation:

> He had no doubt that the guilty parties were young men drawing rations for one, that their rations did not last them more than a day & when hungry went off alone to kill cattle.[4]

The situation became so bad that the agent organized an Indian police force for the primary purpose of patrolling the herds and stamping out the killings. But rather than ending the practice, this action simply resulted in additional arrests and made the lawbreakers more cautious. For the next three years, the spasmodic killings continued, with the Cochrane Ranch being the main loser. Then in 1893 some young men turned to two seasoned veterans for help. Big Rib and Black Rabbit both had served jail terms and were familiar with the ways of the law.

These two men organized a gang of cattle killers to feed the hungry on the reserve. They showed them how to scout the southwest corner of the reserve to look for Cochrane cattle. At night, a team of young men would kill a chosen animal, butcher it, and carry the meat back to their camps. Sam Steele of the North-West Mounted Police was convinced they were killing 350 cattle a year in this fashion.

But all good things must come to an end. The following year, the men began fighting among themselves, and one of them informed on the whole gang. Eighteen Indians were arrested; the two leaders turned Queen's evidence and were released, while the others got sentences ranging up to two years. That wholesale arrest, plus an improvement in rationing, saw cattle killing reduced to a mere trickle.

Cattle killing also occurred among the Metis, many of whom were dislocated after the Riel Rebellion of 1885. Some fled to Montana, where they started small farms or looked for work on ranches and towns. Others turned to cattle killing to provide food for their camps.

In 1894, a trio of rustlers set up operations on the American side of the Sweetgrass Hills, taking horses and cattle from both sides of the line. The three men—Joseph Delorme, William Belcourt, and John Sayers—threatened to burn out anyone who informed on them and to kill anyone who tried to arrest them. A Montana rancher who was losing stock to the raiders posted a cowboy to watch their movements, but he became so frightened by their bullying that he managed to be somewhere else whenever a raid took place.

In spite of the threats, both the American and Canadian authorities were determined to stop the rampage. Commented Superintendent R. Burton Deane:

It was intimated that the half-breeds were in the habit of occasionally crossing the international boundary in their nefarious pursuit and, as we had no means of watching their settlement in Montana, the settlers were re-

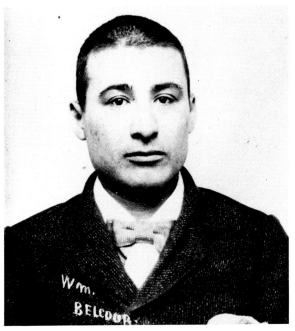

William Belcourt was one of a trio of outlaws in the Sweetgrass Hills, rustling cattle on both sides of the line. The Mounted Police arrested him in 1894, but when he proved to be fifteen hundred feet inside the United States at the time, he was released. However, American authorities caught him rustling two years later and sentenced him to five years in Deer Lodge Penitentiary. *Powell County Museum & Arts Foundation/189*

quested if possible to give us notice of their coming to Canadian soil.[5]

The persistence paid off, and in April, Corporal Dickson at the Writing-on-Stone detachment received a tip that the trio were on their way to Canada. After extensive searching, he finally found them at Halfbreed Coulee, about ten miles from the post. At that point the boundary line was supposedly marked by a pile of buffalo bones; the Metis were camped a short distance to the north. Explained Deane:

When day dawned, Corporal Dickson first of all secured the half-breeds' horses and hid them at a short distance . . . Presently two of them started off to bring in their horses. Taking the precaution to arrest the man who was left in camp before he could reach his fire-arms, Corporal Dickson then discharged the rifle and guns which he found in the camp, and the reports brought back the other two men who were easily secured.

When the Mountie searched the camp he found the remains of a calf and a cow, the latter bearing the brand of the Circle Ranch. It had been shot in the head with a rifle. He then marked the place where the arrest had occurred and took the prisoners to Lethbridge for trial. A surveyor was sent out to measure the exact location, and to everyone's surprise the arrest had taken place twenty-two chains inside the United States. The bone-pile marker was not on the border after all. There was no way the Canadian government could prosecute the cattle killers, and a judge concluded that their offence was not an extraditable one so the men were set free.

It must be remembered that cattle were the *raison d'être* of the ranching industry; they were like

$200
REWARD !

The undersigned promise to pay $25 each towards the above reward, for any information that will lead to the conviction of any one killing or stealing cattle belonging to any of them, (convictions against Indians excepted) :

Alberta Ranche.	H. M. Hatfeild,
F. W. Godsal,	C. Kettles.
L. Sexton,	A. M. Morden,
North Fork Ranche,	Stewart Ranche.

Cattle rustlers were a constant problem. In 1895, a number of ranchers offered a reward for the arrest of anyone ("Indians excepted") caught killing their stock. *Macleod Gazette, 22 March 1895*

cash on the hoof. Therefore, they were logical prey for the unscrupulous and fair game for anyone easily tempted. A calf missed in the roundup and weaned from its mother could be awfully enticing to a small-time rancher. A butcher running a shop in a ranching area might easily find a cowboy to bring him a beef in the middle of the night with no questions asked. And a homesteader barely making ends meet could convince himself that a big rancher would never miss a little calf.

The big outfits practised their own form of cattle rustling, although they didn't see it that way. This was the branding of mavericks found during the spring or fall roundup. A maverick was any cow or horse not carrying a brand. In the early 1880s, the Wyoming government decided that mavericks could be sold to the highest bidder and the proceeds used to pay the expenses of the roundup. This never became the law in Canada, but the big ranchers liked the idea and followed it. In addition, unbranded heifers were killed during the roundup to provide meat for the camps.

The losers in this practice were the little guys—small ranchers and homesteaders with a few head of cattle. If their stock happened to be grazing when a bunch of cowboys came through on the roundup, they were in danger of being swept away with the rest of the range cattle. And if the calves had been weaned but not yet branded, they ended up with the rest of the mavericks.

When Judge Charles Rouleau heard a cattle-rustling case in Calgary in 1895, he bitterly attacked the practice. He pointed out that two big ranching organizations, the Circle Ranch and the High River Stock Association, were appropriating any mavericks found in the area south of Calgary. The Circle Ranch rounded up and branded any mavericks found south of the Bow River and east of the Calgary-Macleod Trail, while the High River organization took anything west of the trail. Judge Rouleau faced the question head-on and said,

If the ranchmen think that they can make a law of this kind to suit themselves it is time they were disabused of any such idea, and he further intimated that if any person doing such an act were brought before him, and the evidence showed him that these parties had placed their brands upon or had sold an animal that did not belong to them, he would not hesitate to punish them severely for it.[6]

However, every big roundup in western Canada continued to gather and brand mavericks. Any suggestion that these cattle become the property of the Crown was immediately greeted with derision. When G.W. "Doc" Fields, foreman of the Walrond Ranch, heard this he commented, "Queen Victoria is a Joe Dandy if she gets e'er a maverick off the WR range."[7] No one challenged the practice in the courts until 1903, when two German settlers near Medicine Hat each lost an unbranded animal to the Plume Creek roundup. In one instance, the settler went to the roundup and tried to recover his steer, but according to the police, "The captain of the round-up pooh-poohed his claim, admittedly took no steps to ascertain whether the claim was well founded or not, and the steer was in due course sold by auction as a maverick (or unbranded animal) for $19." The other settler fared equally as bad, his heifer selling for $16.50.[8]

The Mounted Police had always been concerned about branding mavericks as it could become a means of stealing. Superintendent Deane explained the process:

I will assume that the rounding-up has been completed, and the cattle are gathered at the rendezvous in readiness for the cutting out. The first class of animals to be cut out are the cows with calves. That is an operation that requires great care, and in a properly conducted round-up only the most capable and knowledgeable and best mounted men are al-

Large and small ranchers united in 1893 to offer a $500 reward for the capture of cattle rustlers. *The Calgary Herald,* 3 November 1893

$500.00 REWARD.

The undersigned will pay a reward of $500.00 to any party giving information that will lead to a conviction of any person or persons killing, branding or otherwise illegally handling cattle bearing the following brands:—
THOS. CURRY

3	Conrad Bros.
O	W G Conrad.
44	Glengarry Ranch Co.
⊞	Winder Ranch
I	New Oxley Ranch Co, Ltd
20	Browning Bros.
WR	Walrond Ranch
IV	Maunsell Bros
⊡	Maunsell Bros
Ū	F. S. Stimson
••	Alexander Ranch
Z Z	F W Godsal
♔	W D Kerfoot
ℳ	John McDougal
⊞	W Bell-Irving
℞	James Rogers
X̄Y	Herbert Samson
X̄	Herbert Samson
ᴐC	William E Cochrane
⊟	Ronald Greig
76	C. A. C. & C. Co.
a7	A E Cross
P	George Emerson
Z	Quorn Ranch Co.
C	Cochrane Ranch Co,
♡	George Ross
75	W C Wells
Q	John Quirk
99	John Ware.
25	Hull Bros & Co.
2	Hull Bros & Co.

98

lowed to enter the herd. Two men apply themselves to each cow and calf, riding on each side and a little behind the animals, which are quietly conducted out of the day-herd (as it is called), and headed towards the "cut" which they are intended to join.[9]

However, the process did not always run that smoothly, and often the calf became separated from its mother. If this was accidental, then the cow was left with the main herd until it could be united with her calf. Deane suspected that some of these actions were deliberate, particularly when cutting out cattle owned by a small rancher who was not represented at the roundup. In that instance, cows and unbranded calves were held separately until the end of the roundup, at which time the calves were sold and the money went to the stock association.

After the two Germans had laid their complaint, James Crawford, captain of the roundup, was arrested and charged with theft. The cattle associations were outraged. The Western Stock Growers Association, Medicine Hat Stock Growers Association, and Maple Creek Stock Growers Association joined forces to hire P.J. "Paddy" Nolan, an outstanding Calgary criminal lawyer, to defend the accused. The judge was A.L. Sifton, later premier of Alberta.

Witnesses claimed that the sale of mavericks had been in effect since the formation of the first stock associations and followed a long-established principle. They said that unbranded stock on the open range was too much of a temptation, that a brand signified ownership, and that the stock associations had the right to dispose of

In 1895, the High River Stock Association was willing to pay $100 for the conviction of anyone stealing its members' cattle. *Calgary Weekly Herald, 10 September 1895*

any unbranded stock they found during the course of a roundup. Judge Sifton disagreed. He pointed out that the procedure had never been legalized and that no law required a person to brand his stock. He found Crawford guilty but gave him a suspended sentence and ordered reparation to the two German settlers.

Earlier in the ranching era, this decision may have had far-reaching effects, for it questioned the absolute authority of the roundup captain and the legality of certain aspects of the roundup itself. However, by 1903, settlers were already carving up the big leases, and the golden era was almost at an end. In the few years that were left for spring and fall roundups, cowboys simply had to be more careful when cutting out stock and to keep cows and calves together so they would not be accused of stealing.

Meanwhile, cattle rustling continued unabated during this period. One of the most common methods of stealing cattle was to alter the brand so it could not be recognized or to make it conform to the thief's brand.

The Mounted Police gave an example of such an instance in 1904 when four hundred young dogies from Manitoba were unloaded at Maple Creek. When a storm hit, some wandered away before they could be branded. A rancher named John Lawrence and one of his cowboys, A.J. McConnell, saw this as an excellent chance to make some easy money and rounded up thirteen head of the strays. Six of the calves were branded with JL (Lawrence's

---

$100 Reward

THE High River Stock Association will pay a Reward of $100 for the conviction of any person or persons stealing, illegally branding or making away with any cattle or calves belonging to members of the Association

J. W. FEARON,

jy31-w3m   Sec. H. R. Stock Ass'n.

brand), and seven with 7-11-7 (seven eleven seven), a purely fictitious brand. If they had been caught with the stolen cattle, the latter brand could not be traced to them. When the time came to sell the stolen stock, a line would be burned across the top of the first 7 and the bottom of the 11, creating McConnell's TU7 brand. However, when the rancher learned that McConnell had also applied the fake brand to some of his cattle he had him charged with theft. It may have been a dumb thing to do, but Lawrence warned McConnell not to reveal their scheme as no one would believe him and "he had money enough to buy the police and friends enough to fix up evidence in his favor."[10]

Meanwhile, the owners of the lost stock were searching the prairies and some weeks later they discovered three of their dogies carrying the JL brand. McConnell, who was serving four years, agreed to testify in exchange for immunity. Here was an opportunity to get his revenge. When details of the scheme were revealed, Lawrence was convicted and also received four years. Some people were shocked when the "respectable" rancher was convicted of rustling, for he had a huge spread and already owned between twelve thousand and fifteen thousand cattle. But others had had their suspicions about him for years. A policeman heard the following conversation between two ranchers after the verdict was rendered:

"Well, Joe, what do you think of this?"

"It would have done more good, Pete, if it had happened fifteen years ago."[11]

There were several ways of altering a brand, the most common being to use a running iron or acid. A running iron could be an ordinary branding iron with the end removed or a "round iron," made by cutting a wagon iron in two and using the rounded end. According to L.V. Kelly, "This implement was exceptionally simple of concealment, as it could be slipped inside a long boot-leg and kept out of sight until necessity or opportunity for its use arose."[12]

In some instances, a rustler registered a brand that was similar to one used by a large outfit that ran its stock in the area. In this way, the transformation of an "L" into a "U" could be performed by the simple application of a red-hot running iron. The only way the police could know for sure whether the brand had been altered was to kill the animal and check the inside of the hide. Invariably, the original brand would show through while the added section would not.

Another means of "acquiring" an animal was to apply a hair brand. This process involved cutting or scraping along the lines to be added and rubbing the area with acid. This burned the skin and created an effect similar to a running iron. Its advantage was that it did not require the tools or branding fires and lasted long enough for the thief to dispose of the critter.

The Circle Ranch was the subject of a rustling scheme in which brands were being altered. Belknap "Ballie" Buck, foreman of the Circle outfit, heard gossip that a rancher named Edward Holmes was rustling stock and altering the distinctive O brand to 7UK. He tipped off a former Circle wagon boss, W.S. Hill, who had a ranch nearby, and asked him to keep an eye on the man. On the pretext of looking for strays, Hill went to the Holmes Ranch and saw a heifer bearing the 7UK brand that he recalled seeing two months earlier with the Circle brand. He and one of his cowboys, Jim Fuller, put the place under surveillance. A short time later, the heifer was driven into Holmes's corral and early the following morning the two men saw Holmes and a cowhand kill and butcher it.

Satisfied with what he had seen, Hill went to the corral, pulled a revolver on the rustler, and told him he was under arrest. Holmes wanted to go in the house "to wash his hands" but the wagon boss refused; he was wary in case Holmes was going for his gun.[13] They loaded the evidence into a wagon, picked up Ballie Buck at the Circle, and delivered the rustler to the Mounted Police. He got five years in the penitentiary for cattle rustling.

In the 1890s, a gang east of the Cypress Hills developed a handy scheme for rustling cattle. They had a small "ranch" about twenty miles from a large lease that was being shared by two cattle companies. These two firms often relied on the other to do the range work, so a lot of calves missed the spring roundups and wandered the range un-branded. The rustlers had chosen their spread carefully. It offered good cover and a nearby coulee led to a creek bottom. There they built a cabin, corrals, and stable close together, while some distance away was a large closed-in shed and on a nearby hill was another corral.

The routine was simple. Two cowboys rode out in the morning while a third stayed behind to watch for visitors. When the rustlers found a herd of cattle with their unbranded calves, they rounded up about a dozen and frightened them into a stampede. As they ran, the cowboys turned them in the direction of their camp and kept them running by firing shots into the air. Gradually the cows dropped out one by one until only the calves were left.

This young stock was driven west until the riders came in sight of the corrals on the hill. By prearranged plan, any time visitors arrived at the camp, the third rustler found an excuse to hang a couple of red blankets on the corral fence. These could be seen for miles and warned the others not to come in. They stayed on the range until the blankets were removed or until after nightfall, when they quietly herded the calves into the closed shed. According to rangeman Hugo Maguire, "The calves would never bellow in the dark shed, and the visitor would leave next morning never knowing there was a calf on the ranch."[14] Later, the calves were branded and sold. There is no indication that the gang was ever caught.

Unlike horse thieves, who could travel long distances at great speed and market their stolen goods far from the scene of the crime, cattle rustlers had to ply their nefarious trade in their own areas since the stock could not be moved quickly or easily.

Witness the case of Arthur Collyns and Romain Gervais, two cowboys working on a ranch a few miles from the Bar U. Their boss was C.T.G. Knox, a Calgarian who left the care of his stock to the two men. However, he became suspicious when his calf crop fell from 106 in 1895 to 75 a year later. Conditions had been good and other ranches had done well, so the sharp drop seemed unusual. Local gossip was that the two men were applying their own brands to some of the calves and placing them in their herds.

One day in the spring of 1897, Fred Stimson, manager of the Bar U, noticed two Hereford steers carrying Knox's brand; one of them had a unique white star on its forehead. Two months later he saw them again; this time, Knox's bar brand on the hip had been converted to a fictitious Lazy P and Collyns's 8D brand had been added to their ribs. During a roundup that summer, Knox's cattle were taken to the Bar U corrals, where the two steers were cut out and the rest driven to a sale at the HL Ranch. A week later, Collyns claimed the two animals as his own. Stimson immediately notified the Mounted Police and both Collyns and Gervais were arrested.

During the trial, the police testified to the discovery of 8D and P branding irons belonging to Collyns. Also, one of A.E. Cross's cattle had been found with the A7 brand obliterated and covered with an 8D. In the end, there was not enough evidence to convict Gervais, but Collyns was found guilty of cattle rustling and lost on appeal.

One of the natural alliances in a cattle-rustling scheme was between a cowboy and a butcher. Stealing a cow might be fairly simple, but marketing it without being caught was another matter. If a dishonest butcher was willing to buy the stock from an equally dishonest cowboy, then everybody was happy—except the owner of the beef.

One such case occurred at Fort Macleod in 1904. A butcher named Richard Train had an abattoir near Rocky Coulee, from which point he not only sold direct to local farmers but also provided beef wholesale to Claresholm and Granum. After a while, people became suspicious about his source of beef and notified the police. They kept a watch on the place, and one evening they apprehended Train and two cowboys just as they were killing two beef animals. Both had been stolen from the Bar U by a cowboy named A.F. Blunden, but the butcher had been smart enough to get a bill of sale from him. Though they could not get Train on that charge, a search of his slaughterhouse revealed a pile of cowhides with the brands cut out of them.

These cowboys are skinning a beef on the prairie near Milk River. Rustlers sometimes worked the same way. In a short time they could kill a cow, butcher it, and pack the meat away by wagon or packhorse. *Glenbow Archives/NA–777–28*

Two partially burned pieces found in a stove were enough evidence to leave him wide open for prosecution.

Perhaps the most famous and controversial cattle rustling/butcher case occurred at Fort Macleod in 1903 when Charles "Hip-O" Johnson was charged with cattle stealing. He had come to southern Alberta ten years earlier, settling on a ranch near Slideout. This is when he registered the O brand on the left hip, giving him the nickname of "Hip-O" or sometimes "Hippo." At the turn of the century, he opened a butcher shop in Fort Macleod, where he became one of the community's most popular merchants.

By 1903, cattle rustling had reached such epidemic proportions that the local stock association hired a detective to root out the thieves. The only problem was that their choice, W.W. Foster, was himself a shady character. He apparently had stolen a horse from the Powder River Ranching Company in Wyoming, had been connected with hold-ups, served time in American jails, and had been blacklisted by stock associations across the line. Witnesses described him as "a bad character," and "unprincipled" with an "evil career."[15]

Realizing that rustlers often worked in collusion with local butchers, Foster got a job at Hip-O Johnson's and, according to his testimony, "butchered many cattle some of which did not belong to Johnson." In particular, he said Johnson killed a cow bearing a JO brand. So he reported it to the stock inspector. The next day the Mounted Police searched the slaughterhouse and found the hide. Johnson was committed for trial, but some local people were so convinced of his innocence that they arranged for his escape.

Armed with tools, Johnson removed the bars from his cell door, crawled through the hole, knocked out the guard, and escaped. He crossed the line into the United States, changed his name to William Caldwell, and worked for ranchers in Wyoming, Colorado, and Oklahoma before settling near Belt, south of Great Falls. The stock association offered a thirteen-hundred-dollar reward for his capture, but it was reduced to two hundred dollars a year later. Meanwhile, Johnson's wife and family stayed at the ranch. Although they kept in touch with him, he couldn't return home, not even when his son drowned in a nearby lake.

Finally, in 1908, five years after his escape,

Deputy Sheriff Kirsch recaptured Johnson and he was extradited to Canada. At the trial, three main witnesses testified against him. The first was Foster, the shady stock detective. Then there was Bland Herring, owner of the JO cow, who said he had never sold the animal. And finally a respected rancher, E.H. Maunsell, representing the stock association, who had gone to the slaughterhouse with the police when the arrest was made.

For the defence, rancher J.M. Bratton said that he had examined all the hides at Johnson's slaughterhouse and, contrary to Foster's statement, found they tallied with the records. Hip-O's son Jesse testified that at the time Foster had slaughtered the JO cow, his father was out of town. This was corroborated by D.L. Mudiman, who said Johnson was at his farm that day buying pigs.

One of the most interesting witnesses was A. Jensen, of Great Falls, who had been Johnson's employer while he worked in Montana. Jensen "testified to Johnson's good habits and excellent character since employment with him. Foster's reputation, he understood, was exceedingly bad." Several Fort Macleod businessmen testified next, all swearing to the butcher's good standing in the community. However, in the end, the judge chose to believe Foster, and Hip-O Johnson was sentenced to four years in the Edmonton penitentiary.

Many were convinced that Johnson had been framed. They believed that Foster was so anxious to keep his job that he stole the cow, butchered it when Johnson was away, and then reported it to the stock association. The real truth will never be known, but the people of the area, led by E.H. Maunsell, signed a petition and succeeded in having the sentence reduced to two years.

Meanwhile, stockmen continued to complain about rustlers and the losses they were causing.

The *modus operandi* is very simple. The cattle rustler rides the ranges with a running iron strapped to his saddle and generally in stormy weather and picks up the unbranded cattle, and more often calves which have arrived at the age to be easily weaned from their mothers. It

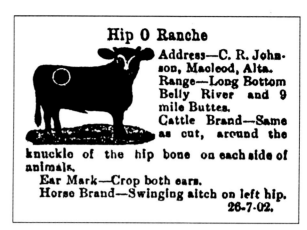

Charles Johnson had been a respectable rancher and butcher before being accused of stealing cattle. His brand gave him the nickname of Hip-O Johnson. Friends believed he had been framed. *Macleod Gazette, 27 March 1903*

is only a work of a few minutes for these experts to rope the calf and drive it to some place where it is held till it would not be claimed by the mother, or recognized by the owner.[16]

Unlike other aspects of nineteenth-century ranch life, cattle rustling did not disappear when the big ranches were broken up. It remained—and is still today—one of the biggest headaches of western ranchers. Only the methods have changed. Where rustlers once raided unguarded herds on the open range, now they use trucks and cattleliners to steal stock from deeded lands or community pastures. Cattle usually go straight to slaughter or, if unbranded, they end up at an auction yard bearing someone else's brand. The details may vary, but in the eyes of a cowboy, a rustler is still a rustler.

OUTLAWS

Not all cowboys were honest, generous souls who would give the shirts off their backs to people in need. In fact, there were some who would steal another man's shirt or anything else that wasn't nailed down. The cowboy's way of life provided excellent opportunities for a criminal. He was free and unencumbered, able to wander from job to job with no questions asked. He was often laid off in the fall and had time on his hands until spring. He had a skill—particularly if he was a horse breaker—that meant he always had a job to fall back on or a place to hide out when he needed it. He was accustomed to a rugged life, so being holed up for weeks in the hills or travelling day and night to escape his pursuers was no great hardship. And the ranching territory was so sparsely populated and close to the border that many of his crimes went unpunished. Admittedly, the lawbreakers were in the minority, although there were enough of them on the Canadian frontier to make life interesting.

But the Canadian West was not like the American West—either the real one or the imaginary one of pulp fiction. Canada had no lynchings of horse thieves, gunfights at the OK Corral, crooked sheriffs, or gunfighters travelling from town to town looking for trouble. On the other hand, the Canadian West was not entirely docile; it had its share of horse stealing, cattle rustling, bootlegging, theft, general mayhem, and murder.

There was a noticeable difference in the presence of law in the American and Canadian West. Americans were not essentially a lawless people, but if they found themselves in a situation where the law was ineffectual or nonexistent, they had no hesitation in making their own rules. This is what happened on the frontier. In some areas, the only jurisdiction was the army, and its mandate was limited. As the ranching industry became established, marshals and sheriffs were elected, but there was no way they could control the flotsam and jetsam of a disrupted society that spread across the American frontier after the Civil War. As a result, horse thieves were lynched and cowboys settled their arguments with six-shooters. Men were governed more by their attitudes of right and wrong than by the dictates of the law.

The Canadian West was entirely different. Here, the law preceded settlement, the North-West Mounted Police arriving while the territory was still

controlled by Indians and traders. By the time the ranching industry moved northward across the international border, the principle of Queen's justice had taken hold and virtually everyone accepted it. There was no need for people to make or enforce their own laws. And because settlement came later in western Canada than in the western United States, the misfits of the post–Civil War period were noticeably absent. Western Canada's main misfits were remittence men and political appointees from the East.

This is not to say the Canadian West was dull. It wasn't; it simply lacked the violence of the American West. Over the years, a number of the larger ranches had their share of cowboys who had been in trouble in the United States. Fred Ings noted that most of them respected the law when they came to Canada. "I have known and ridden with several chaps who were wanted for depredations across the line," he wrote, "but while here they led decent, law-abiding lives, and were fine fellows."[1] L.V. Kelly noted that when authorities broke up the notorious Kingfisher Gang in Texas in 1888, a number of its members came to Canada "where they proved splendid stock-hands and became respectable and honored citizens."[2]

One of the most famous "bad men" to work in Canada was Harry Longabaugh, the Sundance Kid. He had been a cowboy in Wyoming when he was first arrested in 1887 for stealing a saddle. After serving time he joined up with "Butch" Cassidy and other outlaws to rob a bank, and when things got too hot for him Longabaugh fled to Canada. He found work as a horse breaker at the Bar U Ranch in 1890 and later worked at the H2. During his time in Canada the Kid was a law-abiding citizen and was described as a "thoroughly likeable fellow . . . a general favourite with everyone, a splendid rider and a top notch cow hand."[3]

During the winter of 1891-92, the Kid became a partner in a saloon at the Grand Central Hotel in Calgary. There are unverified accounts that Butch Cassidy visited him during that time. In the spring, a dispute arose between the Kid and the saloon keeper over wages. "The Kid, behind the bar when

The most famous outlaw to visit Canada was the Sundance Kid, seen here with the Hole-in-the-Wall Gang. *(Left to right):* Harry Longabaugh (the Sundance Kid), Will Carver, Ben Kilpatrick, Harry Logan (Kid Curry), and Robert Parker (Butch Cassidy). *Denver Public Library/F13281*

the row started, vaulted over and before his feet hit the floor his gun barrel was jammed in his partner's middle."[4] There was no gunplay, but once the Kid collected his money, the partnership dissolved.

The outlaw left Calgary a short time later and went to work for the N Bar N Ranch in Montana where he joined a gang that was rustling cattle on both sides of the border. Later in 1892, the Kid helped rob a train at Malta, Montana, and likely hid out in Canada until things quietened down. Afterwards, he moved farther south where, with the "Wild Bunch," he held up a number of trains and

banks before moving to Texas and finally to South America. It is believed he was killed in Bolivia in 1908 after a payroll holdup. Fred Ings reflected the feelings of many Alberta cowboys when he wrote, "We all felt sorry when he left and got in bad again across the line."[5]

Canadian examples of "real" gunfights, where both parties were armed and shooting at one another, are few and far between. More common were situations where only one party was armed, or in one instance where a man had a gun and a handful of billiard balls. A "typical"

Canadian gunplay occurred at a Metis fiddle dance in Calgary in 1886. The gathering took place in Ellis's hall, an old restaurant on the southern edge of town. It was mostly a Metis affair, and since there was a noticeable shortage of women, each man had to wait his turn and danced about every third dance. However, one of the cowboys, John Bertrand—known locally as the Black Kid—ignored the social graces and stayed on the floor for ten straight dances. For this, Hank Forbes, another cowboy and former detective for the South-West Stock Association, roundly chastised him.

The Black Kid responded by slugging the detective and knocking him down. An angry Forbes stomped out and went to his camp for his gun. As soon as he appeared at the door of the hall, the Kid dived to the floor and tried to escape by crawling through Forbes's legs. While he was in this exposed position, Forbes fired twice, the first bullet going through the Kid's hat and the second striking the floor. The Kid managed to reach the door and was fleeing around a corner when Forbes fired again. This time, the bullet grazed the Kid's side. With a howl, he fell to the ground, at which point Forbes walked up to him and fired a fourth shot at close range. This should have killed him. But Forbes was such a poor shot that the bullet merely grazed his unarmed opponent's forearm. By this time the crowd was pouring outside, so Forbes hurried away into the night. Next morning, the police heard that he was already on his way to his former stamping grounds in Montana.

As far as more traditional gunfights were concerned, there were only three cases reported in Canadian cowboy country. There may have been others, but if there was no loss of life the incidents likely never reached the ears of the Mounted Police or the press. Two of the recorded ones happened in the same year, 1885, while the third occurred just after the turn of the century.

The first was a vicious confrontation that occurred on 9 July and was the only one to result in a death. The principals were Ben Hale and Robert Casey. Hale was a working cowboy employed by O.S. Main, who had a large ranch near Fort Macleod. Hale was in Medicine Hat on his way to the Teton River in Montana to meet his boss on a cattle-buying trip. Casey had been a cowboy in Montana, then worked as a stagecoach driver out of Fort Benton for William Rowe. One winter he got lost in a blizzard near Twenty-Eight Mile Spring and wandered the prairies for nine days. By the time someone discovered him, his legs were so badly frozen that he became a partial cripple. Unable to ply his usual trade, he opened the Brunswick Hotel in Medicine Hat, where he was known to provide a bit of contraband whisky besides his room and board.[6]

Hale and Casey were old friends from their cowboy days. While Hale was in town, the two men decided to have a horse race "to settle a wager as to the respective merits of their horses."[7] When Casey won the bet, Hale claimed the race hadn't been a fair one, but he was shouted down by their cowboy friends.

They did a lot of drinking that night, so next day no one was feeling in the best of spirits. Hale had to leave for Montana, so Casey and another cowboy from the O.S. Main Ranch, Norman "Charlie" Macauley, decided to accompany him as far as Four Mile Lake and camp for the night. Along the way, Hale again raised the argument about the horse race and continued to claim his horse was the best. When they got to a settler's cabin at the lake, Hale demanded a second race. He bet a hundred dollars that he could beat Casey in a marathon race from Four Mile Lake to Kipp's ranch in Montana. Casey was just as vociferous in claiming his horse had already won the previous day's race fair and square.

Both men were becoming so infuriated that Macauley stepped in and tried to calm them, but Casey turned on him and spat, "Shut up, you son of a bitch or I'll kill you." Furious, Macauley grabbed the hotel man by the throat and released him only when Hale pulled a gun. "I've got the drop on you, Charlie," he said ominously. "Let him alone." Macauley drew his own gun but had second thoughts and returned it to its holster without ever cocking it. He decided he'd had enough; Macauley mounted his horse and rode back into town.[8]

Meanwhile, Hale and Casey went into the settler's house, where the argument broke out again. This time, Casey challenged his opponent to a gunfight, so they went outside, revolvers in hand. One of the witnesses was convinced that Casey was bluffing and that he changed his mind when he saw that Hale was prepared to go through with the duel. Casey threw his gun on the ground and said he didn't want to fight. Hale also cast his gun aside, cursing and swearing at the other man and calling him a coward.

Eventually they both recovered their guns, and according to a witness:

> Mr. Casey put his in his pocket, saying he did not want any bother. Ben asked him to come out on the Prairie and fight with revolvers. Mr. Casey said he did not wish to have any bother, he had cooled down. Ben would not let it drop but kept wanting to fight with revolvers.[9]

Casey then said something to Hale that the others didn't hear, but whatever it was, they were fatal words. Hale cursed and said, "We might as well have it out," and shot Casey in the chest.[10] Although Casey was armed, he hadn't had time to draw. When he reeled towards the house, Hale shot him in the shoulder and then in the back. Casey fell on a bed just inside the door. As he lay there dying, Hale came in and apologized and asked for forgiveness. He said, "You know, you vexed me to it or I wouldn't have done it."[11] Casey simply replied, "I'm killed, I'll die," but forgave his one-time friend.[12]

Then, as if putting a lie to their whole argument, Hale decided to take Casey's horse for his escape across the border, commenting to the settler that it was the best one. He threatened to kill the settler and his family if they tried to stop him, saying "he'd lief die for the lot as one." He added, "Tell them if they follow me, they'll have to ride fast," then spurred his horse and rode out of sight.[13]

Casey died the next morning. The coroner determined that the first shot to the chest had been the fatal one. Meanwhile, Hale easily made it across the line before a pursuit could be organized, so a

warrant was issued for his arrest. Sergeant Jones of the Mounted Police went to Fort Benton to locate the wanted man, but he "telegraphed to Superintendent McIllree that although Sheriff [John J.] Healy knew where to find Hale, he would not interfere, unless a reward were offered. Ben Hale is therefore still at large."[14]

Those who saw the killing were adamant that liquor was not a factor. Although the men had a bottle of whisky with them, one of the witnesses was convinced that, "They were not very drunk. They knew what they were doing."[15] Afterwards, someone asked the settler why he didn't do something to stop the gunfight. "Do something?" he replied. "If you had seen him with a gun . . . and blood in his eye you wouldn't have done anything but look helpless."[16] Hale was never caught.

Interestingly, the Hale-Casey encounter was probably the inspiration for an article that appeared in the *Chicago Times-Herald* in 1901. A journalist travelling through Medicine Hat likely heard a garbled version of the fight and wrote a wild article about a shootout between "Bulldog" Kelly and a man named Malone. In his version, the two men had a disagreement over cards (not a horse race) and when they wanted to kill each other, the Mounted Police suggested a duel. Next morning they met on the "Tortured Trail" outside of town where they galloped towards each other like two knights of old. In the savage shoot-out, both horses were brought down, the guns were emptied, and the men finished the fight with knives. Both were carted off to the hospital with numerous wounds. When they woke up, they so admired each other's fortitude that they decided to be friends. The whole thing was, commented the *Medicine Hat News*, an "improbable yarn."[17]

The second 1885 gunfight happened about 16 July at the Walrond Ranch, northwest of Fort Macleod. Two cowboys, Joe Thompson and Charlie Wright, had been at loggerheads for some time but their disagreements had never resulted in violence, only harsh words. On the day in question, Thompson was in the stable saddling his horse to go out on the range when Wright stomped in, angry and irritated over a problem he had just encountered. Thompson should have left him alone, but he couldn't resist complaining about some stories the other man had been circulating about him.

Wright was in no mood to argue; instead, he drew his revolver and tried to smash his adversary over the head. Thompson pulled back and offered to take on Wright in a bare-knuckled fight. But, as he later wrote, his opponent was a gunman, not a boxer:

> He said he was no fighting man, and walked out of the stable, having the revolver in his hand cocked all the while. He then shot at me and I returned the fire by pulling my revolver and shooting at him.[18]

Wright ran for cover and two more shots were exchanged. Then, taking aim through a small window in a shed, Wright fired a third time, hitting his adversary in the left shoulder. As the wounded man fell to the ground with a howl, other cowboys who had been attracted by the gunfire rushed to the scene and disarmed both men. According to the press,

> Immediately after the shooting, in which both men displayed an abundance of that quality known as sand, Wright bid a tender farewell to his old stamping grounds and mounting a horse, struck out for Montana.[19]

The Mounted Police surgeon in Fort Macleod successfully removed the ball. Wright made it across the line and was never brought to trial.

The third incident involved a cowboy who was more at home with a lariat than a gun, and had built up quite a reputation as a colourful lawbreaker in the Fort Macleod area. His name was Joe Gallagher, son of Mike Gallagher who had joined the North-West Mounted Police in the 1870s. When the father's term expired, he had taken his discharge, married his childhood sweetheart, and started a ranch on the outskirts of town. When the blizzard of 1886-87 almost wiped him out, he turned from ranching to mixed farming. The couple had five children; the four girls all married well and settled down, but the boy was a maverick. His father may have been a farmer, but as soon as Joe left school he became a cowboy.

His first brush with the law occurred in 1900, just after he turned twenty. While drinking in Fort Macleod he got into a swearing match with one of the citizens, which led to his arrest by Constable Dooley, a man described as "a plump and good natured Irishman."[20] The policeman was escorting him to the barracks when Gallagher suddenly broke loose and mounted his horse, which was tethered nearby. The fugitive galloped away for a few hundred yards then, taking his lariat, he made a loop and dashed forward to rope the Mountie. The constable ducked into a doorway at the last moment and the lariat merely knocked off his forage cap. The *Gazette* commented that if the policeman had been caught it "would in all probability have ended that gentleman's career once and for all."[21]

Constable Dooley took cover while Gallagher rode up and down the street, challenging him to come out. Instead, the policeman contacted the barracks for help and two Mounties, both new recruits, came to his rescue. Seeing that he was outnumbered, Gallagher rode to the edge of town while several more police and a Peigan Indian scout joined in the pursuit. As one of the constables came close, the cowboy turned in his saddle and neatly roped him, jerking him out of his saddle. Reported the *Gazette*,

> The lad in the red coat was as near his death as ever he will be, but the other policemen galloped up and with their pistols they managed to intimidate Gallagher for a minute until the rope was slipped off . . . As it was, he received a nasty twist and has been reported unfit for duty.

Gallagher made a dash for the open prairie, but again he stopped and twirled his rope threateningly in the air. Respecting the cowboy's skill, the posse stayed back; they tried to surround him but

man is on a horse himself.

Gallagher galloped through the hail of bullets to the river, where he crossed and disappeared from view. Believing he would try to get another horse and make a break for the Montana border, the Mounties posted guards at nearby ranches. That night, Gallagher tried to pick up a horse at Robins's Ranch and was finally apprehended.

None of the bullets had touched Gallagher or his horse, although one of the policemen's horses had been struck in the leg. It turned out that the cowboy had been unarmed. Later, the police were disciplined for the unnecessary use of firearms, and Gallagher was let off with a warning. The *Gazette* lamented the incident. While admitting the cowboy had "managed to make more excitement in Macleod than has been seen for many a day," it saw the demonstration as a blot on the town's reputation as a law-abiding community.

But that wasn't the end of Gallagher's career or his ability to create a sensation. Over the next few years, each time he went on a binge he was ready for a fight. While drunk, said the *Gazette*, "his one great ambition is to rope the whole North-West Mounted Police Force."[22]

In 1904, while working on a ranch near

he galloped away again. Meanwhile, a number of prostitutes at a nearby brothel yelled words of encouragement to the beleaguered cowboy. One of the policemen fired his revolver in the air but Gallagher responded by drawing something that looked like a gun and waving it around.

Gallagher now appeared to be determined to hurt someone and as they could not run him down on account of the superiority of his horse, the policemen opened fire at his horse in the hopes of disabling it. But it is not very easy to hit a horse going at full speed, with a heavy revolver, especially when the marks-

Claresholm, he was drinking in the Wilton Hotel when he fired a number of shots through the ceiling of the bar. A couple of days later, he went to a Claresholm restaurant, but because he had been drinking, was ordered to leave. He stomped out, swore at the owner and customers, and left town.

Next morning he was back and tried to get a drink at the Wilton Hotel bar. However the bartender, Colin Tillotson, recalled his last escapade and refused to serve him. Gallagher angrily hurled a barroom chair at him, and when the man rushed off to summon the police, the cowboy helped himself to a quart of Irish whisky. By the time Corporal Hartzog arrived, Gallagher had already gone to the livery stable for his horse. The policeman found him there, but the cowboy spurred his horse and galloped down the street. Then, instead of riding out of town he went back to the hotel, built a loop on his lariat, and tried to lasso the bartender, who was standing outside watching the excitement. But his victim darted inside.

Meanwhile, Corporal Hartzog got a warrant for Gallagher's arrest, found him sleeping in a nearby shack, and put him in jail. That afternoon,

on his return from the outhouse, the prisoner spotted some guns hanging in the hallway.

He made a dash for them and succeeded in getting them from the peg before Hartzog could prevent him. He jammed a couple of cartridges into the revolver before Hartzog came up to him and then ensued a scuffle. During the scuffle Gallagher got the muzzle against the corporal's breast and pulled but the hammer fell on an empty chamber.[23]

The corporal broke free and went for a carbine in the next room while Gallagher fled out the front door, loading the revolver as he ran. Hartzog followed him and, standing at the door, ordered him to halt. Gallagher turned and fired, striking an empty chamber the first time, but then tried again.

This time there was a report and a bullet came whizzing through the air but the leaded messenger of death went wide. Hartzog then got in his work and he fired. The bullet just grazed Gallagher's neck inflicting a flesh wound. Gallagher dropped to his knees and laid the

Joe Gallagher shot up this hotel in Claresholm in 1904 and was later wounded when trying to escape the law. *Glenbow Archives/NA–5257–40*

revolver across his arm that he might get better aim, but Hartzog's carbine spoke again and the bullet went crashing into Joe's arm, shattering the bone in a horrible fashion.

The gunfight was over. Gallagher was immediately rushed to a hospital, where the doctors had to amputate his arm. He was charged with attempted murder and escape from custody, but in view of his injuries was given a suspended sentence. However, he probably got drunk and troublesome again—even with only one arm—for he was rearrested for violation of bonds a year later. This time he wasn't so lucky; he went to jail and died in 1912 at the age of thirty-two. The press referred to the unfortunate reveller as a "knight of the lariat" and dubbed him "Cowboy Joe."[24]

Among Canada's cowboy population were several who had lived by the gun in the United States but were perfectly content to abide by Canadian laws. A good example was Al Martin, who worked for several outfits around Lethbridge before the turn of the century. He was reputed to be one of the best shots on the range. When visiting "Hod" Main's ranch, he demonstrated his skill by hitting a tomato can at twenty-five yards, using a gun in his left hand. When the can was kicked into the air, he shot it again with the gun in his right hand. He did this three times to show it was no accident.

Martin was always law-abiding while living in Canada, yet he was a known gunman. In Texas he had killed a gambler who tried to draw on him, then shot a sheriff and two deputies who wanted to arrest him. Afterwards he moved to Montana, where a tough cowhand wanting to build a reputation drew on him and was shot for his trouble. Subsequently, Martin shot and killed a man named Frenchy in a saloon on the Little Muddy after the man had stabbed his friend to death. "Martin came to Alberta and lived here for a long time," said a man who had been at Little Muddy. "He kept out of trouble, made many friends, and exhibited his guns only in feats of marksmanship."[25]

Another man with a shady past was Charlie "Bowlegs" Buckley, who had been wagon boss for the TL outfit in Montana. In 1885, he came to Canada with a bunch of saddle horses for the Bar U and stayed on at the ranch. Later, he returned to Montana and was gambling in a bar in Dupuyer when he met an old adversary, a man named Laird. When Buckley offered to buy drinks, Laird asked to be included, but Buckley told him to drink from the creek "like the rest of the dogs."[26] Humiliated, Laird got his gun and killed Buckley on the spot.

Then there was a Bar U cowboy named "Lucky Bill" Brady who had been hired in 1902 with no questions asked. He was good at his job, got along well with the others, and loved to play poker. One day, the crew had to trail a herd of cattle to Montana. Just before they crossed the border, Lucky Bill claimed he had lost his wallet at the previous camp and had to go back for it. That night, when the outfit made camp near Browning, two marshals rode up and asked the foreman if he had a man named Bill Brady in his employ as they had a warrant for his arrest. The foreman answered, "There is no such a man with my outfit. You can look them over."[27] Brady wisely stayed north of the line and was waiting for the Bar U riders when they returned.

Western etiquette demanded that a person's name or place of origin not be asked unless he volunteered it. If he simply said, "I'm Slim," or "Just call me Tennessee," this was a clear indication that he would not welcome any embarrassing questions. Such men often were veteran cowhands and welcome on any ranch. They came, they worked, and they left with no one ever really knowing who they were. For example, rumour had it that a man named Glasgow who lived on a small spread south of Pincher Creek in the 1890s was an American outlaw. According to one story, he was sitting in the Pincher Creek bar when a tough-looking cowboy walked in; the man had obviously ridden for miles and was bone tired. This cowboy took one look at Glasgow, wheeled in his tracks, and rode away. No one knew why, and certainly no one had the nerve to ask Glasgow what was going on.

Another interesting person was a High River cowboy named Walter Kesee, said to have been a

"Slippery Bill" McCombe was photographed with this group of riders at a general roundup in 1901. He is to the right of centre sitting in a saddle astride a friend's back, holding a rope in the air. Friends believe he was lured to the United States and murdered by an old enemy named Walter Kesee. *Glenbow Archives/NA–1035–3*

desperado in Texas. He used an alias of Frank Collins, and according to Fred Ings, he likely had "many other names that we never heard of."[28] Kesee came to Canada about the turn of the century looking for "Slippery Bill" McCombe, a foreman for Pat Burns, who had double-crossed him in a deal in the United States. Slippery Bill promptly hired Kesee as one of his cowhands in order to keep an eye on him, realizing that fear of the Mounted Police would prevent the Texan from resorting to open gunplay.

Ings described Kesee as "long and lean, with a sharp-featured face . . . I knew him to be a gambler and that he boozed quite a lot . . . He was apt to flare up and be quarrelsome when drinking, and he carried a knife like a Mexican, and I do not doubt that he would have used it in a fight. He was the type of bad man who clung close to the national border . . . A quick get-a-way was always kept open."[29]

Because Slippery Bill was a good judge of livestock he was sometimes called upon by other ranchers to buy their cattle. One day, William Fares, a Bar U investor, wanted Bill to travel through the country, looking for likely stock. In spite of warnings from his friends, Fares gave Bill a wad of money so that he could make the purchases in cash. The fall roundup was underway when Slippery Bill started on his rounds. And though it was the busy season, Kesee suddenly quit his job and disappeared. A short time later, Slippery Bill and the money also dropped out of sight.

The story was pieced together later. Apparently Kesee knew he could not get his revenge on Slippery Bill as long as they were under the watchful eyes of the Mounted Police, so he plotted to lure his victim back into the United States. When Kesee learned that Bill was travelling around with a large amount of cash, he made a quick trip across the line where he recruited a "flashy woman" as his accomplice. According to Ings, Kesee arranged for her to meet Slippery Bill.

He fell for her wiles, and they got him to Seattle. Then they did him in, for we never heard of Slippery again; and Fares never saw a penny of his money nor had he any cows to show for it.[30]

Of course, there were some cowboys who were simply bullies and braggarts. These men often showed their worst side when they went to town and had several shots of whisky inside them. Then they wanted to shoot up the town, beat up innocent bystanders, and generally act obnoxious. In 1906, for example, the Mounted Police received a complaint that an armed man named Charles "Cowboy Jack" Monaghan was terrorizing customers at a bar in North Portal, a border town near Estevan. When Corporal Hogg arrived at the saloon he found it full of cowboys, with Monaghan obviously their leader. When the troublemaker resisted arrest, a barroom brawl erupted between the two men. The cowboys cheered for their leader but did not interfere in a fair fight. When it was over, the corporal had Cowboy Jack in handcuffs; he was a bloody mess and needed the attention of a doctor. Fortunately, the cowboy had been unarmed at the time of the melee. He later confessed to the doctor that if he had had his gun "another death would have been recorded in Canadian history."[31] Later, Corporal Hogg received a twenty-five dollar bonus for actions above and beyond the call of duty and a new scarlet tunic to replace the old one, which was too saturated with blood to use.

In 1912, a former Lethbridge city detective, Pat Egan, was almost killed when he came up against a Texas cowboy named Dick Christian. A year earlier, while Egan was still on the force, he had arrested the cowboy for starting a fight in the Lethbridge Hotel. The Texan later complained that Egan had been unnecessarily rough, but no action was taken. A couple of months later, Egan arrested him for theft but the charges were dropped; as a result Christian rightly or wrongly became convinced that the detective had it in for him. Meanwhile, Egan was having troubles of his own. He was charged with accepting payoffs from brothel owners and was dismissed from the force.

After the fall roundup Christian came into town again, this time with a bunch of his friends, vowing to get even with the ex-cop. The two adversaries first met on the street near the Alexandra Hotel at which time they began swearing at each other. Later, while Egan and two friends were walking near the Bank of Commerce, the Texan yelled at him. One of Egan's companions stated,

We barely turned our heads, Egan answering that he didn't want anything to do with Christian. We had probably taken a couple of steps when we heard a deafening report. Pat grabbed his side, yelling, "My God, he got me." He staggered a little, but straightened up. He seemed in a sort of frenzy, saying, "Where's my gun? If I only had a gun!"[32]

A policeman who witnessed the incident quickly disarmed the Texan and placed him under arrest. Egan was taken to hospital with a stomach wound and for a time there were fears that he would not live. Meanwhile, the police learned that Dick Christian's name was an alias. Also, the man had been in Montana for four years where he had punched cattle. "During that time," said a reporter, "he became notorious as a gun man when aggravated, and his escapades led to the climate of the border state becoming too warm for him, and causing his removal to Alberta."[33]

Egan recovered from his wounds, testified against the cowboy, and had the satisfaction of seeing him sentenced to three years in a penitentiary. As for Egan, he was reinstated on the force a short time later.

In another incident, a poker game south of Calgary in 1888 turned ugly when one of the players, a cowboy, thought he was being cheated. He drew his gun, at which point,

most of the party remembered that they had urgent business engagements down stairs about that time and hastened to fulfil them while the hero of the day cooly gathered up his chips and, presenting them to the cashier, got his money. He then "stood the drinks" for the crowd and left the premises.[34]

Cowboys usually settled their disputes with fists, but a 1904 disagreement between a cowboy and rancher at Pincher Creek went beyond that. The cowboy was known locally as Jesse Hindman, a big sullen man who "had quite a criminal record, and several aliases, and was 'wanted' in the U.S."[35] He worked as a horse breaker and because of his surliness he was not popular in town.

One day he was in the pool room at the Arlington Hotel when an elderly rancher, "Rattlesnake Pete" McEwen, tripped on a bench and fell against Hindman, knocking them both down. Angrily, the bronc buster, who was on his back at the time, drew his revolver and fired from the hip, narrowly missing the rancher's head. The bullet lodged in the ceiling, where it remained for many years as a reminder of the "Wild West." Regaining his feet, Hindman then struck Rattlesnake Pete with the butt end of the revolver, knocking him out.

Two pool players quickly disarmed the cowboy but he still wasn't through. Impulsively, he grabbed a number of billiard balls and began throwing them at everybody in the room. Most of the men made it safely outside, except for "Georgia" Jordan, who was struck in the kneecap and crippled for several weeks. When Hindman ran out of billiard balls, the others piled on him, beat him up, and ordered him out of town.

However, the Mounted Police heard about the melee and arrested the cowboy a short distance along the trail. At his trial for "assault with intent to cause grievous bodily harm," he swore he had never struck Rattlesnake Pete with his revolver,[36] and as the evidence was inconclusive, he was released. When the doctor who was treating the rancher heard this, he reported to the police that Rattlesnake Pete's head wounds could only have been caused by a gun butt. Based on this new evidence, the Mounties arrested Hindman on a charge of perjury, for which he was sentenced to five years in the penitentiary.

"Rattlesnake Pete" McEwan, seen here with his wife and child, was almost killed by an outlaw named Jesse Hindman in 1904. McEwan was a rancher in the Pincher Creek district. *Glenbow Archives/NA-102-7*

But probably the most entertaining "gun fight" ever to occur in Canada happened in Fort Macleod about 1892 between rancher Lew Murray and a cowboy named Leeper. They had met during the summer and after a violent argument threatened to kill each other if they ever crossed paths again.

Some time later, Fort Macleod was full of cowboys who had come in from the roundup, and the booze was flowing freely. During the course of the day, some playful cowboys discovered that Leeper was drinking at the Macleod Hotel and Murray was at the Queen's. Neither knew the other was in town. The cowboys, always ready for a practical joke, sent one group to keep company with the cowboy and another to the rancher, while Billy Stewart acted as the go-between. He started by telling Leeper the

nasty things that Murray had said about him the last time they met, then went over to the Queen's and told the same stories to the rancher.

White-hot rage soon took possession of the two, and they talked darkly of dire happenings if only the other could be met with, Stewart and the two parties of cowboys sympathizing with each wronged individual and telling just how to kill most painfully and disgracefully.[37]

Meanwhile, they quietly lifted the men's revolvers, removed the bullets, and returned them to their holsters. Then Stewart convinced Murray to visit the other hotel while the other cowboys cleared a path inside the bar so the men would have a clear view of each other.

Lew Murray was tricked into a fake gunfight by cowboy friends at Fort Macleod in 1892. He is seen here with other foremen of the southern Alberta roundup in 1901. *(Left to right):* Walter Watt, Howell Harris, Jim Fuller, George Ross *(in front)*, Lew Murray *(standing)*, Jack Glendenning *(in front)*, Joseph "7U" Brown, and Charlie McKinnon. *Glenbow Archives/NA–748–43*

The door swung open in the drinking-room of the Macleod hotel. Murray stepped in and swung his eye down the line of the counter, encountering the black gaze of Leeper just as the latter recognized the newcomer. The big guns leaped like magic to the ready hands, they stepped into the clear, and advanced slowly, the "clickety-click" of the futile hammers on their weapons indicating just how earnest they were.

They were almost chest to chest before they realized their guns were empty. Then, as they both flipped their weapons to use as clubs, the other cowboys intervened and amid the gaiety of drunken laughter, "patched up a truce that remained unbroken, if strained."

Since the beginning of the cattle industry in the early 1880s, relations between homesteaders (or "nesters") and ranchers were a constant source of trouble. Men like John Glen and Sam Livingston had started farming before there were surveys or land patents. When the leasing system began in 1882, the homesteaders discovered that some of their lands were situated within blocks claimed by such ranching companies as the Cochrane and Walrond. Although regulations stated that these settlers were entitled to a half section of land, they had trouble getting their patents and were harassed by ranchers. Other settlers who arrived after the leases had been issued believed they had the right to homestead any Crown land they wished, but when they moved onto ranching leases they ran into trouble. Some ended up in court, others were bought off, and still others were forcibly evicted.

In 1885, Sam Livingston said, "For the present I defend my claim as my neighbours do, behind my Winchester. Unless the land is all opened up for homestead entry all must either fight for our rights or leave the country and if I am compelled to leave, I will leave marks on the trail behind me."[38]

Some ranchers relented and surrendered parts of their leases to settlers but others were adamantly opposed. Dr. Duncan McEachran, manager of the Walrond Ranch, led the opposition. Whether by instruction or just because they didn't like "nesters,"

the cowboys from this ranch constantly harassed settlers on their range and tore down some of their buildings. In addition, McEachran used the courts and his Ottawa connections to prevent settlers from getting homestead patents and from cutting hay on adjacent lands. Claude Gardiner noted, "My ranch is right in the middle of the Waldron [sic] lease; they are a big company and own about 10,000 head of cattle . . . I am glad to say [they do not] trouble me much but they certainly make themselves unpleasant to some of the neighbours."[39]

Sometimes the settlers fought back. Dave Cochrane intimated he would set fire to the Walrond range if they didn't buy him out. Ed Paisley, another settler, made such violent threats against the manager that he was arrested and fined. And in 1893, a frustrated settler fired a shot through McEachran's window but escaped apprehension.

Even when the leasing regulations were changed in 1896 and homesteading was encouraged, hostility between ranchers and settlers continued. In 1902, a man named Sevill took possession of a quarter section of land used by the Medicine Hat Ranch as a part of its range. To add insult to injury, the land also contained the ranch's summer headquarters; this became the settler's new home. Legally, there was nothing the ranch company could do, and at the fall roundup, Range Boss M. Margeson had to ask permission to use the corrals for branding calves.

When the settler's dog began to harass the cattle during branding, an argument broke out between Margeson and Sevill. When the homesteader raised his whip in anger, the cowboy threw a loop over him, pulled him off his horse, and dragged him across the prairie for some fifty yards. Although unhurt, Sevill had the man arrested. The judge may have sympathized with the cowman, but he noted that "the charge was the first of the kind to come before him in the Northwest, that in a stock country the offence was one which should not be encouraged." Margeson was fined one hundred dollars.[40]

A couple of years later, a deadly confrontation occurred in the Neutral Hills, north of the Bow.

According to old-time cowboy Ivan Inman:

I can only recall one instance where gunplay came into the action. One rancher attempted to enforce the trespass law armed with a shotgun, and a new homesteader armed with a six-shooter was not about to be convinced that he did not have the right of entry. The unfortunate incident ended with serious consequences: a loss of one eye to the rancher and a two year jail term to the other.[41]

Most of these troubles resulted from human frailties such as anger, pride, and drunkenness. Some of the participants were just plain bad while others responded instinctively to situations that confronted them. In this way, they were probably no different from townspeople or farmers, except that a cowboy with a gun on his hip or a carbine in his saddle had all the potential of being as dangerous as a rattlesnake. And if he had the inclinations of a snake, the consequences were sometimes serious.

ADVICE TO YOUNG MEN

IN 1890, A YOUNG COWBOY NAMED RICHARD CAMPBELL
WAS CONVICTED OF HORSE STEALING AND
SENT TO STONY MOUNTAIN PENITENTIARY. WHILE THERE,
HE WROTE A LETTER, WHICH THE *CALGARY TRIBUNE* PUBLISHED,
WARNING YOUNG MEN TO STAY ON THE STRAIGHT AND NARROW.
IT SAID, IN PART:

My advice to all young men and boys is "To obey their parents or guardians, and to be ruled by their counsel." (A potent reason for my fault, I did not do that.) And again not to drink whiskey and smoke cigars to make them look tough, and take delight in being praised by the vicious and simple-minded, and last but not least, be industrious and clean-mouthed.

"Hard-hearted wretch," "He don't care," etc., were the encomiums lavished on me by many while some did not hesitate to express their opinions yet more broadly to my face. Some asserting that I should get more than my share of the law's vengeance. I shall not attempt to exculpate myself, but I must say, and I hope to be believed, that it was "six of one and half-a-dozen of the other." I own the sentence just: the argument that we were once honest has no effect for if every once-honest man were pardoned there would be few where I am now.

Mac and I are in cells next to each other. The cells are about 8 ft. long by 4 ft. wide, with brick walls painted, the bottom half red, and the top half white-washed, entered by a steel gate and furnished with table, stool, bed, blankets, brush, dustpan, spittoon, wash basin, etc.

There are about 70 convicts here. We wear a decent check suit, which would not be out of place in a public street. The building is not fenced in by a wall but is surrounded by the cottages of the guards. The food is very decent, porridge for breakfast twice a week, two plugs of tobacco a week for 1st class men, also a lamp to the same. The dinners are varied, tea consists of bread and tea. We always get enough.

Calgary Tribune, 25 November 1890

THE NEW WEST

THE EARLY RODEO COWBOY

THE FIRST RODEO EVENTS IN CANADA
WERE SPONTANEOUS ACTIVITIES HELD ON WORKING RANCHES.
WHEN AN ITINERANT HORSE BREAKER CAME TO A SPREAD,
COWBOYS GATHERED AT THE CORRAL TO WATCH THE FUN.
SOMETIMES A LOCAL RANCH HAND EVEN TRIED TO COMPETE BY TAKING ON
ANY BRONCS THE PROFESSIONAL BUSTER COULDN'T TAME.

Also, if two cowboys had an argument about their prowess with a rope or wrestling a steer, a contest was the best way to settle it. And if the cowboys were bored on a Sunday afternoon, what better way to pass the time than to demonstrate the skills of their profession?

On a roundup, one outfit would sometimes match its best bronc buster or roper against another, with plenty of money riding on the winner. In town, after the men were paid, an inebriated cowman bragging about his skill could find himself challenged to a match. Much to the delight of the locals, two men might square off in a competition, and the winner would be the hero of the day. At other times, a braggart might be shamed into putting on a solo demonstration and occasionally proved that his drunken claims were perfectly true. During the 1880s, some cowboys dared Frank Strong, manager of the Strong Ranch, to ride a steer bareback along the main street of Fort Macleod while attired in a morning coat and top hat. The bets were placed and the whole town came to watch. Strong mounted the lunging beast in front of the Queen's Hotel and succeeded in riding it for more than a block before being knocked off by the eaves of a low building.

Horse races and riding events were common on Sunday afternoons at Ed Barker's ranch near Cardston in the 1880s. On one occasion, spectators bet on who could stay on a longhorn cow the longest. The victor would be rewarded with ten gallons of whisky. There were two competitors, Dicky Bright and a cowboy named Hocking. A couple of wild cows were driven into a corral and saddled, and each man waited for the other to mount; meanwhile the cows stood bawling and swishing their tails in anger. Finally, Hocking put a foot in the stirrup and swung aboard. He held on while the enraged cow made two frantic jumps before throwing the cowboy over her horns. Bright suffered the same fate but as he had mounted a few seconds after his competitor, he was still in the saddle when Hocking was thrown. On that basis, onlookers declared that Bright was the winner.

Barker commented that such animals usually weren't saddled for this event. The most approved method of riding cattle is to put on a big pair of Mexican spurs, then drop on the cow face to tail, lie full length with legs locked under the neck, with hands dropped down the flanks with a secure hold on to the loose skin of the flanks with each hand. The only objection to this mode is that you cannot see where you are going.[1]

The United States recorded its first rodeo in 1847 when Spaniards coming into Santa Fe "contest[ed] with each other for the best roping and throwing, and there [were] horse races and whiskey and wines."[2] In the 1870s and 1880s, rodeo events occurred sporadically all through cattle country. Often they were one-time events that took place at an agricultural fair, horse race, or as an impromptu performance when a roundup crew came to town.

Prescott, Arizona, claimed to have started the first annual rodeo in 1888, with Cheyenne following nine years later. In 1891, Miles City, Montana, had a show for the Montana Stock Growers Association, the first in that state where prizes were given. Many cowboys who came to Canada, then, were not only familiar with rodeos but had probably competed in them. For example, noted horse breaker Frank Ricks had been champion bronc rider at the state fair in Sacramento, California, in 1878.

The earliest known rodeo in Canada occurred at Fort Macleod in the autumn of 1891 at the conclusion of the local agricultural society's first fall fair. There were two events: steer roping and bronc riding. The I.G. Baker Ranch provided the wild Texas longhorns, and Billy Metcalf of the Trefoil Ranch, Moss of the STV outfit, and Johnny Read of I.G. Baker were the competitors. Each was given two steers.

Moss drew his first steer, a big roan that ran like a deer. He tried twice to rope the beast, but it jumped the fence and got away. Metcalf caught his steer at the east end of the grounds, but his rope broke and the steer escaped. It dashed against the fence, broke through, and darted across the prairie with the cowboy in hot pursuit. Metcalf finally caught up with it at Craig's Ranch and roped it several times, but on each occasion the rope broke.

Next was Johnny Read.

Johnny herded his steer, so as to give the crowd a good view. He caught him just about where the race track turns into the home stretch, and threw him on the broad of his back a moment later. The pony braced himself, and held the steer there while Johnny got down and had his victim quickly tied up. Time 4:15.[3]

On his second attempt, Moss tied his steer in 5 minutes 23 seconds, while Metcalf's next try took 5 minutes 12 seconds. Read didn't need a second calf; his time was fast enough for him to be declared the winner.

There were only two competitors for the bronc riding event—Johnny Franklin of the Strong Ranch, and Billy Stewart of Cornish Cattle Company. An ex-Mountie described the event:

Two horses were produced for them, one a 3 yr. old, lean, wiry and every inch a pitcher. Stewart had him saddled in a loose box and stayed with what, up to the time, was the worst bucking for height and vigor I ever saw. He pitched four feet in the air every time and never stopped till he was brought up at the fence the other side of the grounds.[4]

Johnny Franklin was given a big black stallion to ride. Although impressive in appearance, the horse stood quietly while the bridle and saddle were put on. The crowd was even more disappointed when Franklin mounted with no trouble and started on a seemingly peaceful ride.

Frank Ricks won the bronc-riding title in Sacramento, California, before coming to Canada in 1880. He worked for the Mount Royal Ranch, and later managed the L & S outfit. *Glenbow Archives/ NA–3046–4*

Emboldened by his gentleness, his rider touched him with the spur and the transformation scene began and all other pitching I ever saw was child's play. He wriggled in the air like an eel, always coming down with his head in a different point of the compass to where it pointed when the buck began. The crowd screamed and the fur flew for ten solid minutes and but for losing his hat, I bet Franklin never left the saddle by a quarter of an inch.[5]

Both rides had been so sensational that the judges were obliged to call the competition a draw.

Born in Texas in 1863, Franklin had worked for several big outfits in the Dakotas, Wyoming, and Montana before coming to the Fort Macleod district in 1889. He found a job with the Strong Ranch, but the foreman, knowing nothing about Franklin's ability, put him to work night herding. After a while, word of Franklin's reputation reached the ranch so the foreman asked him if he could break some horses needed as Mounted Police remounts. "Johnny modestly replied he *thought* he could, was willing to *try*," said his old friend Harry Sharpe.[6]

After witnessing Franklin's skill in the saddle, the foreman promoted him to range rider at seventy-five dollars a month and put him in charge of the ranch's horse herd. At times, this meant breaking as many as fifteen horses a day. After Strong died, Franklin took over the place and

One of the best-known bronc riders in Canada before the turn of the century, Johnny Franklin came to the Macleod area in 1889 and worked for the Strong ranch. Though he became a prosperous rancher and businessman himself—operating a slaughterhouse and butcher shop at Macleod as well as running his ranch—bronc busting remained the love of his life. *Glenbow Archives/NA-2359-1*

began breaking horses for other ranches. After his marriage in 1895, he concentrated on his ranching business, often making a good profit by buying wild horses and breaking them for riding.

Bronco busting was the love of his life. He once made a bet that he could stick silver dollars in his stirrups and hold them under his boots until his ride was finished. He performed so smoothly that he scarcely left the saddle during the animal's wildest gyrations and finished the horse-breaking job with the dollars still in place. Another time, instead of participating in a bucking contest in honour of a visit by Sir Frederick Haultain and the lieutenant-governor of the Territories, he put on a solo performance, riding the worst outlaw in the bunch for fifteen minutes until it gave up.

In 1912, when Franklin was almost fifty, Guy Weadick invited him to judge the bronc-riding events at the first Calgary Stampede. L.V. Kelly recorded the following conversation:

"Say, Johnnie," said a friend to the sturdy old cowman, "how are you going to make a decision if two men should tie?"

"I'll just ride both them horses myself," he said.

"That's the only way to find out which bucks hardest."[7]

In later years Franklin turned to raising and running race horses. He owned a number of prominent racers, including *Irish Lad, Miss Stilton* and *Carabosse*, the latter having been imported by the Prince of Wales. However, he was always remembered for his uncanny skill in breaking horses to saddle.

Rodeo came to Calgary in 1893 when George Lane organized a steer-roping contest for the city's annual fair. The idea arose after an argument as to who was the best roper. Among the names put forward were Lane, John Ware, and Bill Todd. Carson & Shore, a local firm, donated a tooled saddle worth one hundred dollars as first prize and silver-mounted spurs and bridle for second.

Lane drew the first steer but had difficulty roping it, and four minutes elapsed before he was able to raise his hands in victory. Todd came next; he gave a thrilling performance, beating Lane with a time of 2 minutes 51 seconds. Then came Ware, riding a pony without a bridle; he caught his steer with his first loop just as the animal came out of the chute. The cowboy jumped off his horse, threw the animal, and had it tied in 51 seconds. According to James Smart, the record-breaking crowd cheered because Ware, "who was rated as the best bucking horse rider in Canada at that time, was very popular with the populace."[8]

For the next few years, Fort Macleod and Calgary dominated the rodeo scene in Canada. Each fall, Fort Macleod featured races, steer roping, and bronc riding. There were two kinds of races. One was a cowboy race, which featured hands from the local ranches. The other was an Indian race, usually bareback, with contestants from the Peigan or Blood Reserves. In a few instances, an Indian working for a ranch might compete in a cowboy race, but this was rare. An English spectator watched the Fort Macleod excitement in 1894:

> I got a safe position on top of a fence . . . They had several steers in a corral. The boy who is going to rope is on his horse waiting outside. They let out one steer and when it is clear of the crowd and running away, they sing out "go!" The cowboy takes after it, catches it round the head with his lariat, throws it down and ties its legs together so it cannot get up . . . A lot depends on your horse as while you are tying the steer's legs, the horse has to keep the rope tight and hold the steer down.[9]

Johnny Read won the event with a time of 2 minutes 12 seconds.

Calgary also had a repeat performance of steer roping and bucking contests in 1894, with the southern cowboys of Fort Macleod pitted against those of the Calgary–High River district. Representing the south in the bucking event were Johnny Franklin, Billy Stewart, B. Cunningham, and P. Roach, while John Ware, Mike Herman, and M. Mallett upheld the north's reputation. The front runners were soon eliminated, and Billy Stewart and Mike Herman squared off for the final prize of three hundred dollars. This time the local boy was victorious and Herman walked off with the money.

In the steer-roping competition, John Ware was the odds-on favourite. He succeeded in roping his steer in record time, but he didn't tie the rope securely and the animal broke free. "There was great disappointment among the crowd," commented a

Mike Herman (left) won bronc-riding and steer-roping competitions in 1894 during a contest between Fort Macleod and Calgary cowboys. He is seen here at the Winnipeg Stampede in 1913 with A.F. Bryson (centre) and Clem Gardner. Glenbow Archives/NA-1029-3

At the first Territorial Exhibition, held in Regina in 1895, Duncan S. McIntosh had his picture taken when he won the steer-roping contest. Riding *Sox*, he roped and tied the steer in 2 minutes 10 seconds. *Glenbow Archives/NA–902–1*

reporter, "John having been backed pretty heavily to win."[10] Instead, Mike Herman triumphed again, tying his steer in 2 minutes 8 seconds. He was followed by B. Cunningham, 4 minutes 29 seconds, and T.C. Lusk, 4 minutes 50 seconds.

During the 1890s, the roping and riding demonstrations in cattle country continued, and in 1895 the cowboys went to Regina for the first Territorial Exhibition. It extended over much of the week with such entrants as Johnny Franklin, Billy Stewart, Lew Murray, Duncan McIntosh, Jim Patterson, George McKay, S. Reid, "Billy the Kid" Welch, and a local cowboy known as Gopher Dick. However, the whole exhibition was poorly organized and the cattle so badly handled that they were in no condition to run. During the first couple of days, Stewart was the only roper to get a decent run from his steer and win any money in the semi-finals. The final championships went to Billy Stewart for bucking horse and Duncan McIntosh for steer roping.

Rodeo took on an international flavour in May, 1900, when some Montana cowboys passing through Calgary with a herd of horses bet one hundred dollars they could produce a bronc that no Canadian cowboy could ride. Some Calgary people, led by R.G. Robinson of the Chipman Ranch, Mayor James Reilly, and a man named Meldrum, immediately accepted the challenge. The Montana cowboys brought one hundred horses to the contest, held at Calgary's exhibition grounds. Representing the United States were Hi Loomis and Jake Ralstin; Canada had Birnie Fairheller and Lee Marshall, both from the Chipman Ranch. However, Fairheller was kicked by a horse shortly before the show and had to withdraw.

To start the contest, the Montana cowboys picked an outlaw from their bunch that had never been ridden. Marshall had to ride this animal to decide the bet. The horse bucked wildly and took a terrible fall, but Marshall stayed with him to the end, easily winning the hundred dollars. According to the press, "The Montana riders admitted that they had fairly lost their bet and will go back with a better opinion of Alberta broncho twisters than they brought in with them."[11]

Finally, to entertain the crowd of more than three hundred people, the riders each drew three mounts for an exhibition of horsemanship. Loomis rode the first three, then Ralstin followed with two horses and a mule. "The mule was a terror to buck. He jumped all the fences in sight and finally bolted for the stables with [Ralstin] still on his back."[12] The last horse ridden by Marshall turned out to be the wildest bronc of the bunch, far surpassing the performance given by the prize-winning mount. Near the end of the bone-shattering ride, just when Marshall thought he had tamed the outlaw, he suddenly threw up his head and struck the cowboy in the face with the bridle, cutting him badly.

By 1900, Lee Marshall was part of the new breed of cowboys who were taking over from Franklin and Ware. Born in Texas, Marshall had arrived in Alberta with his parents in 1895 at the age of seventeen. They settled in the Springbank district, west of Calgary, where Marshall hired on with the Chipman Ranch, worked for two years at the Bow River Horse Ranch, and returned to the Chipman outfit just before the turn of the century.

According to an acquaintance,

He had, by this time, attained his full manhood—six feet, two inches in height, straight as a whip and weighing 170 lbs. He was as supple as a cat and blessed with good looks, having dark eyes and hair and perfect teeth. When mounted on a flashy horse he made a perfect picture.[13]

Over the years, Marshall had demonstrated his skill as a bronc rider and soon became something of a showman. A popular Sunday pastime for Calgarians was to ride out to the Chipman Ranch to watch the cowboys in action. Marshall obliged by putting on riding exhibitions and showing his skill as a roper. The weekly entertainment stopped only when a valuable horse named *Shannon*, which Mar-shall was riding, crashed into a corral fence and perished.

Immediately after the defeat of the Americans in 1900, Milton Dowker, a small-time rancher who was supplying beef to the Indian Department, approached Marshall and Fairheller. Dowker was aware of the success of Wild West shows in the United States and invited the two cowboys to join his new company—the Canadian Wild West Show. This was probably the first such outfit in Canada. The entire troupe was made up of Dowker, who was a trick rider; Fairheller, who went under the name of the Alberta Kid; and Lee Marshall. They had a number of bucking horses and steers, as well as *Merry*, Dowker's trick riding horse.

The show was obviously patterned after American performances although its first efforts were quite amateurish. In Winnipeg, the show started with Marshall riding *Black Death* and giving demonstrations of roping steers and horses. His "work in lassoing steers, etc., while on horseback and throwing them into position so that they could be branded was very clever," said a reporter.[14] He was followed by the Alberta Kid, who rode a bucking horse, first with saddle and then bareback.

Dowker then offered a twenty-five-dollar prize to the winner of a horse race, inviting anyone from the audience to join. Two took part, but the Alberta Kid won handily. Other features of the show included a tug-of-war and a wrestling match by Marshall and the Alberta Kid, both on horseback.

When they completed their show in Toronto, Dowker decided to sell his stock rather than pay the shipping costs back to Calgary. He found a ready buyer in a local promoter who decided to put on his own "Wild West" show to demonstrate how to tame horses. He hired some local equestrians who, suitably dressed, looked almost like cowboys. But there the resemblance ended, for one rider after another landed in the dirt. With the crowd booing and hooting, the manager stopped the performance and then hired Marshall and the Alberta Kid—who were in the audience—to take over.

Dowker was back in Calgary in 1901 at which time he was contracted to put on his Wild West show at the annual exhibition. The Alberta Kid had left the troupe so the promoter—now calling himself "Professor" Dowker—brought in Billy Stewart and Johnny Douglas to work with Lee Marshall. The show had come a long way in a year. In particular, it featured a cattle-rustling act, which was described as follows:

> The first to appear on the scene was the rustler, with a cow and calf which he was trying to get away; then came the cow boys and considerable shooting took place; the boys finally roped the thief, dragged him to a pole, strung him up and filled his body full of lead.[15]

The program ended with bucking exhibitions featuring all four cowboys in the troupe.

By 1902, the promoter had become "Wild West" Dowker, and the show included steer roping, wild steer riding (with saddle), bronc riding, hurdle jumping, and the popular cattle-rustling act. Like many Wild West shows, it was a combination of rodeo and vaudeville.

Lee Marshall's skill in the saddle came to the attention of American promoters, who asked him to join "Buffalo Bill" Cody's Wild West Show. He was on a circuit at Pittsburgh in the summer of 1903 when his saddle horse reared backwards and fell on him, pinning him beneath the saddle horn. Just before he died, he said, "Tell the folks back home I died game."[16] He was twenty-seven years old.

The year 1900 saw Medicine Hat enter the rodeo field with a steer roping event added to its fall fair. Prizes of $10.00, $6.50, and $3.50 were offered, but because of rain, sleet, and high winds there was only one winner, Will Hargrave, who roped and tied his steer in 1 minute 30 seconds. The following year, the prizes were reduced to $10.00 and $5.00.

In addition, towns sometimes organized impromptu events to give distinguished visitors a feeling of the Old West. In 1901, a rodeo was held in Calgary to honour the Duke of Cornwall and York, later to become King George V. Others in the royal party included Lord Minto and Sir Wilfrid Laurier.

It turned out to be a thoroughly enjoyable afternoon, with the cowboys, horses, and steers putting on their best show for the dignitaries. Bert Pierson, a cowboy for the Chipman Ranch, won the bucking horse competition and Vic Smith the steer roping.

A year later, Medicine Hat put on a similar show for James de Rothschild and Hon. Vere Ponsonby, two peers on a world tour. F.L. Peacock arranged for a bronc-riding competition at his ranch a short distance from town. He had recently received a herd of wild horses from Montana. Commented a spectator,

> One unbroken gelding and a couple of untamed buckers were selected in the bunch, and the men from over the seas given an exhibition of what "cutting out" means. This work was performed very skilfully by Messrs. E. Kelly, H. Sullivan, and J. Whelan, American cowboys who came over with the bunch.[17]

O. Sanderson rode each horse after it had been saddled, while H.H. Ross gave a demonstration of roping a running horse by its front feet and bringing it down for saddling.

Once Medicine Hat had discovered the delights of rodeo, it became a hotbed of the sport, equalling or surpassing any efforts made by Fort Macleod and Calgary. By 1904, the prize money for roping had increased to one hundred dollars, with seven cowboys joining the fray. But it was no contest, for Les Richardson had the best time for both steers, 56 and 63 seconds. No one else was even close to him. And Addison Day provided the entertainment for the show when he roped and threw his steer, leaped off his horse, and was surprised when the animal jumped to its feet. Cowboy and steer glared at each other for a moment, then Day got back on his horse and roped the steer again. This time it stayed down. However, it all took so long that Day was out of the money.

In the years that followed, such Medicine Hat district cowboys as Jim Taylor, Orville McCullough, Frank Nichols, and George Armstrong of Maple Creek became leaders in Canada's rodeo sport.

GRAND COWBOY TOURNAMENT.

CALGARY,
Friday June 23, Sat. JUNE 24

Roping and Riding Contests.
Novelty Races.

SPECIAL PRIZES.

ROPING—1st Prize, $200.
2nd prize, $75.

RIDING—1st Prize, $100.
2nd prize, $25.

Address all communications to
C. J. CRESWELL,
Calgary.

Nichols brought a wealth of experience with him, for he had been the steer-roping champion of Texas, while Armstrong made a name for himself in rodeo at Denver and other American centres.

In 1907, a number of these cowboys, led by Taylor and McCullough, attempted to form a circuit to offer rodeo at Calgary, Edmonton, and other centres. They had more than fifteen hundred people at their first show in Medicine Hat, but a poor crowd at the second offering ended their grandiose plans. Three years later, Addison Day picked up the idea and gathered some of the best cowboys and bucking stock of the period. In 1910 and 1911, his show featured such riders as Emery Legrandeur, Tom Three Persons, George Armstrong, Art Whitney, Sol Bulyea, and Len "Red" Parker. Among his stock were such famous bucking horses as *Scar Head, Rooster, Maple Creek Black,* and *Grey Ghost.*

Besides offering local events, the Day outfit travelled to Winnipeg in 1911 to take part in their exhibition. The most outstanding performance was a ride by Parker on *Scar Head.* Until that time, no one had ever successfully ridden this notorious outlaw. The press reported that "the horse was in good shape and gave a magnificent exhibition of the possible evolutions of a cayuse, but not once was the rider in danger of losing his seat."[18] According to a cowman,

> "Scar-Head" was to go on for a decade as the top bucking horse of the old Day string. He was a very short-haired, slim-legged bay, weighing about 1,100 pounds, with a thin tail carried high. His head was wide between the eyes, with several conspicuous scars.[19]

During the early years of the twentieth century, rodeo became a common, albeit irregular, event in many centres such as Lethbridge, Maple Creek,

This advertisement in the *Lethbridge News* on 9 June 1905 was one of Canada's earliest rodeo announcements.

These were the champion rough riders and ropers of southern Alberta in 1908. *(Left to right, back):* S. Fallon, J. Black, and R. Kellogg; *(centre):* T. Stockton, Milt Irwin, Jeff Davis, and E. Allie; *(front):* F. Perkins. *Glenbow Archives/NA-1171-7*

Moose Jaw, Raymond, Gleichen, Cardston, High River, and Pincher Creek. For example, the village of Irvine introduced rodeo in 1906 in an effort to catch competitors on their way to the summer fairs at nearby Medicine Hat. Lethbridge had bronc riding at its summer fairs in 1908 and 1909. And in 1909, Fort Macleod offered "the bucking horse championship of Alberta."[20] The town of Raymond held its first rodeo—which it called a "stampede"—in 1902 under the leadership of Ray Knight, de-

scribed as "Canada's Buffalo Bill."[21] He also promoted the event in Lethbridge, Magrath, and other centres after 1912. A number of places were inspired to experiment with rodeos after the Calgary Stampede and either held separate competitions or incorporated them into their agricultural fairs. These events usually featured only saddle bronc riding and wild steer roping, although occasionally a steer-riding event (with saddle) may have been added for its entertainment value. There were very few experts in the latter class; most demonstrations were marked by rapid departures from the steers' backs.

In 1908, a new feature—steer wrestling—was added to western Canadian rodeos, probably as a result of a visit by Miller Brothers's 101 Ranch Wild West Show. Instead of roping and tying the steer, a cowboy jumped from his horse, grabbed the animal by its horns, and wrestled it to the ground. Once this was accomplished, he held the steer down by holding its lip between his teeth. He then signalled his success by raising his arms. Albert Nimmons recalled performing this feat at Calgary:

Take the steer decoratin'. We used to call it hoolihanin'. We'd drop the steer on his horns, toss him over, then grab his upper lip with our teeth and throw up our hands to show we were done. The critters would snort and blow right smack in your face![22]

It was Bill Pickett, the famous black cowboy from the Miller Brothers show who invented this feature. Eventually it became known as "bulldogging" because if a bulldog attacked a steer, it would lower its head to fight it off; the dog would then sink its teeth into the animal's lip, pull back, and cause the steer to fall. As this new event became popular, steer roping gradually died out.

Addison Day of Medicine Hat began to promote rodeos about 1910, taking a troupe to Winnipeg a year later. He is seen here on *Dude* while serving as arena director for the 1919 Calgary Stampede. *Glenbow Archives/NA–3164–33*

At the time of the great 1912 Calgary Stampede, the number of rodeo events were limited. The only competitions being offered were saddle and bareback bronc riding, steer roping, and bulldogging, as well as vaudeville-type relay races, trick riding, fancy roping, and fancy riding. Not until later years were calf roping, steer decorating, wild cow milking, wild horse racing, barrel racing, and chuckwagon racing added to the list. The distinctive feature about the 1912 Stampede was that women were able to compete in all the events. These were almost all Americans who were part of the vaudeville circuit.

The 1912 Stampede thrust Canada into international rodeo. Competitors from the United States and Mexico mixed with local cowboys to put on a spectacular show. The next Stampede was held in 1919 and four years later it became an annual event. By this time, a third generation of Canadian cow-

boys was on the scene. The era of Johnny Franklin and John Ware had blossomed in the 1890s; Lee Marshall and Milton Dowker had come and gone during the early years of the twentieth century; and now Canada had produced a new crop of competitors. These included such people as Tom Three Persons, Clem Gardner, Emery Legrandeur, "Red" Parker, Harry Bray, and Dug Wilson. In later years, they would be followed by Herman and Warner Linder, Pete Knight, Ray Knight, Pete Bruised Head, Slim and Leo Watrin, Pat and Toots Burton, Floyd Peters, Pete Legrandeur, Fred Gladstone, and the hundreds of other cowboys and cowgirls who contributed to the sport.

The tradition of rodeo in Canada, therefore, is more than a century old and has become a well-established part of sporting, cowboy, and social life. Men like Addison Day, Ray Knight, and Milton Dowker were, in effect, the Guy Weadicks of an earlier generation.

MARKETS AND MANGE

Cattle shipments were an excellent way for cowboys to expand their horizons. If they talked to the right people, they could get free passage in exchange for looking after the stock. This gave them a chance to see eastern Canada and perhaps go by cattle boat to England. Travelling on a train or boat was not the same as rounding up stock on the prairie, but the work still required an intimate knowledge of wild cattle that only the cowboy could provide with any level of efficiency and understanding. This skill also was the means by which English-born cowboys were able to make rare visits home that otherwise might never have occurred.

Once the eastern Canadian markets opened in 1886 and British markets a year later, cowboys were required to add one more task to their routine—driving the cattle to the nearest shipping point. At Lethbridge during the 1895 fall roundup, in one week alone twenty-four hundred head were shipped on nine trains, with another shipment planned as soon as the Pincher Creek roundup was over. In that year, some forty-five thousand head were sent by rail from the West to supply the fresh beef market.

A Scot who witnessed an 1895 shipment of range cattle described it to his readers in Inverness:

A cloud of dust on the prairie, some three miles distant, announced their approach, and as they drew near, it was seen that they were in charge of 10 cowboys, all well mounted ... When the cattle first leave their usual feeding ground, where they were bred and reared for four, and sometimes five years, they become restless, and averse to being driven, and a certain number of cowboys are told off to watch alternately, for three hours during the night, to prevent a stampede.

Occasionally a refractory heavy bullock will make a dash for liberty, and it is really surprising with what rapidity he gets over the ground for a short distance, but the expert riders—who almost live in the saddle—are after him like the wind, and the fleet, well trained horses soon bring him to book.[1]

The Scot also observed the skill of the cowboys in herding the cattle into a corral and through the chutes to the boxcars. He concluded, "The cowboys of Alberta are a superior class of young men in the prime of life, really 'fine fellows,' many of them of good family, well educated, and, as a body, warm hearted and generous to a degree, and always ready to do a kindly turn to a friend or a neighbour in need."[2]

However, cowboys weren't always available for railway and boat shipments so problems arose when unemployed drifters were used; they were often brutal to animals they didn't understand. This, coupled with a highly inefficient rail system and avaricious ship owners, exposed the traffic to criticism.

By 1890-91, the British public was being bombarded with accusations of inhumane practices

CALGARY STOCK YARDS AND SHIPPING DEPOT.

Cattle destined for British markets were held in these stockyards in Calgary. From there they were loaded onto boxcars and then cattle boats. This engraving appeared in *The Calgary Herald,* 30 September 1893.

relating to cattle shipments from Canada. Complaints were encouraged by the British cattle industry, which was trying to protect its interests against foreign competition. Its proponents knew that the British public could be counted on to rush to the defence of dumb animals. In response to these criticisms, the Imperial government set up a committee to look into the charges. One of the most negative accounts of cattle shipments was written by Nele Loring, a British agriculturist who owned a ranch near Fort Macleod. His article was published in the influential magazine *Nineteenth Century,* and reprinted in the *Live Stock Journal* and in a number of English newspapers.[3] Loring's initial impression of the cattle drive was favourable. He met a dozen cowboys as they drove 940 cattle from the foothills to loading chutes near the CPR line in October, 1890, and was impressed with their work. He joined them in their tent camp about seven miles from the corrals and noted how the night hawks kept watch on the herd. Next morning, the remuda was driven in and cowboys selected the horses they would need for their work. The cattle were to be moved in three separate

trainloads, 227 to be loaded and shipped that day. He wrote:

> Good cow-hands work their cattle with a wonderful absence of fuss and noise, and it was a pretty thing to see the way in which these steers were separated from their companions and moved off towards the railroad.

As they approached the corrals, the lead cattle changed direction, causing the whole herd to mill about in a circle. When they became thoroughly agitated, they broke free and scattered over the range. The cowboys rounded them up and placed a number of tame cattle in the corrals as decoys, but when one of the greenhorn cowboys yelled at them, they stampeded again. "Your genuine cowboy," said Loring, "never shouts at his cattle. It is permissible to curse cattle, but this should be done in a conversational tone of voice." On the third try, the cattle were finally driven into the corral, but the foreman delayed the loading for two hours to allow the excited cattle to cool down.

The cattle train consisted of thirteen boxcars,

each with about three inches of gravel on the floor to provide a foothold. As a boxcar rolled into place, the cowboys cut seventeen or eighteen cattle from the herd, drove them into a chute and up a ramp into the car. Throughout the loading, some tried to turn back, others resisted entering the chutes, while a few steers attacked the riders. As the cowboys continued to struggle with the cattle, the scene, according to the writer, became "more magnificent but less businesslike."

At last the cattle were safely on board. Loring was in charge of the train, with three cowboys helping him. "My men were," he said, "fortunately for me, Englishmen, and of gentle birth, although very wild and woolly in appearance." Loring climbed into the caboose at the end of the train, where the cowboys stayed, and was amused to see that the walls were covered with pictures of actresses—nineteenth-century pin-ups.

He noted:

In the first fifty miles or so, none of the cattle lay down, but tremendous fights took place. In several cases we found some single steer glori-

ously holding one end of the car against all comers, and now and then charging from end to end and causing a general scrimmage among the occupants.

As they travelled, the cowboys had to check the stock every time the train stopped for water or coal, or at a siding to let another train pass. Armed with prod poles, their job was to make sure all the cattle were standing and to jab those lying down. At night when the train made a temporary stop, one cowboy walked with a lantern on one side of the boxcars while the man on the other side peered through the slats to check the animals. Then, as the train started, the cowboys jumped on board and walked along the runways on top of the boxcars until they reached the window of their caboose. Sometimes, when the cowboys found themselves at the far end of a violently rocking train, they had to either crawl along the tops on their hands and knees or simply hold on until reaching the next stop.

After travelling for twenty hours, the train reached Moose Jaw—"a hideous collection of dirty wooden houses, standing drearily huddled to-

Corrals at Crane Lake, Saskatchewan, served the big ranches shipping cattle to eastern Canada and overseas. *Glenbow Archives/NA-3375-7*

gether on a boundless stretch of inhospitable prairie." This was the first rest stop for the cattle. The corrals were muddy from recent rains, and, according to Loring, the hay was "the merest rubbish, evil-smelling and black with mould." The cattle were unloaded and left to rest all day, but young boys from town showed up to taunt and harass the animals, completely destroying their tranquillity.

All the cattle survived the first leg of the journey, although one was found lying down in the boxcar, its body covered with bruises and horn wounds. Believing it could not survive the rest of the trip, Loring sold it to a bystander for a fifth of its value.

The next day took them to Swift Current—two cattle being trampled to death on the way—and the next to Winnipeg. "At every stopping-place," said the writer, "we found the cattle lying down in greater numbers, and more difficult to rouse; while, at the same time, those still on their feet grew more vicious to their weaker companions."

East of Winnipeg, the cattle train was constantly shunted onto sidings and left there for hours while other trains went by. The next stopping places at Schrieber and North Bay presented major problems with water, feed, and harassment by the locals, but finally the train reached the docks at Montreal. According to Loring:

> The cattle which, eleven days before, I had seen in their pride on the prairie, sleek, fat, and well-looking, were now mere ghosts of their former selves; their sides had fallen in and their backbones had come out, their legs were in many cases sore and swollen, and most of them had raw bruises on their quarters.

After being held for two days in the corrals, the cattle were taken to a waiting ship. It was a two-year-old steamer, about 750 feet long and 75 feet wide, with a round bottom and flat sides. Its load consisted of 730 cattle on the upper and lower decks plus regular cargo. There were four rows of wooden pens erected on each deck, the two in the centre being back to back. A false floor of one-inch boards sat an inch off the bottom for drainage. There were no stalls; cowboys simply tied the cattle in place, secured by a rope tied to their horns. On the upper deck was a crude plank roof to protect the cattle from the weather.

Loring was appalled at the way the dock workers treated the cattle as they were being loaded, "shouting furiously, and beating them about the eyes and nose with heavy sticks. This sort of treatment seems barbarous enough when it effects its object, but it becomes doubly revolting when, as is certainly the case with range cattle, it only bewilders the patient."

Loring and two cowboys (the third went back west) secured the ropes but found the cattle were so closely jammed together that they had no place to go. The result was that if a steer laid down, it risked being trampled to death. Ensuring that the animals remained on their feet kept the cowboys busy the entire journey.

Luckily, they encountered no storms during the trip. But the fact that the boat was round-bottomed assured them a rough voyage.

> The cattle, slipping helplessly backwards and forwards as the vessel rolled, threw their whole weight at times upon the head boards, several of which soon broke . . . In this way we soon had steers loose in the alley-ways, and steers loose in the pens, and steers trampling on each other in all directions.

As a result, it was often unsafe for the cowboys to work with the cattle. Only when the sea calmed and the rolling stopped were they able to get the animals back in their pens, get the weaker stock on their feet, and throw the dead ones overboard. Despite these conditions, Loring admired the work of the cowboys—both those working for him and others on the boat. He said they were often seasick, worked amid a terrible stench, and "their food was slopped by the dirty hands of a . . . cook's mate into a large pan, over which they had to scramble for their meals."

When the boat finally arrived in England, the

The polo player at right is Albert E. Browning, a Fort Macleod rancher who was in charge of a cattle train in 1890. He disputed claims that the trains were poorly managed. The others in the polo team photo are *(left to right)* Montague Baker, Stanley Pinhorn, and E.M. Wilmot. *Glenbow Archives/NA-967-26*

stock was emaciated, haggard, and dispirited. All but one rangy steer. It knocked over a dock worker "and stood there, a gaunt but still imposing skeleton, looking around with an air of pained surprise . . . then turned, cocked his tail in the air, and galloped as gaily as might be after his companions into the abattoirs."

To counter Loring's negative article, the *Canadian Gazette* published an account by Albert E. Browning, who had been a rancher in the Fort Macleod district for five years and had been placed in charge of a cattle train in 1890.[4] It was carrying 225 steers for the Cochrane Ranch and left the siding at Strathmore about the same time as Loring's train. Browning was assisted by a young English cowboy and two greenhorns.

They arrived at Moose Jaw with no problems, but Browning agreed that the corrals there were a disgrace. By the time he was ready to reload the cattle he wished he had the railway supervisor there "in the middle of that mud with a few 'western long horns' charging about." From Moose Jaw to Winni-

peg there were a few problems with cattle lying down, but they were easy enough to raise when the train stopped for water for its boilers. Winnipeg was crowded with cattle—too crowded—but the hay and water were good. Like Loring, Browning ran into trouble east of Winnipeg with the train frequently being shunted onto sidings, but they used the time to good advantage "running along the train at each stop, finding a few down at each time and not at all at others."

Every hour or so we were able to work the whole train. By sending an assistant along the top of the cars as the train slackened speed, I was enabled to begin at the front end and work back, and the balance of us worked from the back end forward, and in this way it required but a few minutes.

Browning also had trouble with boys harassing the cattle at the rest stops, and sightseers proved a constant nuisance. During this part of the trip, he lost only two steers when the train started with a jerk and they were thrown to the floor. His train reached Montreal with the stock in good shape for the ocean trip. Browning's part of the journey was over and he was back on the southern range before winter.

The same year that these opposing viewpoints about cattle shipments were being presented by a Canadian rancher and a British agriculturist, the Imperial committee was holding meetings in England "to enquire into the treatment of live cattle on the Atlantic ocean cattle ships."[5] In fact, Loring's article had probably been written at the urging of those who wanted strict controls enacted. Even before the Imperial committee's report was issued, the anti-competition lobby must have realized that

the Canadian and American cattle would not be stopped by attacking the shipping procedures. Fortuitously for them, when the *S.S. Huron* docked at Liverpool with a load of Canadian cattle, the regular veterinarian was ill, so a medical health officer who "has gained some notoriety of late in connection with the question of meat inspection"[6] examined the stock. He declared that one of the animals had pleuro-pneumonia and ordered that the entire shipment be destroyed. Canada, however, was free of that highly infectious disease. Later, a veterinarian said they had been suffering from only a mild form of "corn disease." However, erring on the side of caution, the British government placed an embargo that prohibited the importation of live cattle. This meant that cattle had to be slaughtered as soon

These cattle are being held in corrals at Drowning Ford Ranch, north of Medicine Hat, in preparation for dipping. An outbreak of mange at the turn of the century meant that each year half a million cattle had to be dipped in a solution of sulphur and lime. *Glenbow Archives/NA–2003–3*

as they came off the boat. No cattle could be brought in for breeding purposes, nor could they be held in corrals and fattened until they recovered from the effects of the journey. Regardless of whether the embargo was necessary or not, it certainly had a negative effect on ranching in western Canada.

While the country may have been free of pleuropneumonia, western cattle did suffer from other diseases, including blackleg and lump jaw. Infected stock were usually killed right away, but Indians sometimes showed up to see if they could have the meat, infected or not. This was graphic evidence of the starvation that existed on many reserves.

In 1904, there was an outbreak of blackleg among cattle on the Rosebud River. Cowboy Johnny Martin recalled,

One morning, I rode south to where our cattle ranged and everywhere were dead yearlings. In a few days most riders were also finding dead young cattle so the veterinarian at Gleichen was asked to diagnose the trouble. When he was told that only yearlings were dying and that a front shoulder would puff up and crackle when touched with the hand, and was black when scored with a knife, he knew without coming to see the dead animals that the disease was blackleg.[7]

Injections were available to combat the outbreak but ranchers also had their own cures, including tying a copper wire to the dewlap or bleeding the animal. The Indians had another remedy. According to Martin,

When the Blackfoot Indians found out about the fat yearlings dying at Rosebud they came out and had a sure cure for blackleg. They cut the animal's throat just before it died, removed the infected front quarter and had a good wholesome carcass that was enjoyed by the hungry natives.[8]

Similarly, Dick May recalled Sarcee Indians

coming to his ranch near Bragg Creek to butcher a cow infected with lump jaw and take the meat home.

In 1896, the first serious outbreak of mange occurred among cattle along the Little Bow. This skin disease was caused by parasites and made the animal's hair fall out in great patches. In 1899, the first dipping vats were constructed at Kipp, Goose Lake, and at Spring Creek in the Medicine Hat district. For a while, ranchers thought they had the disease under control, but by the turn of the century it had become a major problem. In 1904, the federal government enacted compulsory dipping and divided the West into fourteen mange districts. Scores of vats were constructed throughout the ranching region and massive amounts of sulphur and lime were imported to control the disease. In that year alone, more than a half million cattle were dipped once and of these four hundred thousand required a second dipping. Yet thousands of animals perished when they went into the winter in a weakened condition because of the disease.

Mange added a new element to the roundup procedure and considerably altered the duties of the cowboy. After being gathered up, the cattle were taken to the dip and herded into corrals, then into a crowding pen, and finally forced down an incline into a long vat filled with a heated mixture of sulphur, lime, and water. The cattle had to swim through this pungent concoction for some sixty feet before climbing into a pen where they stayed until most of the liquid had drained off and back into the vat. From there they were turned loose, but if a second dipping were needed, they were close herded for a couple of weeks and the whole process was repeated.

Some dips were built by large ranches for their own use while others were community projects. As Ballie Buck recalled, "All the cattle outfits were getting hit by this mange. The Circle let all who wanted bring their herds to our tanks on the Little Bow. We figured if we could stop the mange in the whole country it would benefit us and everyone."[9] It was a smelly, dirty job that turned many cowboys into labourers and mechanics. Supplies of sulphur

Cattle are readied for dipping at Bull Springs, in eastern Alberta, about 1904. They are being driven into chutes that lead to the dipping vats. *Glenbow Archives/NA-3375-4*

and lime had to be hauled from town; the donkey engine used to heat the liquid required constant attention; and the dip often needed repairs. Cowboy "Bud" Cotton observed that the chemical mixture "permeated our skins and we were almost pickled in it."[10]

He was involved in a roundup that brought twelve thousand head of cattle to the dip north of the Bow. They were divided into three separate herds and each animal had to go through the dip twice over a ten-day period. Most of the trouble came in handling calves and their refractory moth-

ers. Calves were often balky and sometimes a cowboy had climb into the corral and wrestle an obstinate critter into the dip. With an angry mother nearby, this could be a dangerous exercise. Cotton recalled:

One cowboy got into the pen and had successfully manhandled all but one lone calf over the slippery metal-floored jump-off pen into the dip. Peeved, sweating and intent on manhandling this lone kicking and squirming dogie, the rider didn't realize until too late that the

"Ballie" Buck *(right foreground)* supervises cattle being dipped for mange. Because of its size, the Circle Ranch had its own dipping vats. In other areas, the federal government built vats at various locations to serve the smaller ranchers. *Glenbow Archives/NA-286-4*

cut-gate man had accidentally let mother cow into the pen too. She sure was on the prod. There was just one howl; a frantic leap for the crossbars failed, and the cowboy disappeared with a splash into the tank of dip, the cow right behind.

Frantically, the crew dragged out the well-dipped cowpoke. The only consolation he got was a few dry remarks to the effect, "Well, boy, you sure-all won't get the mange now."[11]

On another roundup, Jim Gladstone of the Blood Reserve was having problems with a skin rash that wouldn't go away. Finally, one of the other cowboys laughingly suggested that he go through the dip. Jim thought it was a good idea so he covered himself with the mixture, but the pain was so excruciating that he almost passed out. However, much to his surprise, his skin problem was completely cured.

Fred Kanouse, one of the original cattle owners in Canada, had a dramatic way of treating mange. He had bought an unbranded horse from an Indian, and, because it showed signs of mange, he got it cheap. Kanouse's treatment was to apply generous quantities of kerosene to the afflicted areas of

Cowboys had the messy job of mixing quantities of sulphur, lime, and water. They had to heat it, feed it into the chutes, and make sure the cattle were thoroughly doused with the noxious concoction. *Glenbow Archives/NA-3929-9*

the unfortunate animal. He then took his iron and applied a brand to the wet horse. L.V. Kelly describes what happened next:

> As he pressed the white-hot iron to the horse's side there was a flash—and then a sheet of flame went dashing across the prairie. The forgotten mange ointment had asserted itself. Before the horse died he had ignited a half-mile of dry grass, and a great fire that necessitated the services of all the men at hand threatened the town for some time, but was eventfully extinguished before any real damage was done.[12]

Like the British embargo, the mange epidemic had a disastrous effect on the ranching industry. The whole area along the border was placed under quarantine and no cattle were allowed to be imported from the United States until they had been examined. This also was true of the thousands of dogies being brought in from Mexico. The free and easy days of open borders and unlimited ranges

were past. Some smaller operators got out of the business entirely while others scaled down their operations to cope with the changing conditions. This of course, included the cowboy.

END OF AN ERA

The golden age of the Canadian cowboy did not come to a sudden halt. In fact, some people say it never really ended; it simply changed. Be that as it may, a sequence of events around the turn of the century played havoc with the ranching industry, destroying many of the huge spreads and changing the role of the cowboy forever.

A number of factors were involved, including markets, disease, and weather, but the primary reason was the losing battle ranchers waged against settlers. From the beginning, there had always been a few homesteaders who complained about the large leases and the inability of individuals to gain title to Crown lands. However, as long as the Conservatives held power in Ottawa, they stood firmly behind the industry. Such men as Member of Parliament Donald W. Davis lobbied long and hard on behalf of the ranchers. As a result, homesteaders made a few gains but were never able to make the inroads into the leasing system that they wanted.

The settlers achieved a concession in 1886 when the government changed the leasing system to give homesteaders a chance to settle on those Crown lands not under the "closed" twenty-one-year leases of 1881. This, however, had little effect on the big spreads, most of which remained under the old system. The real crunch came in 1896 when all the large leases were cancelled; ranchers were permitted to buy 10 percent of their leased land at $1.25 an acre and to apply for new leases for the rest of their land. The government also passed a regulation to protect the streams and springs, thus preventing homesteaders from cutting ranches off from their essential watering places.

Some of the more affluent ranchers bought the maximum amount of land available and were successful in leasing much of the remainder. But there was nothing to stop homesteaders from coming onto the leases and filing on land wherever they liked—as long as they did not block the ranchers' access to water. Over the next few years, barbed wire fences began to appear through the length and breadth of ranching country. "Ballie" Buck of the Circle Ranch recalled the problems this created:

> It seemed like we were getting close to a shooting war. My boys would cut homesteaders' fences anytime our cattle got caught in one of their corners. Then we'd have heck to pay. Several times I had to send a man to fix their fences. A few times the nester had shot our cattle and let them lay.[1]

To add to the frustration, the Circle corrals used on the range during the spring and fall round-ups began to disappear. It didn't take the cowboys long to find out that homesteaders were using them

for firewood. C.J. Christianson recalled, "When I came to work for the Circle in 1905 there wasn't a corral left, just places where they had been. The corral posts were cut off at the ground level with axes."[2] As a result, the cowboys had to brand their calves on the open prairie.

Old-time rancher Bob Newbolt had no use for either homesteaders or fences. For years he had followed a well-established trail across the prairies to Calgary, and when homesteaders began to fence it off, he simply ignored them. Time after time, when settlers found their wires cut and the trail reopened, they knew that Newbolt had been through.

A further blow to the ranching industry occurred in 1896—the same year the leases were cancelled—when the Liberals swept the Conservatives from power. Not only had the big companies lost their political support, but the new minister of the interior, Clifford Sifton, was intent upon populating the West with immigrants as quickly as possible. He was obviously thinking of farmers, not ranchers, when his land agents descended upon Germany, Ukraine, Poland, and the Scandinavian countries, as well as farming areas in the United States. As the fertile lands of central Alberta and Saskatchewan were taken up, immigrants began flowing into ranching country in increasing numbers.

Some ranchers responded to the problems by moving farther north and east into areas not yet available for homesteading. Lands along the Red Deer River that had been used only occasionally were now leased, while in Saskatchewan several new companies arrived, some from the crowded ranges in the United States. Among them were Tony Day and Frank Cresswell's Turkey Track outfit, the famous Matador Ranch, Beresford's Mexico Ranch, Jeffers Cattle Company, and Smith & Mussett Cattle Company.

A.J. "Tony" Day was an old-time cowman from Texas. He had started the Turkey Track brand in southern Texas just after the Civil War and gradually moved north to Nebraska, Oklahoma, and Dakota Territory. In 1895, he became a partner of Cresswell, an Englishman. By the turn of the cen-

Spencer Brothers were one of the last big outfits to operate in the area southwest of Medicine Hat. In 1900 the brothers were arrested for smuggling cattle into Canada, but they were so politically influential that the matter was never resolved satisfactorily. The company was sold a few years later. This is a view of Spencer Brothers's roundup in 1899. *Glenbow Archives/NA–2927–1*

tury, the Dakota range was becoming too crowded, so in 1902 Day hired Hugo Maguire, a Maple Creek cowboy, to scout out a possible range in Canada.

Maguire showed them the Mule Creek and Big Bend country and suggested a headquarters site near Rush Lake in the Swift Current area. Within weeks, the two ranchers had made the necessary arrangements. Recalled Maguire:

Mr. Day and Mr. Cresswell had not lost any time. Mr. Cresswell went to Texas to round up and ship five thousand cows and heifers to Billings, Montana, while Tony Day contacted Archie McLean of Winnipeg and contracted for eight thousand yearlings and two-year-old steers and then went to South Dakota and shipped some men and six carloads of saddle horses to Rush Lake.[3]

Joe Cose was sent to Billings with saddle horses for the trail drive to Canada while "Tennessee" and other cowboys stayed at the Rush Lake camp to receive dogies arriving from Winnipeg. These were given the Turkey Track brand, then moved south to Whiskey Creek where they were close herded all summer. Meanwhile, other crews set to work to erect corrals, barns, and various buildings at the Canadian ranch. When they were ready, Day and Cresswell asked Maguire to show them the way to Montana so they could fetch the Texas cattle.

I got my bed and necessary articles together and with my two horses I went along, they taking turns riding with me. The cook gave us some sour-dough bread, coffee and bacon. We each took along a tomato can and made our own coffee and cooked the bacon on meat sticks, and when I had located them on the Malta trail in Montana, I returned to our camp in Canada.[4]

A few weeks later, the Texas cattle arrived with Joe Cose as the trail boss. They were accompanied by a crew of American cowboys, many of whom stayed in Canada. Among them were Charlie Franklin, Ed McPherson, and Sib Jones. By the end of 1903, the Turkey Track was running thirty thousand cattle and seven hundred horses on its range.

The Matador Ranch moved to Canada in 1904 after operating large spreads in Texas, Colorado, and Montana. Like Day and Cresswell, the Matador people saw the northern prairie as an excellent place to finish cattle that were shipped in from their American ranches. These arrived "in bond" and after two years on the range they were returned to the United States and sold in Chicago.

The Jeffers Cattle Company moved from Madison, Montana, in 1905 with fifteen hundred cattle and one hundred horses, settling near Cypress Lake. According to T.B. Long, who scouted out the ranch site, "several years growth of grass rippled in the wind, knee deep to a horse as far as the eye could see."[5] The Jeffers stock was taken by rail to Havre and then driven overland to Canada. Smith & Mussett, a Kansas outfit, arrived just weeks before

winter with thirty-two hundred head of Manitoba dogies, which they turned out north of Maple Creek.

These new ranches, located in the short grass country, had experienced several wet years and offered ideal range conditions. At that time, the rush of homesteaders had not yet penetrated the area. Closer to the foothills, however, several large ranches were being besieged so they scaled down the size of their operations, dispensed with their large crews of cowboys, and restricted themselves to deeded land. The example of F.W. Godsal, owner of the North Fork Ranch, was typical. He had started ranching near Pincher Creek in 1882 but realized that times had changed.

My lease was about the first to be invaded by settlers, and I saw that it would be impossible to keep them off . . . I therefore accepted the inevitable and told Ottawa that I would throw open about nine-tenths of my lease (keeping what I had under fence) provided they would reserve from settlement certain springs and watering places on the river.[6]

Ranchers experienced another setback in 1901, when prairie fires devastated huge parts of the range. In October, an American newspaper com-

BUNCH OF BEEVES IN CALGARY STOCK YARDS.

An artist sketched cattle awaiting shipment at the Calgary stockyards. *The Calgary Herald, 30 September 1893.*

mented, "The whole country north of the Great Northern railway is one vast sheet of flame as far as the international boundary line and north, covering hundreds of miles."[7] In that same month, another fire burned the prairie between the railway and the South Saskatchewan west of Medicine Hat, while a third one destroyed the winter range in the Plume Creek area.

But the worst fire erupted near Gleichen when a man named Dan McNelly carelessly threw away a match after lighting his pipe. The flames swept south and west, covering some fifty square miles of grazing land as far south as the mouth of the Bow. According to the Mounted Police,

> Nothing could escape it, and horses, cattle and wild animals were burnt to death or left so injured that they died shortly after . . . In the river bottoms along the Little Bow there are bunches of horses and cattle burned to death; others were so badly injured that they had to be destroyed.[8]

By the time it was over, the Bar U had lost fifteen thousand dollars in property and stock; Pat Burns three thousand, T.C. Langford, five thousand, and George Ross, two thousand. The police superintendent considered the fire "the most destructive that has, to my knowledge, ever visited the North-west."[9] Considering the depressed market prices and other problems, it was an unwelcome visitor.

As ranches were reduced in size or went out of business, the need for the old-time cowboy sharply declined. As well, many small-time ranchers were raising their own families and had children old enough to assume the duties of cowhands. Many of them were so adept at their trade that they became to twentieth-century Canadian ranching what the Texan had been to the nineteenth. An American cowboy, watching a roundup on the Little Bow, noticed the skill of the local cowboys in cutting out the stock and roping the calves. "Don't those Canadian sons-of-bitches ever miss?" he asked admiringly.[10] These Canadians had known no other life than that of a cowboy, and they learned well from the old hands—mostly American—about the ways and mores of the North American cowboy. In fact, so many Alberta and Saskatchewan ranch boys picked up the slow Texas drawl that it became recognized as part of the speech pattern of the Canadian cowboy.

By 1902, people were already talking about the end of the ranching era. In that year, Mounted Police Superintendent Gilbert Sanders pronounced that "the days of the big rancher are numbered."[11] And a writer admitted that even south of Medicine Hat the open range was changing. Whereas in the past it was exclusively ranching country, now men were going into business to "combine ranching and farming and dairying."[12]

With immigration, new towns began springing up all over the range. A common expression among merchants was, "I would rather have half a dozen farmers as customers than a 20,000-acre ranche."[13] In many cases, local boards of trade turned their backs on ranching, proclaiming it a dying industry that was giving way to the homesteader and farmer.

E.J. "Bud" Cotton saw obvious signs of change when he rode through the area northwest of Medicine Hat in 1906 after being hired on by the Turkey Track outfit. One day, when travelling from the northern part of the range with "Curly" Hunter and Jim Finch, he came to a new railway town just as a trainload of settlers arrived. He described the scene:

> Down where the settlers' freight cars had been shunted, bedlam reigned as the newcomers busily unloaded. Horses and cows were led down improvised ramps. Men, women and youngsters toted wagon gear and household effects. Loud-voiced commands rang out as each family piled belongings on the bald prairie . . . In an incredibly short time, tents were up and stovepipes smoking, wagons were assembled and animals staked out. What had been chaos a short time before now resolved itself into a typical railhead camp of pioneers ready to travel to their visioned homes somewhere over the hill.[14]

The next day, as the three cowboys rode across the open range, they helped a stranded settler with a broken wagon wheel. Farther on they came to a "soddy" living in a house built into the side of a coulee. In front were the detested "barb wire gate in the fence of sagging wire and spindly willow pickets."[15]

The following day they reached a long valley littered with homesteaders' shacks, some made of rough boards, others tarpapered. And there was so much barbed wire that the cowboys were forced to follow along a road allowance past a few ploughed fields. Not until they had cleared the valley did they reach their destination, the large McCann Ranch at Antelope Lake.

The life of the rancher was further complicated in 1903 when cattle prices fell so low in Britain that some companies were unable to profitably sell their stock. For some, it was the last straw and they got out of the business altogether. One of the first to go was the Bar U, sold to a partnership of cattle dealers Gordon, Ironsides & Fares and George Lane in 1902. A year later, stock dealer William R. Hull bought the Oxley Ranch, and in 1905 the Cochrane Ranch was turned over to the Mormon church. In several instances, the ranches were bought by men or firms with large interests in the meat-packing industry, while in others, like the Cochrane Ranch, the Mormons wanted the land primarily for farming purposes.

Finally, the winter of 1906-07 finished the devastation that homesteaders, depressed prices, and leasing regulations had begun. The season started with prairie fires that ravaged huge areas of grazing land, to be followed by rain in October and early November. On the night of 15 November, the rain turned to snow, and by morning the temperature had dropped to -15°F. Up to three feet of snow was dumped on the prairies during the space of a few hours. A brief thaw followed, adding another layer of crust to the snow. After that the temperature plummeted, and one blizzard followed another throughout the rest of the winter.

There had been seasons like that before—although perhaps not quite as bad. What set this one apart were two factors: fences and ranges overstocked with dogies. During the winter of 1886-87, for example, cattle were able to drift with the storm, some ending up on the ranges in Montana. But by 1906, hundreds of miles of fences blockaded the land. Also, the earlier herds had been local cattle, raised on the plains and accustomed to winter conditions. Many dogies, imported months earlier from Ontario and Mexico, were entirely unfitted for the savage and unremitting storms. Not only that, but few ranchers had enough hay to carry them for more than five or six weeks.

A Pat Burns outfit was taking a herd of twenty-three hundred steers north to a feedlot on the Highwood River when the first blizzard struck them. They were still sixty miles from their destination at the time, so they had to close herd the stock at night and managed only about fifteen miles a day into the face of the wind and sub-zero temperatures. They had a chuckwagon and bed wagon but no tent, for it had been blown to pieces when the storm first struck. Recalled one of the cowboys,

> The balance of that trip was a nightmare. When we hit the settled, fenced country, known as the Gladys Ridge, we were in road allowances. Behind the two wagons, pulled by four horses each, came 70 saddle horses, then the herd of 2,300 steers. You can imagine what this did to a foot-and-a-half of fresh snow. The drags of that herd [the ones at the end] were sliding on ice from one side of the road allowance to the other and became so sore-footed they could hardly move.[16]

The cowboys were forced to abandon seventy weaker stock along the way, and each night they tried to find an empty granary or shack to hole up in. When they finally got to the mouth of the Highwood, the herd was split, some going to winter quarters and about three hundred to the packing plant.

Farther north, when the storm began, Jack Morton took three days to move his cattle from his CX Ranch to Horse Shoe Canyon, a distance of twenty miles. His cowboys drove a herd of range

The winter of 1906–07 marked the end of the big-time ranching era. These cattle died on the Shaddock Ranch, east of Calgary, in the spring of 1907. The starving animals had broken down a fence around a haystack and stayed there until they perished. *Glenbow Archives/NA-1636-1*

horses to break a trail through the snow; a four-horse sleigh loaded with hay followed, and at the rear the cattle were strung out for a half-mile. Luckily, Morton had bought a lot of hay from homesteaders and had stored it in the protective canyon, so the stock there wintered well. However, the ones that stayed at the CX weren't so fortunate. When Johnny Martin went to the ranch to skin some dead animals, there were a hundred in the feedlot and before he finished, another hundred had died. "We finally left," he said, "as it was hopeless to keep up with the dying cattle."[17]

By the middle of December there was an acute shortage of hay, and even some ranches with stacks found them completely drifted over. The cattle had no recourse but to wander south, and there was nothing the ranchers could do to stop them. The northern herds drifted to the main line of the CPR, where many perished along the fences. Others broke through and streamed onto the Little Bow range, where they were joined by cattle from the Highwood district. Where possible they wandered across the open prairie, but often they were obliged to follow road allowances; from there they broke into homesteaders' yards and ate their supplies of hay. Near Fort Macleod, Charlie Brewster and his wife spent much of the winter fighting off starving cattle from the Red Deer River. "They almost walked over his buildings," said a family biographer, "and desperately tried to get at his small feed stack. He and Annie spent many hours in the bitter cold urging the moaning animals past their home. No matter how much they loved animals, there was nothing they could do for the suffering herds."[18]

The year 1907 started with another blizzard, and soon dead cattle were piling up against fences and in coulees, while emaciated beasts were wandering through towns like Fort Macleod, Gleichen, and Maple Creek. In Medicine Hat, the town fathers decided that any cattle within the city limits would be shot to put them out of their misery; the stronger ones would be fed as long as there was hay, and the rest would be sent on their way to oblivion. At Fort Macleod, the town water carrier dragged a frozen carcass to the dump each time he returned from his deliveries.

The carcasses of dead cattle poke through the snow on the Bow River Horse Ranch, west of Calgary. *Glenbow Archives/NA-2084-24*

There was another blizzard on 5 February but a day later a chinook swept the western part of the range, sending the temperature up to 50°F. The eastern part of the range, however, did not have any chinooks to relieve the misery. In November, the same blizzard that swept the Alberta plains blew east but from then on, the sub-zero temperatures lingered, bringing one storm after another. At first, many ranchers thought they had enough feed, but when there was no letup they soon ran short. As a result, their cowboys were forced to remain in the saddle for days at a time driving the cattle to available feed and water.

Ed McPherson and another cowboy were sent out by the Turkey Track at the start of the season to establish a winter camp at the west end of Wood Mountain. "Very soon," McPherson recalled, "the snow got so deep that a horse would bog in it crossing a coulee and we had to dig him out or tramp the snow around him so he could get out

himself. Finally we could get no further than a half mile before the horse played out. My chum played solitaire while I read every scrap of paper we had in the dug out . . ."[19]

T.B. Long had to round up the stock each morning along the wooded areas of the White Mud River and drive the cattle to the ranch to feed. As soon as they were finished, they were quick to get off the open plains and back into the protected valley. Next morning the whole routine was repeated. Long recalled,

After many many attempts to hold my cattle on the home range I finally had to give up and leave them on the range of their own choosing. All I was accomplishing was the wearing down of their strength as well as my own . . . My face became brown and was continually peeling from the many frost bites. I was as hardened in to the cold as a man could get.[20]

At the beginning of February, Long bought some hay from a settler named Nelson on Dry Coulee, fifteen miles from the ranch. There was no way of moving it, so Long, fellow rancher Fred Garrison, and their cowboys cut out three hundred of the strongest animals and prepared to drive them to the stacks. The weather was good when they started so they took their time; a sleigh was used to break a trail and the cattle were strung out behind. But they were only part way to their destination when another blizzard struck and visibility dropped to less than fifty feet. They were in rolling country without landmarks and soon any sign of a trail was lost. Long said,

About three o'clock in the afternoon we got together to discuss our chances and it was a grim meeting. We all knew that at best we had a fifty-fifty chance for survival. We talked the situation over thoroughly and we all agreed that we had one chance and one only, this being to drift with the wind which, we prayed had not changed directions. If we came out above Nelsons, in the bottom of Dry Coulee, we would hit his sleigh road and be able to follow it in. If we were to bear too far west and come out below Nelsons we would be lost.[21]

They rode with the wind at their backs and had almost given up hope when at last they struck the sleigh road. Soon they were sitting in front of Nelson's roaring fire. When they returned to their own ranches, Garrison discovered he had lost half his calves in the storm; they were bunched up at a fence corner, frozen to death.

Winter held the Maple Creek country in its grip until early April. By that time many cattle that hadn't frozen to death were scattered over the range as far south as Montana.

Many stories of bravery and pathos have come out of the winter of 1906-07 and its aftermath. A woman travelling to Calgary noticed some cattle standing in the snow, and when she returned they hadn't moved. When she investigated, she found they were frozen stiff, still on their feet. Near

Cypress Hills, the carcass of a cow was seen in the top of a tree where it had died before the snows melted. And at Coaldale, a cowboy looked into an unused railway shed and found it crammed with dead cattle, all standing up.

On the Red Deer River, Billy MacLean, a cowboy on the Douglass Ranch, was hauling hay for the cattle when the first storm struck. The morning had been warm and pleasant but when the wind changed, it started to snow, and the temperature dropped. When MacLean didn't return for lunch, Charlie Douglass went looking for him. At the stacks, the team was still in the corral but there was no sign of the cowboy. In spite of the full-blown blizzard now raging across the plains, Douglass found his man wandering aimlessly on the open range. The wind was blowing too hard to ride directly into it so they made their way to the river and followed it until they could reach the ranch. MacLean surely would have perished had he not been found; within three hours, snow had drifted completely over the back of the ranch house.

Others weren't so lucky. Lee "Dad" Brainard had come into the Hand Hills area with one thousand head of cattle just two months before the bad winter. His seventeen-year-old son and a crew of cowboys put up corrals and a shack for the winter, but there was no way they could hold the cattle once the blizzards struck. Within three weeks, there was two feet of snow with a double crust that made grazing impossible. Each morning the cowboys and the Brainards were out, driving the cattle back to their range. One day the stock drifted so far that the crew could not make it back to the home place that night. Fortunately, they saw the light of a homesteader's shack through the driving snow and headed for it. When they took count, Brainard and his son were missing. The cowboys went back into the storm and found the old man barely alive on the lower strand of a barbed wire fence, while nearby his son had frozen to death.

That same winter, Nat Scofield, a cowboy at the Mexico Ranch, left to visit friends at the McCord & Wilkinson spread. Three weeks later his horse wandered into a ranch with no saddle but trailing a rope. Next spring they found Scofield's body. He had laid down with his saddle as a pillow and died on the prairie.

Perhaps the most graphic description of the winter was provided by historian L.V. Kelly.

One day in January the citizens of Macleod saw what appeared to be a low, black cloud above the snow to the north, which drew slowly, draggingly nearer until it was seen that a herd of thousands of suffering range cattle were coming from the north, staggering blindly along the road allowances in search of open places in which to feed.

A steady, piteous moaning filled the air as the suffering creatures drew close, feeble, starving, skinned from the knees down by sharp snow-crusts and by stumbling and strug-

gling to arise, hair frozen off in patches—naked, mangy steers, tottering yearlings, and dying cows. Straight into the town this horde of perishing brutes slowly crawled, travelling six and eight abreast, bellowing and lowing weak, awful appeals which no one was able to satisfy. There were Bar U and other Northern cattle and their numbers were so great that it took over half an hour for them to pass a given point.

Right through the town they dragged themselves—exhausted animals dropping out every minute to fall and die as they lay, the route through the town being marked with a string of carcasses—past the hotels, the stores, the staring people on the sidewalks, out into the blackness of the prairie beyond, where they were swallowed up and never heard of again.[22]

Rancher Claude Gardiner and a cowboy helper named Blaire feed starving cattle on the Wineglass Ranch, west of Fort Macleod, in the spring of 1907. These were the remains of the herd that survived the winter. *Glenbow Archives/NA-4035-22*

The spirit of cowboy life is reflected in this bronc riding scene at a roundup on the Milk River in 1912. Photographer A.E. Brown entitled it "Riding a Bad One." *Glenbow Archives/NA-777-14*

When spring finally arrived, the ranchers began to count their losses. Tony Day rode out from the Turkey Track and in the first two miles he found two hundred carcasses. Another five hundred cattle were dead in the river bottom, and eighteen more had perished when they pushed inside a log shack looking for food and shelter. By the time Day had finished his count, the Turkey Track had lost eighteen thousand head. The few that were left were fattened and sold, and the ranch closed forever.

The Bar U outfit lost 15,000 head. Wilkinson & McCord lost 3,000 and left the country. The Smith & Mussett outfit started the winter with 3,200 dogies and ended up with 250. The Glengarry Ranch went from 4,000 to 2,500. Bob Patterson lost a third of his 1,500. High River Trading Company, which ran 1,200 cattle on the Red Deer, had 75 in the spring. Smaller ranchers suffered as well; a rancher named Powlett saw his herd shrink from 640 to 33. The stock associations estimated that the Calgary district lost 60 percent of its stock; Lethbridge, 50 percent; and Pincher Creek, 25 percent. Losses along the Red Deer and in the Maple Creek areas were equally depressing. In total, some $11 million in stock perished.

The following summer, a cowboy in the middle of branding looked up at the sun and cried, "Where in damnation were you last January?"[23] It was all over. Perhaps the influx of immigrants had already ended the cowboy era, but the winter had made it a dramatic certainty. Even the secretary of the Western Stock Growers Association admitted in 1908 that "no one at all familiar with the ranching industry will hesitate to state that it is in a condition of rapid decline; dying as decently and as quickly as its financial obligations will permit."[24] The curtailment of the free range and closure of the big cattle companies meant there was no longer a place for the kind of itinerant cowboy who could tour the ranches to break horses, work the roundups, or spend winters in a lonely line cabin.

In 1913, writer W.A. Tait, who had known the Cochrane Ranch in its palmy days, penned a eulogy to the cowboys who had worked there over the years:

> The cowboy's day on the Cochrane ranch is past, for the open range of southern Alberta is no more. The eye sees no more herds of countless cattle roaming the broad prairies; it sees no round-ups; it sees no marvellous displays of horsemanship; it sees no feuds between the employees of different ranches; it sees no resistance to the advance of the iron horse and the encroachment of the settler; it sees no tearing down of barbed wire fences of those who would despoil the range by turning the sod upside-down.[25]

Of course, neither cowboys nor ranches disappeared entirely. The Circle outfit stayed around for another three years, while other ranches like the McIntyre and Ross carried on through the rest of the century. Yet as early as 1913, an old-time rancher was convinced that cowboys of that day were nothing like the men of old. He observed cynically:

> What one of them would stay all night with frozen feet, watching a herd, as I knew one of the old time boys to do? None. The duties which the present-day cowboy thinks are paramount are not the interest of his ranch, but the necessity of getting into town as often as possible, wearing chaps, riding through the streets, and getting as drunk as possible.[26]

The introduction of irrigation and early-ripening wheat meant that many areas previously unsuited for farming were now put to the plough. The remaining ranches tended to rely more on deeded land and less on leases. Not only that, but the wild range stock gave way to tamer, beefier breeds that offered no challenges like those presented by the rangy Texas longhorns. After 1907, roundups continued but often with only one outfit involved. For a few years, reps came from other ranches, but even this practice died away as fences and community pastures became the norm.

Interestingly, much of the spirit of the western cowboy has persisted because of a well-intentioned effort to bury it. In 1912, Guy Weadick promoted the first Calgary Stampede as a tribute to the memory of the cowboy. The implication was that this phenomenon of the saddle had ceased to exist, except in the hearts of the old timers and the skills of the rodeo performers. In fact, the Stampede revived that western spirit to such an extent that the public would not let the Old West die and, in doing so, have perpetuated the image of the Canadian cowboy.

CROWDED OUT

H. LAKE OF RAYMOND, ALBERTA, WAS INSPIRED TO WRITE
THIS POEM IN 1903 AFTER READING THE FOLLOWING NEWS ITEM:
"SEVEN OF THE OLD TIMERS OF THE PINCHER CREEK DISTRICT
HAVE MADE PREPARATIONS TO LEAVE THEIR HOMES,
AND WITH THEIR CATTLE ARE GOING INTO THE RED DEER DISTRICT
TO FIND OPEN RANGE. 'CROWDED OUT' IS THE TERM THEY USE
TO DESCRIBE THEIR CONDITION."

Go gather up the cattle, boys
We'll have to make a change
For the fences and the farmers
Have spoiled the open range.

The big-horns and the heifers
Must be brought in right away,
We start our journey northward
At the breaking of the day.

I hate to leave the old home, boys,
'Tis where the babies came,
'Tis here I brought the Missus, boys,
When first she took my name.

'Twas here I made my money, boys,
Thank God I made it straight,
But we're smothered by the farmers
'N we'll have to pull our freight.

They're coming fast and faster, boys,
'N when the spring commences,
They'll block the open prairie
With their cursed cruel fences.

They'll cut the great broad bench land
With their tearing ripping ploughs
'N work their darned old ditchers
To drain away the sloughs.

They'll run their starving dogies
In twenty acre lots,
'N bunk their blooming slavies
In Columbia rough-board cots.

You say I'm mighty bitter, boys,
I hardly think that's strange,
There was lots of room for farming East,
They might have saved the range.

But they've come, that's all about it,
'N I know they'll do their best,
To make themselves a living and
To hell with all the rest!

So gather in the cattle, boys,
The range out here is done,
And we'll trek for open country,
'Fore the coming of the sun.

NOTES

THE PRAIRIES BECKON

1. George M. Grant, *Ocean to Ocean: Sandford Fleming's Expedition through Canada in* 1872 (London: Sampson Low, Marston, Low & Searle, 1873), 113.

2. John West, *The Substance of A Journal During a Residence at the Red River Colony, British North America In the years* 1820–1823 (Vancouver: The Alcuin Society, 1967), 29. Diary entry for 1 January 1821.

3. William F. Butler, *The Great Lone Land* (London: Sampson Low, Marston, Low & Searle, 1874), 199–200.

4. John McDougall, *On Western Trails in the Early Seventies* (Toronto: William Briggs, 1911), 152. McDougall identified the miner simply as Spencer.

5. Letter, John Bunn to Richard Hardisty, 14 August 1875. Hardisty Papers, Glenbow Archives.

6. Cecil Denny, "Animals of the Early West," *Alberta Historical Review*, 4:2 (Spring 1956): 24.

7. Hugh A. Dempsey, ed., "The West of Edward Maunsell," Part One, *Alberta History*, 34:4 (Autumn 1986): 4.

8. Ibid., 7.

9. Ibid., Part Two, 35:1 (Winter 1987): 19.

10. Leroy V. Kelly, *The Range Men* (Toronto: Coles, 1980), 128.

11. Hugh A. Dempsey, ed., "The West of Edward Maunsell," Part Two, *Alberta History*, 35:1 (Winter 1987): 20.

12. Kelly, *The Range Men*, 129.

13. *The River Press*, Fort Benton, Montana, 6 July 1881.

COMING OF THE COWBOY

1. Thomas B. Braden, "When the Herald Came to Calgary," *Alberta Historical Review*, 9:3 (Summer 1961): 1.

2. F.W. Godsal, "Old Times," *Alberta Historical Review*, 12:4 (Autumn 1964): 19.

3. Simon M. Evans, "Stocking the Canadian Range," *Alberta History*, 26:3 (Summer 1978): 1.

4. R.G. Mathews in *The Macleod Advance*, 10 March 1908.

5. Kelly, *The Range Men*, 154.

6. Grant MacEwan, *Fifty Mighty Men* (Saskatoon: Modern Press, 1965), 218–19.

7. C.J. Christianson, *My Life on the Range* (Lethbridge: Southern Printing Co., 1968), 84.

8. Harold W. Riley, "Herbert William (Herb) Millar," *Canadian Cattlemen*, 4:4 (March 1942): 164.

9. Simon M. Evans, "Stocking the Canadian Range," 3.

10. Kelly, *The Range Men*, 153.

11. H. Frank Lawrence, "Early Days in the Chinook Belt," *Alberta Historical Review*, 13:1 (Winter 1965): 12.

12. *Macleod Gazette*, 24 December 1885.

13. Ibid.

14. Ibid.

15. The Military Colonization Company was founded in 1883 by General T.B. Strange to raise horses for the British army and provide a base from which retired army officers could establish their own ranches. It experienced limited success and was bought by the Canadian Agricultural Coal & Colonization Company about 1887.

16. W.R. Newbolt, as told to Angus McKinnon, "Memories of Bowchase Ranch." *Alberta History*,

32:4 (Autumn 1984): 3. All quotations dealing with Newbolt are from this article.

THE TYPICAL COWBOY

1. Henry Norman in *Calgary Tribune*, 27 June 1888.
2. *Calgary Daily News*, 26 July 1907.
3. W.H. Williams, *Manitoba and the North-West* (Toronto: Hunter, Rose & Co., 1882), 130.
4. Cited in *The Calgary Herald*, 9 April 1885.
5. *Alberta Tribune*, Calgary, 2 July 1895.
6. *Medicine Hat News*, 26 April 1906.
7. *Winnipeg Daily Times*, 6 May 1884.
8. H.A. McGusty, "An Englishman in Alberta," *Alberta Historical Review* 14:1 (Winter 1966): 13.
9. Ibid.
10. W. Lacy Amy, "Broncho-Busting as a Pastime," *The Badminton Magazine of Sport and Pastimes*, London, 36:215 (June 1913): 684.
11. "Bill Watt" in *Mosquito Creek Roundup* (Nanton: Nanton & District Historical Society, 1976), 49.
12. *Medicine Hat News*, 7 January 1904.
13. Ibid., 31 March 1904.
14. Ibid.
15. *Calgary Daily News*, 26 July 1907.
16. Tom Ward, *Cowtown* (Calgary: McClelland & Stewart West, 1975), 139.

FAR FROM HOME

1. *Lethbridge News*, 27 January 1897.
2. Laurie Johnson in *Big Hill Country* (Cochrane: Cochrane & Area Historical Society, 1977), 318.
3. *They Came to Wood Mountain* (Wood Mountain: Wood Mountain Historical Society, 1969), 45. All references to McPherson are from this source.
4. *Medicine Hat News*, 12 July 1906.
5. Ibid.
6. See Michael Klassen, "'Hell Ain't a Mile Off': The Journals of Happy Jack," *Alberta History*, 38:2 (Spring 1990): 1–12.
7. *Macleod Gazette*, 23 June 1885.
8. David H. Breen, biography of John Ware in

Dictionary of Canadian Biography, vol. XIII, 1901–1910, (Toronto: University of Toronto Press, 1994), 1074.

9. Mary Terrill, "'Uncle' Tony Day and the 'Turkey Track,'" *Canadian Cattlemen*, 6:1 (June 1943): 8.
10. *Leaves from the Medicine Tree* (Lethbridge: Lethbridge Herald Publishing Co., 1960), 314.
11. *Lethbridge News*, 5 June 1908.
12. Frederick William Ings, *Before the Fences* (Calgary: McAra Printing, 1980), 19. This may have been the famous Bill Pickett.
13. Ibid.
14. Dallas Banister Wright, "James C. Alcock of Okotoks, Alberta," *Canadian Cattlemen*, 16:1 (January 1953): 37.
15. *Blackwood's Edinburgh Magazine*, 163:987 (January 1898): 14.
16. Mary E. Inderwick, "A Lady and her Ranch," *Alberta History*, 15:4 (Autumn 1967): 2.
17. Ibid.
18. Evelyn Cartier Springett, *For My Children's Children* (Montreal: Unity Press, 1937), 116.
19. *Montreal Star*, 3 October 1906.
20. Ibid.
21. "James Ford Family" in *Mosquito Creek Roundup*, 103.
22. "Louie Hong," in *The Gleichen Call* (Gleichen: Gleichen United Church Women, 1968), 220.
23. Claude Gardiner, *Letters from an English Rancher* (Calgary: Glenbow Museum, 1988). All references to Gardiner are from this source.
24. *They Came to Wood Mountain*, 32. All references to Ogle are from this source.
25. Gardiner, *Letters from an English Rancher*, 40–41.
26. Joe Mitchell Chapple in the *National Magazine*, reprinted in *The Calgary Herald*, 13 August 1907.
27. *Lethbridge Herald*, 26 July 1930.
28. *Lethbridge Herald*, 26 April 1930.
29. *Lethbridge News*, 27 January 1897.
30. Thomas H. Whitney, "Rambling with an Old-timer," *Canadian Cattlemen*, 5:2 (September 1942): 79. All quotations from Whitney are from this source.

RANCH AND TOWN LIFE

1. *Medicine Hat News*, 6 April 1905.
2. "Memoirs of an Itinerant Cowhand," *Canadian Cattlemen*, 5:3 (December 1942): 125.
3. *Medicine Hat News*, 6 April 1905.
4. *Calgary Tribune*, 16 January 1889.
5. *Today* magazine, London, as quoted in *The Calgary Herald*, 5 July 1901.
6. *Macleod Gazette*, 30 November 1886.
7. Springett, *For My Children's Children*, 94.
8. James H. Mitchell, "Archibald Mitchell," *Fort Macleod–Our Colourful Past* (Fort Macleod: Fort Macleod History Book Committee, 1977), 378.
9. *Mosquito Creek Roundup*, 78.
10. John Higinbotham Papers, file 20, vol.A, p.100, M517, Glenbow Archives.
11. *Calgary Daily News*, 26 July 1907.
12. Higinbotham Papers, 120–21.
13. Gardiner, *Letters from an English Rancher*, 34.
14. *Macleod Gazette*, 31 December 1891.
15. Williams, *Manitoba and the North-West*, 131.
16. *Manitoba Free Press*, 29 August 1883.
17. George Shepherd, "The Oxarat-Wylie Ranch," *Canadian Cattlemen*, 5:1 (June 1942): 35.
18. George Shepherd, "Tom Whitney of Maple Creek," *Canadian Cattlemen*, 4:9 (March 1942): 156.
19. John J. Martin, *The Prairie Hub* (Strathmore: Strathmore Standard, 1967), 11.
20. *Mosquito Creek Roundup*, 113.
21. "Hugh McDonald" in *Taming the Prairie Wool* (Glendale: Glendale Women's Institute, 1965), 148.
22. Charles Drage, *Two-Gun Cohen* (London: Jonathan Cape, 1954), 25.
23. *Macleod Gazette*, 24 November 1885.
24. *Calgary Tribune*, 7 October 1885.
25. *Lethbridge Herald*, 23 August 1930.
26. James H. Gray, *Red Lights on the Prairies* (Toronto: Macmillan of Canada, 1971), 156.
27. *Morning Albertan*, Calgary, 19 October 1906.
28. *Calgary Daily News*, 26 June 1907.

ROUNDUP

1. *Fort Macleod Gazette*, 1 July 1882.
2. Fred Ings called it "the first big roundup." See Ings, *Before the Fences*, 21.
3. Kelly, *The Range Men*, 178.
4. *The Calgary Herald*, 13 May 1887.
5. Alfred E. Cross, "The Roundup of 1887," *Alberta Historical Review*, 13:2 (spring 1965): 24.
6. Ibid., 26
7. Ings, *Before the Fences*, 23.
8. *The Western World*, May 1894, 120.
9. *Calgary Daily News*, 27 July 1907.
10. Helen Parsons Neilson, *What the Cow Said to the Calf: Stories and Sketches by Ballie Buck* (Gig Harbor, WA: Red Apple Publishing, 1993), 84.
11. *The Western World*, May 1894, 120.
12. Nele Loring, "Five Thousand Miles with Range-Cattle," *Nineteenth Century*, 29 (April 1891): 649.
13. "Memoirs of an Itinerant Cowhand," 153.
14. Ibid.
15. Ibid.
16. "Hugh McDonald" in *Taming the Prairie Wool*, 147–48.
17. S. Evangeline Warren, "Seventy South Alberta Years" in *Prairie Patchwork* (Lethbridge: Southern Alberta Writers' Workshop, 1980), 34.
18. "Slim" Marsden, "Midnight Stampede," *Canadian Cattlemen*, 4:2 (September 1941): 63.
19. *Lethbridge Herald*, 26 April 1930.
20. Ibid.
21. *Edmonton Bulletin*, 22 June 1907.
22. Ibid.
23. *Calgary Weekly Herald*, 8 August 1907.
24. Stan Graber, *The Last Roundup: Memories of a Canadian Cowboy* (Saskatoon: Fifth House Publishers, 1995).

DANGERS AND DISASTERS

1. *Medicine Hat News*, 1 August 1906.
2. *Lethbridge Herald*, 21 June 1930; also, S. Evangeline Warren, *Seventy South Alberta Years: The Autobiography of Ernest Herbert Falkland (Bert) Warren* (Ilfracombe, U.K.: Arthur H. Stockwell Ltd., 1960).

3. *Lethbridge Herald*, 21 June 1930.
4. Ibid., 5 July 1930.
5. *Medicine Hat News*, 26 April 1906.
6. Dempsey, "The West of Edward Maunsell," 21.
7. "Memoirs of an Itinerant Cowhand," 101.
8. Kelly, *The Range Men*, 200–201.
9. Ings, *Before the Fences*, 41.
10. *Lethbridge Herald*, 7 June 1930.
11. *Macleod Gazette*, 28 October 1885.
12. Rosa Anderson, "The Prairie Fire of 1886," *Our Pioneers* (Cypress Hills Pioneers Association, n.d.), 6.
13. Ralph Stock, "The Big Prairie Fire," *Wide World*, November 1902. Reprinted in the *Medicine Hat News*, 25 December 1902. All quotations about the incident are taken from this source.
14. Mrs. S. Evangeline Warren, "The Worst Fire I Ever Saw," *Canadian Cattlemen*, 13:7 (July 1950): 38. All references to this event are from this source.

HORSE THIEVES

1. *Alberta in the 20th Century, Volume Two, The Birth of the Province* (Edmonton, United Western Communications Ltd., 1992), 179.
2. Hugh A. Dempsey, ed., *William Parker, Mounted Policeman* (Edmonton: Hurtig Publishers, 1973), 45.
3. Report of Commissioner A.G. Irvine. *Annual Report of the North-West Mounted Police Force for the Year 1884* (Ottawa: Queen's Printer), 14.
4. Ibid.
5. Ibid., 17.
6. *The River Press*, 8 April 1885.
7. Ibid.
8. *Benton Weekly Record*, 8 September 1881.
9. William M. Graham, *Treaty Days: Reflections of an Indian Commissioner* (Calgary: Glenbow Museum, 1991), 10.
10. Ibid., 10–11.
11. Jack Thomas stated that other members of the gang were "Long George" Thompson, Suffolk, and Reid. See Jane Havens, "Mulligan Jack," *Canadian Cattlemen*, 18:10 (October 1955): 23.

12. *The Calgary Herald*, 8 August 1904.
13. Zachary Hamilton and Marie Hamilton, *These are the Prairies* (Regina: School Aids and Text Book Publishing Co. Ltd., 1948), 238.
14. *The Calgary Herald*, 8 August 1904.
15. Hamilton and Hamilton, *These are the Prairies*, 239.
16. *Calgary Tribune*, 18 July 1888.
17. *The Calgary Herald*, 14 October 1901.
18. Ibid., 31 October 1901.
19. *Report of the Commissioner of the North-West Mounted Police Force for the Year 1889* (Ottawa: Queen's Printer, 1890), 110.

CATTLE RUSTLERS

1. *Fort Macleod Gazette*, 3 February 1883.
2. Thomas Bland Strange, *Gunner Jingo's Jubilee* (London: Remington & Co., 1893), 390.
3. Ibid., 401.
4. Report of Indian Agent William Pocklington to Indian Commissioner for January 1890. Blood Indian Agency letter-books. Note: These books are now in the National Archives but were consulted while still at the Blood Agency.
5. *Annual Report of the North-West Mounted Police Force for the Year 1894* (Ottawa: Queen's Printer, 1895), 92–93. All references to this incident are from the same source.
6. *The Calgary Herald*, 19 December 1895.
7. Godsal, "Old Times," 22.
8. William M. Baker, ed., *Pioneer Policing in Southern Alberta: Deane of the Mounties, 1888–1914* (Calgary: Historical Society of Alberta, 1993), 139.
9. Ibid., 140.
10. *Medicine Hat News*, 24 March 1904.
11. R. Burton Deane, *Mounted Police Life in Canada* (London: Cassell & Co., 1916), 102.
12. Kelly, *The Range Men*, 16.
13. *Lethbridge Herald*, 27 May 1908.
14. Hugo Maguire, "Cowboy Tales of 1896," *Canadian Cattlemen*, 15:8 (August 1952): 39.
15. *Lethbridge Herald*, 5 August 1908. All references to this matter are from this source.
16. *Medicine Hat News*, 30 April 1907.

OUTLAWS

1. Ings, *Before the Fences*, 52.
2. Kelly, *The Range Men*, 223.
3. Ings, *Before the Fences*, 52. See also Donna B. Ernst, "The Sundance Kid in Alberta," *Alberta History*, 42:4 (Autumn 1994): 10–15.
4. Vicky Kelly, "Butch and the Kid," *Glenbow*, 3:4 (July 1970): 4.
5. Ings, *Before the Fences*, 52.
6. He sold the business to his brother William just before the shooting.
7. *Winnipeg Daily Times*, 28 July 1885.
8. Testimony of Norman Macauley at Robert Casey inquest. RCMP Papers, RG18, vol. 1823, file 3200, National Archives of Canada.
9. Ibid., testimony of William Culley.
10. Ibid., testimony of Thomas Culley.
11. Ibid., testimony of William Culley.
12. Ibid., testimony of Thomas Culley.
13. Ibid., testimony of William Culley.
14. *Report of the Commissioner of the North-West Mounted Police Force for the Year 1885* (Ottawa: Queen's Printer, 1886), 18.
15. Testimony of William Culley. See Note 8.
16. J.W. Morrow, *Early History of the Medicine Hat Country* (Medicine Hat: Medicine Hat Historical Society, 1923), 29.
17. *Medicine Hat News*, 4 April 1901.
18. *Macleod Gazette*, 28 July 1885.
19. Ibid., 21 July 1885.
20. Hamilton and Hamilton, *These are the Prairies*, 152.
21. *Macleod Gazette*, 14 September 1900. Unless otherwise indicated, all references to this event are from this source.
22. Ibid., 15 July 1904.
23. Ibid. Unless otherwise stated, all references to this incident are from this source.
24. *Where the Wheatlands Meet the Range* (Claresholm: Claresholm History Book Club, 1974), 247–48.
25. Robert Gard, "Alberta's 'Wild Bill Hickock,'" *Alberta Folklore Quarterly*, 2:2 (June 1946), 65.
26. *Leaves From the Medicine Tree*, 272.
27. C.J. Christianson, *Early Rangemen* (Lethbridge: Southern Printing Co. 1973), 26.
28. Ings, *Before the Fences*, 53.
29. Ibid., 54–55.
30. Ibid., 57.
31. *Medicine Hat News*, 23 August 1906.
32. *Lethbridge Herald*, 19 September 1912.
33. Ibid.
34. *Qu'Appelle Vidette*, 19 July 1888.
35. Fred H. Schofield, *Pincher Papers I* (Pincher Creek: Pincher Creek & District Historical Society, 1974), 7.
36. *Rocky Mountain Echo*, Pincher Creek, 8 March 1904.
37. Kelly, *The Range Men*, 267–68. All quotations on this subject are from this source.
38. David H. Breen, "Plain Talk from Plain Western Men," *Alberta Historical Review*, 18:3 (Summer 1970): 8.
39. Gardiner, *Letters from an English Rancher*, 54.
40. *Medicine Hat News*, 13 February 1902.
41. Ivan D. Inman, "The Ranchers Roundup," *Alberta History*, 23:3 (Summer 1975): 1.

THE EARLY RODEO COWBOY

1. *Lethbridge Herald*, 11 November 1905.
2. Letter, Capt. Mayne Reid to Samuel Arnold, 10 June 1847, cited in Clifford P. Westermeier, *Man, Beast, Dust: The Story of Rodeo* (Lincoln: University of Nebraska Press, 1987), 34.
3. *Macleod Gazette*, 27 October 1891.
4. Letter, R.B. Giveen to E.I. Wright, 16 October 1891, published as "An Early Rodeo" in *Glenbow*, 2:1 (January 1969): 2.
5. Ibid.
6. Harry Sharpe, "Our Friend—Johnny Franklin," *Canadian Cattlemen*, 6:1 (June 1943): 35.
7. Kelly, *The Range Men*, 230.
8. *The Calgary Herald*, 30 November 1933.
9. Gardiner, *Letters from an English Rancher*, 22.
10. *Medicine Hat News*, 2 August 1894.
11. *The Calgary Herald*, 15 May 1900.
12. Ibid.

13. *Canadian Cattlemen*, 8:1 (June 1945): 23.
14. *Winnipeg Daily Tribune*, 10 July 1900.
15. *The Albertan*, Calgary, 13 July 1901.
16. *Canadian Cattlemen*, 8:1 (June 1945): 34.
17. *Medicine Hat News*, 17 July 1902.
18. *Medicine Hat Times*, 4 July 1911.
19. R.H. Imes, "Old-Time Bronks and Bronk Riders," *Canadian Cattlemen*, 17:7 (July 1954): 25.
20. *Lethbridge Herald*, 9 August 1909.
21. Ibid., 8 August 1917.
22. *The Calgary Herald*, 16 July 1956.

MARKETS AND MANGE

1. J. Grant Mackay, *Northern Chronicle*, Inverness, Scotland, 4 December 1895.
2. Ibid.
3. Nele Loring, "Five Thousand Miles with Range-Cattle," 648–66. Unless otherwise indicated, all direct quotes are from this source.
4. Alfred E. Browning, "On a Ranche Cattle Train," *Canadian Gazette*, reprinted in *Macleod Gazette*, 13 & 20 August 1891.
5. *Macleod Gazette*, 4 June 1891.
6. Ibid., 18 June 1891.
7. Martin, *The Prairie Hub*, 13.
8. Ibid.
9. Neilson, *What the Cow Said to the Calf*, 92.
10. E.J. "Bud" Cotton, with Ethel Mitchell, *Buffalo Bud: Adventures of a Cowboy* (North Vancouver: Hancock House, 1981), 69.
11. Ibid., 70.
12. Kelly, *The Range Men*, 137–38.

END OF AN ERA

1. Neilson, *What the Cow Said to the Calf*, 92.

2. C.J. Christianson, *Early Rangemen* (Lethbridge: Southern Printing Co., 1973), 87.
3. Hugo Maguire, "Shaunavon Tales," *Canadian Cattlemen*, 13:2 (February 1950): 7.
4. Ibid.
5. T.B. Long, *Seventy Years a Cowboy* (Regina: Western Printers Association, 1959), 9.
6. Godsal, "Old Times," 23.
7. Report from Portal, North Dakota, reprinted in *The Albertan*, Calgary, 26 October 1901.
8. *Annual Report of the North-West Mounted Police Force for the Year 1901* (Ottawa: Queen's Printer, 1902), 68.
9. Ibid., 67.
10. Christianson, *Early Rangemen*, 87.
11. Kelly, *The Range Men*, 336.
12. *Medicine Hat News*, 21 August 1902.
13. *The Calgary Herald*, 2 August 1904.
14. Cotton, *Buffalo Bud*, 25.
15. Ibid., 29.
16. Christianson, *My Life on the Range*, 105.
17. Martin, *The Prairie Hub*, 16.
18. *Fort Macleod–Our Colourful Past*, 164.
19. "Edward McPherson," in *They Came to Wood Mountain*, 48.
20. Long, *Seventy Years a Cowboy*, 17.
21. Ibid., 21.
22. Kelly, *The Range Men*, 377.
23. Christianson, *My Life on the Range*, 35.
24. R.R. Mathews, "The Cattle Business Reviewed," *Macleod Advance*, 17 March 1908.
25. W.A. Tait, "Passing of the Cochrane Ranch," *The Calgary Herald*, 26 September 1913.
26. *Lethbridge Herald*, 20 March 1913.

SOURCES CITED

PRIMARY SOURCES

Amy, W. Lacy. "Broncho-Busting as a Pastime." *The Badminton Magazine of Sport and Pastimes*, London, 36:215 (June 1913).

"An Early Rodeo." Letter, R.B. Giveen to E.I. Wright, 16 October 1891. *Glenbow* 2:1 (January 1969).

Annual Reports of the North-West Mounted Police, 1880–1904. Ottawa: Queen's Printer.

Baker, William M., ed. *Pioneer Policing in Southern Alberta: Deane of the Mounties, 1888–1914*. Calgary: Historical Society of Alberta, 1993.

Braden, Thomas B. "When the Herald Came to Calgary." *Alberta Historical Review* 9:3 (Summer 1961).

Butler, William F. *The Great Lone Land*. London: Sampson Low, Marston, Low & Searle, 1874.

Christianson, C.J. *My Life on the Range*. Lethbridge: Southern Printing Co., 1968.

——. *Early Rangemen*. Lethbridge: Southern Printing Co., 1973.

Cotton, E.J. "Bud," with Ethel Mitchell. *Buffalo Bud: Adventures of a Cowboy*. North Vancouver: Hancock House, 1981.

Cross, Alfred E. "The Roundup of 1887." *Alberta Historical Review* 13:2 (Spring 1965).

Deane, R. Burton. *Mounted Police Life in Canada*. London: Cassell & Co., 1916.

Dempsey, Hugh A., ed. *William Parker, Mounted Policeman*. Edmonton: Hurtig Publishers, 1973.

——. ed. "The West of Edward Maunsell." *Alberta History* 34:4 (Autumn 1986), and 5:1 (Winter 1987).

Denny, Cecil. "Animals of the Early West." *Alberta Historical Review* 4:2 (Spring 1956).

Drage, Charles. *Two-Gun Cohen*. London: Jonathan Cape, 1954.

Gardiner, Claude. *Letters from an English Rancher*. Calgary: Glenbow Museum, 1988.

Godsal, F.W. "Old Times." *Alberta Historical Review* 12:4 (Autumn 1964).

Graber, Stan. *The Last Roundup: Memories of a Canadian Cowboy*. Saskatoon: Fifth House Publishers, 1995.

Graham, William M. *Treaty Days: Reflections of an Indian Commissioner*. Calgary: Glenbow Museum, 1991.

Grant, George M. *Ocean to Ocean: Sandford Fleming's Expedition through Canada in 1872*. London: Sampson Low, Marston, Low & Searle, 1873.

Hopkins, Monica. *Letters from a Lady Rancher*. Calgary: Glenbow Museum, 1981.

Inderwick, Mary E. "A Lady and her Ranch." *Alberta History* 15:4 (Autumn 1967).

Ings, Frederick William. *Before the Fences*. Calgary: McAra Printing, 1980.

Lawrence, H. Frank. "Early Days in the Chinook Belt." *Alberta Historical Review* 13:1 (Winter 1965).

Long, T.B. *Seventy Years a Cowboy*. Regina: Western Printers Association, 1959.

Loring, Nele. "Five Thousand Miles with Range-Cattle." *Nineteenth Century* 29 (April 1891).

McDougall, John. *On Western Trails in the Early Seventies*. Toronto: William Briggs, 1911.

McGusty, H.A. "An Englishman in Alberta." *Alberta Historical Review* 14:1 (Winter 1966).

Maguire, Hugo. "Shaunavon Tales." *Canadian Cattlemen* 13:2 (February 1950).

——. "Cowboy Tales of 1896." *Canadian Cattlemen* 15:8 (August 1952).

Marsden, "Slim." "Midnight Stampede." *Canadian Cattlemen* 4:2 (September 1941).

"Memoirs of an Itinerant Cowhand." *Canadian Cattlemen* 5:3 (December 1942).

Newbolt, W.R., as told to Angus McKinnon. "Memories of Bowchase Ranch." *Alberta History* 32:4 (Autumn 1984).

Sharpe, Harry. "Our Friend–Johnny Franklin." *Canadian Cattlemen* 6:1 (June 1943).

Springett, Evelyn Cartier. *For My Children's Children*. Montreal: Unity Press, 1937.

Stock, Ralph. "The Big Prairie Fire." *Wide World* (November 1902).

Strange, Thomas Bland. *Gunner Jingo's Jubilee*. London: Remington & Co., 1893.

Symons, R.D. *Where the Wagon Led*. Toronto: Doubleday Canada Ltd., 1973.

Warren, S. Evangeline. "Alberta Tales for Alberta Kiddies." *Lethbridge Herald*, a series of 29 articles bylined "W.E.H.F." (Warren, Ernest Herbert Falkland) published weekly from 3 Feb. to 13 Sept. 1930.

——. "The Worst Fire I Ever Saw." *Canadian Cattlemen* 13:7 (July 1950).

——. *Seventy South Alberta Years: The Autobiography of Ernest Herbert Falkland (Bert) Warren*. Ilfracombe, England: Arthur H. Stockwell Ltd., 1960.

——. "Seventy South Alberta Years." In *Prairie Patchwork*. Lethbridge: Southern Alberta Writers' Workshop, 1980.

West, John. *The Substance of a Journal During a Residence at the Red River Colony, British North America in the Years 1820-1923*. Vancouver: The Alcuin Society, 1967.

Williams, W.H. *Manitoba and the North-West*. Toronto: Hunter, Rose & Co., 1882.

SECONDARY SOURCES

Alberta in the 20th Century, Volume Two, The Birth of the Province. Edmonton: United Western Communications Ltd., 1992.

Big Hill Country. Cochrane: Cochrane & Area Historical Society, 1977.

Blackwood's Edinburgh Magazine 163:987 (January 1898).

Brado, Edward. *Cattle Kingdom: Early Ranching in Alberta*. Vancouver: Douglas & McIntyre, 1984.

Breen, David H. "Plain Talk from Plain Western Men." *Alberta Historical Review* 18:3 (Summer 1970).

——. "John Ware." *Dictionary of Canadian Biography* XIII, 1901–1910. Toronto: University of Toronto Press, 1994.

——. *The Canadian West and the Ranching Frontier, 1874-1924*. Toronto: University of Toronto Press, 1983.

Ernst, Donna B. "The Sundance Kid in Alberta." *Alberta History* 42:4 (Autumn 1994).

Evans, Simon M. "Stocking the Canadian Range." *Alberta History* 26:3 (Summer 1978).

Fort Macleod–Our Colourful Past. Fort Macleod: Fort Macleod History Book Committee, 1977.

Gard, Robert E. "Alberta's 'Wild Bill Hickock.'" *Alberta Folklore Quarterly* 2:2 (June 1946).

The Gleichen Call. Gleichen: Gleichen United Church Women, 1968.

Gray, James H. *Red Lights on the Prairies*. Toronto: Macmillan of Canada, 1971.

Hamilton, Zachary, and Marie Hamilton. *These Are the Prairies*. Regina: School Aids and Text Book Publishing Co. Ltd., 1948.

Hanson, Stan D. "Policing the International Boundary Area in Saskatchewan, 1890-1910." *Saskatchewan History* 19:2 (Spring 1966).

Havens, Jane. "Mulligan Jack." *Canadian Cattlemen* 18:10 (October 1955).

Imes, R.H. "Old-time Bronks and Bronk Riders." *Canadian Cattlemen* 17:7 (July 1954).

Inman, Ivan D. "The Ranchers Roundup." *Alberta History* 23:3 (Summer 1975).

Jameson, Sheilagh. *Ranches, Cowboys and Characters: Birth of Alberta's Western Heritage*. Calgary: Glenbow Museum, 1987.

Kelly, Leroy Victor. *The Range Men*. Toronto: Coles, 1980.

Kelly, Vicky. "Butch and the Kid." *Glenbow* 3:4 (July 1970).

Klassen, Michael. "'Hell Ain't a Mile Off': The Journals of Happy Jack." *Alberta History* 38:2 (Spring 1990).

Leaves from the Medicine Tree. Lethbridge: Lethbridge Herald Publishing Co., 1960.

MacEwan, J.W. Grant. *Fifty Mighty Men*. Saskatoon: Modern Press, 1965.

Martin, John J. *The Prairie Hub*. Strathmore: Strathmore Standard, 1967.

Memoirs of the Ghost Pine Homesteaders. Three Hills: Capital Printers, 1954.

Morrow, J.W. *Early History of the Medicine Hat Country*. Medicine Hat: Medicine Hat Historical Society, 1923.

Mosquito Creek Roundup. Nanton: Nanton & District Historical Society, 1976.

Neilson, Helen Parsons. *What the Cow Said to the Calf: Stories and Sketches by Ballie Buck*. Gig Harbor, WA: Red Apple Publishing, 1993.

Our Pioneers. Cypress Hills: Cypress Hills Pioneers Association, n.d.

Raby, S. "Prairie Fires in the North-West." *Saskatchewan History* 19:3 (Autumn 1966).

Riley, Harold W. "Herbert William (Herb) Millar." *Canadian Cattlemen* 4:4 (March 1942).

Schofield, Fred H. *Pincher Papers I*. Pincher Creek: Pincher Creek & District Historical Society, 1974.

Shepherd, George. "Tom Whitney of Maple Creek." *Canadian Cattlemen* 4:9 (March 1942).

——. "The Oxarat-Wylie Ranch." *Canadian Cattlemen* 5:1 (June 1942).

Taming the Prairie Wool. Glendale: Glendale Women's Institute, 1965.

Terrill, Mary. "'Uncle' Tony Day and the 'Turkey Track.'" *Canadian Cattlemen* 6:1 (June 1943).

——. "Medicine Hat Pioneer, William Mitchell, 1878-1946." *Canadian Cattlemen* 9:3 (Dec. 1946).

They Came to Wood Mountain. Wood Mountain: Wood Mountain Historical Society, 1969.

Thomas, Lewis G. *Ranchers' Legacy*. Edited by Patrick A. Dunae. Edmonton: University of Alberta Press, 1986.

Ward, Tom. *Cowtown*. Calgary: McClelland & Stewart West, 1975.

Westermeier, Clifford P. *Man, Beast, Dust: The Story of Rodeo*. Lincoln: University of Nebraska Press, 1987.

Western World, The. May 1894.

Where the Wheatlands Meet the Range. Claresholm: Claresholm History Book Club, 1974.

Whitney, Thomas H. "Rambling with an Oldtimer." *Canadian Cattlemen* 5:2 (September 1942).

Wright, Dallas Banister. "James C. Alcock of Okotoks, Alberta." *Canadian Cattlemen* 16:1 (January 1953).

MANUSCRIPT SOURCES

Richard Hardisty Papers, Glenbow Archives

John D. Higinbotham Papers, Glenbow Archives

Blood Indian Agency letter-books, National Archives of Canada

Robert Casey inquest, RCMP Papers, RG18, Vol. 1823, File 3200, National Archives of Canada

NEWSPAPERS

The Albertan, Calgary

Alberta Tribune, Calgary

Calgary Daily News

The Calgary Herald

Calgary Tribune

Morning Albertan, Calgary

Edmonton Bulletin

Benton Weekly Record

The River Press, Fort Benton

Northern Chronicle, Inverness, Scotland

Lethbridge Herald

Lethbridge News

The Macleod Advance

Macleod Gazette

Medicine Hat News

Medicine Hat Times

Montreal Star

Rocky Mountain Echo, Pincher Creek

Qu'Appelle Vidette

Manitoba Free Press, Winnipeg

Winnipeg Daily Times

Winnipeg Daily Tribune

INDEX